Confucian Concord

Ideas, History, and Modern China

Edited by

Ban WANG (*Stanford University*)
WANG Hui (*Tsinghua University*)

VOLUME 24

The titles published in this series are listed at *brill.com/ihmc*

Confucian Concord

Reform, Utopia and Global Teleology in Kang Youwei's Datong Shu

By

Federico Brusadelli

BRILL

LEIDEN | BOSTON

Cover illustration: Yu Wei Kang. C. 1905. Photograph. https://www.loc.gov/pictures/item/2005687157/.
Library of Congress Prints and Photographs Division. Public Domain.

Library of Congress Cataloging-in-Publication Data

Names: Brusadelli, Federico, author.
Title: Confucian concord : reform, utopia and global teleology in Kang
   Youwei's Datong Shu / Federico Brusadelli.
Description: Leiden ; Boston : Brill, [2020] | Series: Ideas, history, and
   modern China, 1875-9394 ; volume 24 | Includes bibliographical
   references and index.
Identifiers: LCCN 2020017495 (print) | LCCN 2020017496 (ebook) |
   ISBN 9789004434448 (hardback) | ISBN 9789004434714 (ebook)
Subjects: LCSH: Kang, Youwei, 1858–1927. Da tong shu. | Utopias. |
   Universalism. | Confucianism.
Classification: LCC HX811.K36 B78 2020 (print) | LCC HX811.K36 (ebook) |
   DDC 335/.02—dc23
LC record available at https://lccn.loc.gov/2020017495
LC ebook record available at https://lccn.loc.gov/2020017496

Typeface for the Latin, Greek, and Cyrillic scripts: "Brill". See and download: brill.com/brill-typeface.

ISSN 1875-9394
ISBN 978-90-04-43444-8 (hardback)
ISBN 978-90-04-43471-4 (e-book)

Copyright 2020 by Koninklijke Brill NV, The Netherlands.
Koninklijke Brill NV incorporates the imprints Brill, Brill Hes & De Graaf, Brill Nijhoff, Brill Rodopi,
Brill Sense, Hotei Publishing, mentis Verlag, Verlag Ferdinand Schöningh and Wilhelm Fink Verlag.
All rights reserved. No part of this publication may be reproduced, translated, stored in a retrieval system,
or transmitted in any form or by any means, electronic, mechanical, photocopying, recording or otherwise,
without prior written permission from the publisher.
Authorization to photocopy items for internal or personal use is granted by Koninklijke Brill NV provided
that the appropriate fees are paid directly to The Copyright Clearance Center, 222 Rosewood Drive,
Suite 910, Danvers, MA 01923, USA. Fees are subject to change.

This book is printed on acid-free paper and produced in a sustainable manner.

This is for my grandparents.

道洽大同
"The Way is in Harmony with the Great Concord"
Beijing, Temple of Confucius, Main Hall

Contents

Acknowledgments   IX

Introduction   1

PART 1
Roots

1 The Sage and the Unicorn: Confucian Progressivism and Esoteric Classicism   13

2 Indra's Net: Buddhism and the Hidden Face of Kang's Confucianism   42

3 State and Science: The Weight of the West   56

PART 2
Threads

4 Nation: Defending Universalism from the Builders of Borders   85

5 Democracy: "You Don't Wear a Fur in Summer". Between Utopianism and Pragmatism   107

6 Socialism: Confucian Equality, from the Well-fields to the Communes   126

PART 3
Legacies

7 The Red Concord: Kang Youwei and Mao Zedong, Meeting in the Land of Utopia?   147

8 A *Datong* for the Third Millennium: Globalism versus Nationalism   168

  Conclusions   178

  Bibliography   183
  Index   192

Acknowledgments

This book originates from my doctoral dissertation, completed at the University of Naples "L'Orientale" under the supervision of Prof. Donatella Guida. She is the first person I wish to thank: a mentor, an inspiration and a friend, whose guidance has accompanied me in the world of academia ever since.

Prof. Marc A. Matten introduced me to the methodology of conceptual history. In my almost three years as a researcher at the University of Erlangen, he played a fundamental role in the further development not only of the present work, but of my Sinological research in general. Together with them, other friends and colleagues, in Italy and in Germany, contributed to this project with their suggestions, observations and comments: Chiara Ghidini, Luca Stirpe, Lisa Indraccolo, Phillip Grimberg, Anne Schmiedl, Renée Krusche, Michael Hoeckelmann.

The two anonymous reviewers offered some precious hints and equally precious criticism, and the editors at Brill (Qin Higley, Lauren Bissonette and Elizabeth You) made this book possible.

Finally, Ben Young helped with the copyediting in the best possible way.

And Luca deserves a special thanks for his patience, and his support, during my years as a PhD student.

Introduction

1   Kang Youwei and the Call of Prophecy

> Every day the salvation of society was uppermost in my thoughts, and every moment the salvation of the society was my aim in life, and for this aim I am determined to sacrifice myself. Since there were an infinite number of worlds, great and small, I could only console and try to save those on the world where I had been born, those I met along the way, those I had a chance to grow close to. Each day I would call to them and hope that they would listen to me. I made this my guiding principle and my goal.[1]

These words were used in 1895 by the 37-year-old Kang Youwei 康有為 (1858–1927) to describe his intellectual path. At this stage in his life the best was still to come, and his world-saving aspiration had not yet produced its most interesting outcomes.

Kang, who would later become one of the most famous figures of modern Chinese intellectual history, and one of the most widely discussed, was born in Nanhai, Guangdong, into a scholarly family which enabled him to follow a classical course of studies.[2] He was never a quiet student, though. When he was eighteen he became convinced that he had been given the task to "become a sage" and "remake the world." To this end, he adopted the not immodest goal of the reestablishment of the Chinese tradition, and then its projection into modernity. Endowing Confucius with the status of a prophet and breaking open the traditional cyclical flow of history so as to create a "progressive" and evolutionary timeline, thus to a certain extent producing modernity out of tradition and contributing to the opening of a *Sattelzeit* (Saddle-period)

---

1 Kang Youwei, *Nianpu* (1895), quoted in Jonathan Spence, *The Gate of Heavenly Peace. The Chinese and Their Revolution 1895–1980* (New York NY: The Viking Press, 1981), 5–6.

2 The best resource in a Western language for a biography of Kang, mainly drawing on Kang's diaries and autobiography, is still Lo Jung-Pang (ed), *K'ang Yu-wei: A biography and a symposium* (Tucson AR: The University of Arizona Press, 1967). As far as Kang's thought is concerned, the most comprehensive survey in English is Hsiao Kung-chuan, *A Modern China and a New World. Kang Yu-wei, Reformer and Utopian, 1858–1927* (Seattle WA: University of Washington Press, 1975). For a more recent analysis of Kang's philosophy in Chinese, see Bai Rui 白锐, *Xunqiu chuantong zhengzhi de xiandai zhuanxing. Kang Youwei jindai Zhongguo zhengzhi fazhanguan yanjiu* 寻求传统政治的现代转型—康有为近代中国政治发展观研究 (Beijing: Zhishi chanquan chubanshe, 2010).

in China, to borrow Reinhart Koselleck's term, was for Kang the only way to sustain an energetic claim for political reform.[3] Kang responded to the urgent need to redefine a "political order," felt so acutely by Chinese scholar-officials since the mid nineteenth century, after having ostensibly "gathered the deep and more abstruse statements in the classics and in other philosophic works, examined hidden meanings in Confucianism and Buddhism, [and] studied new ideas developed in China and in the West." The final product of such a continent-spanning intellectual journey—a journey which would become *real* in the years following 1898—could be defined as a "new Classicism" or a "modern Classicism," and was the outcome of the interaction between intellectual trends internal to the tradition (Kang having formed his early worldview mainly on the basis of the so-called New Text School of Confucianism) and external challenges deriving from the collision with the West. Kang never intended his philosophical system as abstract speculation, but rather as the rationale for a thorough reform of the imperial institutions, this being the only way to save China from the double threat of internal decline and foreign aggression. The political nature of his reflections was explicitly showcased in his *Confucius as a Reformer* (孔子改制考, 1897), whose title leads us to a major question underlying any study on Kang Youwei, namely: To what degree can we consider him a Confucianist? From an internal point of view (from Kang's perspective) he definitely was a Confucianist. Indeed, he might also be considered the first *real* Confucianist, since in philological circles it is well known that the word "Confucianism" is a misleading translation of *Ru*, and that the latter term might be better understood as denoting Classicism, rather than a personalistic philosophical current—not to mention a cult—wholly devoted to the figure of Confucius himself. As his text from 1897 demonstrates, Kang oriented his Classicism entirely towards the person of Confucius, and his proposal for the establishment of a Confucian Church clearly attests to his understanding of Ruism as the religion of Confucius. In this sense, it is not merely a provocation to suggest that, whereas the label "Confucian" is generally misleading when writing a history of Chinese philosophy, in Kang's case it is a perfect match for his agenda.

Fulfilling the aspiration of any Classicist, in 1895 Kang went to Beijing for the long-awaited *jinshi* examinations: there, he led more than a thousand degree candidates in presenting a petition to the emperor protesting against the Treaty of Shimonoseki, signed that year in the humiliating final act of the war with Japan. This "elite mass protest" signalled his strong political inclination,

---

3 See Luke S. Kwong, "The Rise of the Linear Perspective on History and Time in Late Qing China, c. 1860–1911" (*Past & Present* n. 173 2001: 157–190).

as well as his classical understanding of the intellectual as a politically engaged figure in a new context. A few months later he established the Society for the Strengthening of China and founded a newspaper, edited by his pupil Liang Qichao 梁启超 (1873–1929). In less than three years, having gained the trust of Weng Tonghe 翁同龢 (1830–1904), an influential councillor at the Court, he gained access to the council of Emperor Guangxu 光绪 (1871–1908), the titular ruler who at that time was trying to escape the influence of his aunt, Empress Dowager Cixi 慈禧 (1835–1908). Kang's discourse on the necessity of a pervasive change in the functioning of the Empire—in which he presented the Emperor with a wide range of historical examples of active rulers, like Peter the Great or the Meiji Emperor of Japan—rapidly convinced the young monarch to open the path for reforms: in June 1898 Guangxu issued a series of edicts inaugurating the so-called Hundred Days Reforms. As the label suggests, these were indeed short-lived.[4] Kang had proposed a project of hyper-centralization (in contrast to the decentralizing dynamics at work since the Taiping revolt), intended to restore the power which the emperor had lost through the restructuring of the political order; yet his project ran up against obstacles within and outside of the court, and in September Empress Cixi was able to thwart the reforms. After Ci Xi's coup (or counter-coup), Kang fled to Japan, thus starting his journey across the world. Yet throughout his extensive travels, from Singapore to London, from Rome to Vancouver, from India to Paris, he never abandoned his political agenda. On the contrary, Kang used his connections with Chinese communities across the continents to establish and fund a number of associations working for the establishment of a constitutional monarchy in China (the most famous being the Society for the Protection of the Emperor,

---

4 For a recent and thorough analysis of the 1898 Reforms and their legacy see Rebecca Karl and Peter Zarrow (eds), *Rethinking the 1898 Reform Period. Political and Cultural Change in Late Qing China* (Cambridge MA: Harvard University Press, 2002) and Peter Zarrow, *After Empire. The conceptual transformation of the Chinese state, 1885–1924* (Stanford CA: Stanford University Press, 2012), 24–55; 89–118. The actual role of Kang in the 1898 Reforms has been challenged by some Chinese scholars like Huang Zhangjian and Luke Kwong since the late 1970s, suggesting that the importance of Kang in the 1898 process was more a fabrication by his disciples than a historical fact. See Luke Kwong, "Chinese Politics at the Crossroads: Reflections on the Hundred Days Reform of 1898" (*Modern Asian Studies* 34/03, 2000: 663–695). Wong, after a study of new materials and sources on the 1898 events, has defined Huang and Kwong's work as an example of "conspicuously polemical" revisionism, full of "factual errors" and poorly grounded. See Young-tsu Wong, *Beyond Confucian China. The Rival Discourses of Kang Youwei and Zhang Binglin* (London: Routledge, 2010), 15–17. However, since the *Wuxu bianfa* is not the focus of the present work, which is a study of the Datong Shu and of its connections to Kang's activities after 1898, I will not address the question.

Baohuanghui 保皇會, Vancouver, 1899).[5] Yet in this time of nationalism and republicanism, Kang's views on constitutional monarchism were denounced as conservative attempts to turn back the clock of history. Kang returned to China after the proclamation of the Chinese Republic in 1912, where he started vigorously sponsoring the return of the Manchu monarchs—even taking part in the unsuccessful restoration of the last emperor Pu Yi 溥仪 to the throne in 1917—while at the same time favouring the establishment of a Confucian Church as the national cult of China (unsuccessfully, again). In the last years of his life, Kang nourished his spiritual inclinations more than his political battles; drawing on his lifelong interest in Buddhism, he practiced meditation and deepened his esoteric knowledge. Kang Youwei died in 1927 in Qingdao. Eight years later, a posthumous text was published in Shanghai, shedding new light on the entirety of his thought: the *Book of Great Concord* (*Datong Shu* 大同書), which is the focal point of the present study.[6]

2   The Book: Utopia or History?

Content. In a nutshell, the *Datong Shu* describes the long march of mankind from division to unity. According to the innovative vision of history merely hinted at by Kang's predecessors in the New Text School,[7] but fully developed by the author in this book, the final stage of history is the Age of Great Concord—in Chinese *datong* 大同, a Classical word indicating the attainment of individual equality and social stability.[8] Generally considered a Chinese

---

5 An ongoing scholarly project is researching the activities of the *Baohuanghui* in North America. See the website http://baohuanghui.blogspot.it. A collection of materials related to Kang's involvement into the association's activities is available in Wang Youwei (ed), *Kang Youwei yu Baohuanghui* 康有为与保皇会, (Shanghai: Shanghai renmin chubanshe, 1982).

6 I have translated *Datong* as Great Concord, although a number of different options have been adopted by scholars across the decades, from "Great Community" (Spence, *The Gate of Heavenly Peace*) to "Great Commonweal" (Zarrow, *After Empire*). For a list of possible translations of the original Confucian term, see Laurence G. Thompson, *Ta-tung shu. The One-World Philosophy of Kang Yu-wei*, (London: George Allen & Unwin, 1958), 29–30. As for the Chinese version of the text, I chose the Renmin University Press edition of 2010, edited by Jiang Yihua and Zhang Ronghua. It presents some minor differences in the distribution of parts and chapters with the Zhonghua edition of 1935 used by Thompson. Discrepancies between the two versions, when occurring in translated excerpts, are mentioned in the notes.

7 See below, Chapter 1.

8 For an analysis of Kang's use of the term *datong* as the result of the interaction of multiple sources (traditional and Western), see Zang Shijun, *Kang Youwei datong sixiang yanjiu* 康有为大同思想研究 (Guangzhou: Guangdong gaodeng jiaoyu chubanshe, 1997), especially pp. 17–59. Zang also defines *ren* 仁 as the core of Kang's ideal. On this, see below Chapter 2.

Utopia, the *Datong Shu* actually defies any strict categorization. Even though—from a Koselleckian perspective—the book clearly represents a projection of "modern" ideas into an ideal future (and in this sense has a distinct utopian spirit),[9] defining its literary genre is a bigger challenge. Besides its fascinating and indeed utopian description of the "world of tomorrow" with its technological, political, and social wonders, it also includes significant pieces of historical, political, religious, and scientific literature dealing with the past and the present. Again, Koselleck would find Kang's work to be an interesting complex of *Ungleichzeitigkeiten*, or nonsynchronicities, structured around a teleological view of history.[10] Yet if we adopt Foucault's definition of Utopias as "sites with no real place," "sites that have a general relation of direct or inverted analogy with the real space of Society," and which "present society itself in a perfected form, or else society turned upside down, but in any case are fundamentally unreal spaces,"[11] then the *Datong Shu* is not a Utopia: although it includes many utopian aspects, it cannot be limited to this genre. The world prophesied by Kang is in fact our own world, not another one; not an allegory but a positivist anticipation of what is to come when the laws of history are applied. In other words, the Age of Concord is not presented as a *model* positioned outside of history, but as the natural outcome of the *same* historical dynamics that are at work in the present. In the book there is no break between the survey of the past and the anticipation of the future; in fact, there is no description at all of another space, but only of another time in the same space as we now inhabit. Nevertheless, if we follow Karl Mannheim's suggestion and consider utopias as a "state of mind which tends to shatter the order of things,"[12] then Kang's detailed description of how humans will "shatter" their boundaries does indeed

9 Reinhart Koselleck, *Futures Past. On the Semantics of Historical Time* (New York, NY: Columbia University Press), 2004. Adapting Koselleck's view of modernity to the Chinese case is an interesting challenge. Where would the "saddle period," that he positions for the West in the mid 18th century, begin? Apparently, China experienced a series of conceptual mutations comparable to the Western ones only one century later, from the mid 19th century. However, as argued below in Chapter 1, a modern idea of Time emerged among some Confucian currents from the 18th century, suggesting a sort of synchronicity—although with different success and with different political scopes—opening a possible "global" intellectual and conceptual analysis of the century of the Enlightenment.

10 Ibid. For a discussion of Koselleck's idea of multiple temporalities and historical periodization, also see Helge Jordheim, "Against Periodization: Koselleck's Theory of Multiple Temporalities." (*History and Theory*, 51/2, 2012: 151–171).

11 Michel Foucault, "Des Espaces Autres (1967)." (*Architecture/Mouvement/Continuité*, 1984: 46–49).

12 Karl Mannheim, *Ideology and Utopia* (London: Routledge, 1936), 341. For a use of Mannheim's theory on utopianism on Kang's work, see Cheng Boqing, "*Shijie shehui de Zhongguoshi xiangxiang—Datong Shu zuowei yige wenhua shijian de shehuixue jiedu*

grant the *Datong Shu* the full status of a utopian work. And again, if utopias tend to illuminate the actual fractures perceived by the author in his world, while projecting them onto another plane, then this is the case for the *Datong Shu*. Its utopian nature notwithstanding, however, we could paradoxically define the *Datong Shu* as a "global history" written from the viewpoint of its end, in the (not so distant) future.

At this point, a very brief survey of the book's structure will help.[13] The first chapter of the *Datong Shu* is the most spiritual and purely philosophical: here—with an unmistakable Buddhist nuance—Kang analyses the roots of universal suffering, which he identifies in a set of "boundaries" (*jie* 界) separating men and obstructing their self-realization: sufferings arising from living (incarnation/conception, infant mortality, sickness, aboriginal existence, living in borderlands, slavery, womanhood); sufferings from natural calamities (drought, locusts, fire, floods, volcanoes, accidents, epidemics); sufferings from human relationships (orphanhood, poverty, low social status); political sufferings (imprisonment, taxation, military service, state, family); emotional sufferings (ignorance, hatred, affection, attachments, toil, desires, tyranny); and finally the sufferings caused by "prominence" (from the rich to Buddha himself). All these sufferings are then understood by Kang as originating from nine barriers or boundaries. The central section of the book comprises seven chapters which are presented in different orders in the two editions of the *Datong Shu*, the 1935 Zhonghua edition and the 2010 Renmin Daxue edition based on a manuscript found in 1985 in the Jiangsu Library. They deal with the gradual overcoming of those boundaries as the ideal of Unity (*tong* 同) emerges in a more and more visible manner, progressively destroying the divisions that obstruct empathy and fracture the common body of humanity into smaller and conflictive units. More specifically, the chapters foretell the abolition of the following obstacles: national boundaries;[14] boundaries of class, race, gender, and family distinctions; and economic and administrative boundaries, which will be substituted by an almost communist model of production, and a democratic one-world order which will substitute the States—and more generally

---

世界社会的中国式想象—大同书作伪一个文化事件的社会学解读." (*Jiangsu shehui kexue* 1, 2009: 20–26).

13 To this day, the main text in a Western language dealing exclusively with the *Datong Shu* and presenting the translation of substantial parts of the book is Thompson, *Ta-tung shu*. The introduction, albeit to some extent outdated, is a good summary of the text and of its gestation.

14 On this, see below Chapter 4.

all the political, familial, religious, or social authorities—of the past.[15] Finally, he discusses the general overcoming of any boundary dictated by the existence of physical suffering, with the extension of life expectancy beyond a century and the triumph of medical science (with a sinister foreshadowing of eugenics). Even from this outline it should be clear that the utopian vision of the *Datong Shu* accounts for just a part of the book, as the author engages in an extensive review of the past and the present of humanity before moving to the description of its future.

Dating. The question of when the book was composed is just as intractable as that of defining its genre. Although it was published posthumously, Kang Youwei claimed to have drafted *Datong Shu* as early as 1884 (when he was 28): as we will later observe, in his arguments against republicans he would often cite the *Book of Great Concord* as testimony to his longstanding democratic sentiments.[16] In fact, however, the text Kang actually referred to in these arguments bore a different title: *Renlei Gongli* 人類公理, or *The Common Principles of Mankind*, which is no longer extant.[17] It is certainly true that the basic principles of the *Datong Shu* as they will be presented hereafter (an evolutionary and optimistic vision of history, a concern for equality and empathy, an interest in scientific and institutional development, and a global view on "modernity") had already been elaborated by Kang around 1898. However, the text in its definitive version was probably drafted in 1902, when Kang was in Darjeeling, India (a dating confirmed by Liang Qichao).[18] In 1913 it was Liang himself who forced the publication of the first two chapters of the book, which appeared in Kang's journal *Bu Ren* 不忍. The whole text, though, was voluntarily kept unpublished by the author, as it was—as he would state in his later years—too advanced for that time.[19] Certainly it underwent some minor modifications in the following years, as the abundant references to European or American episodes, facts, and figures may suggest (being the result of Kang's journeys between 1898 and 1912). In conclusion, Che Dongmei provides possibly the best summary of the complex process behind the creation of the *Datong Shu*: its "conceptual embryo" was defined in 1884 and its "first draft" was completed

---

15 On the institutional aspects, see below Chapters 3 and 5; on the economic recipes provided by Kang (and the debate on his "socialism") see below, Chapters 6 and 7.
16 See below, Chapter 5.
17 Thompson, *Ta-tung shu*, 26.
18 *Ibid.*
19 See below, Chapter 5, for the exact quotation.

in 1902 in India, but the final version of the book is the result of the "lifelong adjustments" effected by Kang up to his death.[20]

3 An Intellectual Circuit

This book is not a translation of the *Datong Shu*. Lawrence Thompson provided Western scholars and readers with a partial translation in 1958 (though some of the parts left untranslated by Thompson will be used for the present study). Nor is it intended to be a summary or analysis of the book's narrative content, or a description of Kang's utopianism *per se*. The *Datong Shu* is not a minor work, and the purpose of this study is not to rediscover it nor to rescue it from oblivion; indeed, much has been written on Kang's *magnum opus* (with the number of studies in Chinese increasing noticeably since the 1990s).

As fascinating as the content of the book may be, then, my intent is to view the *Datong Shu* from a wider perspective. More specifically, I try to see Kang's book as an "intellectual circuit" in which the author addresses some of the key issues of modernity through a vast and diverse set of cultural and political materials, which ultimately thwart any strict division between "traditional" and "modern," Western or Chinese concepts. Kang's teleological linearity—his unwavering commitment to the advancement of China, and of the world, toward a brighter future—will also be used (against Kang's own intentions, probably) to challenge any linear and "ordered" interpretation of China's modern intellectual evolution(s).

The book will try to answer some of the following questions.

What does the *Datong Shu* tell us about Chinese utopianism and its political implications? How is it related with late Qing and early Republican concerns and currents of thought, such as Esoteric Classicism, Heterodox Confucianism, the New Text School, the revival of Buddhism, the emergence of Statism, and the rise of nationalism? How consistent and significant are the Western influences in the text? Can we easily separate the Chinese and Western components in the construction of Kang's utopian view? And is Kang's devotion to Classicism and to Chinese tradition at odds with his vision of a world where homosexuals can marry and women have the same rights as men?

Is Kang's "Statist" recipe for a stronger China—fully on display during the failed Hundred Days Reform—at odds with the *Datong Shu*'s one-world dream? Or is it just its antecedent on a smaller scale? What, in other words,

---

20   See Che Dongmei, "Datong Shu chengshu shijian kao 大同书成书时间考." (*Jiangnan xuekan* 5, 1999).

INTRODUCTION

is the relationship between Kang's utopianism, his political platform, and the rise of nationalism? How, moreover, can we coherently position Kang's escape to Utopia within his political production, considering the watersheds of 1898 and 1912? And, again, under its prophetic tone does the *Datong Shu* veil those very same themes addressed in the harsh political debate that saw Kang on one side and Republicans and Nationalists on the other, on the eve of the Xinhai Revolution?

Finally, we may ask: since its publication, what legacy has the *Datong Shu* left for Chinese intellectuals? What connection might we trace between Kang's utopia and Mao's own utopian view of *datong*? (Without forgetting Sun Yat-sen's personal contribution to the construction of a modern concept of *datong*.) Is the "global" projection of Confucianism as portrayed in the *Book of Great Concord* of any significance in relation to the political and intellectual challenges faced by China in the twenty-first-century?

In the first part of this book I try to uncover the roots of the *Datong Shu*, focusing on the emergence of a linear and progressive vision of history within the Chinese tradition, and more specifically discussing Kang's Buddhist and Western influences, and his adherence to the New Text School.

Then I follow some of the threads running through the *Book of Great Concord*: its significance in Kang's image of China as a potentially *universal* model of civilization, more than a nation built on *ethnic* premises; the (apparent) contradiction between the *Datong Shu*'s dream of global democracy on the one side, and Kang's defense of the Imperial system during the Revolution on the other; and the role of religion, which Kang in the *Datong Shu* viewed as an obstacle to the attainment of Supreme Peace, yet saw as a useful tool for legitimacy in the Reform years. In analysing some of the major themes conveyed by the book (from religious reform to socialism, from the praise of science to the view on democracy), I often try to adopt a "global intellectual" perspective, focusing on how the dynamics shaping the cultural history of the so-called long nineteenth century were refracted through Kang's works.

In the third part, finally, I turn to the legacy of the *Datong Shu* and of Kang's interpretation of Classicism in general. First I focus on the Communist and anti-Communist interpretations of Kang's socialism, and then I address the use of Kang's theories and/or suggestions in the most recent debates on Chinese identity and the role of China on the global stage.

PART 1

Roots

∴

CHAPTER 1

The Sage and the Unicorn
Confucian Progressivism and Esoteric Classicism

"Begin at the beginning," the King of Hearts advises Alice. Lewis Carroll's words, as simple as they seem, are always a valid methodological prompt, even when the matter in hand is the posthumous work of a Confucian philosopher. Unsurprisingly, the beginnings of the world of tomorrow envisioned in the *Datong Shu* are rooted in an intellectual legacy drawn from the past: Kang's teleological view of history—which makes him a participant of Koselleck's *Sattelzeit*, specifically in its Chinese version—is intertwined with his idealized portrait of Confucius the reformer. Linearity, although not stretched to the utopian dimensions of the Great Concord, was the framework for Kang's reforming agenda of 1898. But again we may ask: from where did Kang retrieve his portrait of Master Kong as an uncrowned king (*suwang* 素王), as a prophet urging intellectuals to abandon their passive acceptance of the status quo and to act *in* and *for* society?

Rather than being a late imperial extravagance or a desperate effort to adapt Confucianism to a new context dominated by Western intellectual, economic, and political forces, Kang's reformism, and its inherent utopianism, are deeply rooted—at least in Kang's own perception of his philosophical endeavour—in an authentically Chinese debate originating in the late imperial age. By this token, Kang Youwei is simply the last major figure in a long line of intellectuals who had questioned the late imperial orthodoxy and, often indirectly, the Qing political order. The so-called New Text School, an interpretive tradition of Chinese Classicism which had been consolidated during the eighteenth century thanks to the efforts of some prominent members of the local gentry in the Jiangnan region, was Kang's main source of inspiration for his Confucian agenda. The prophetic profile of Confucius and the use of *datong* as a political project was not a sudden invention by Kang. So our question then becomes: from where, in turn, did the New Text School draw its inspiration? What political and social issues did its proponents veil under some apparently innocuous philological quibbles? What were the School's premises and purposes? And why did Kang choose to affiliate himself—although in way that preserved significant autonomy, as will be argued in this chapter—to that lineage? In short: where does Kang Youwei's thought, which found its concluding form in the *Datong Shu*, really begin?

Lewis Carroll would have been delighted to discover that it begins—with a unicorn.

1 The Annals of Lu, from History to Prophecy

> Fourteenth year of Duke Ai. In the spring, a unicorn[1] was captured on an imperial hunt in the West.[2]

This reference to the year 481 BC is an extract from the *Annals of Lu*, or *Spring and Autumn*, which is, according to a venerable tradition, the only Confucian Classic actually written by the Master himself. As is well known, the *Annals* record events such as title accessions, marriages and deaths, military campaigns, diplomatic treaties and alliances, droughts, floods, and other notable happenings during the reign of twelve dukes of the State of Lu from 722 to 481 BC, all in slightly more than sixteen thousand words. Ostensibly a concise (and rather dull) succession of dates and facts—like the catching of the unicorn—during the Han dynasty, it later began to be interpreted as something more valuable and complex than a simple chronicle.

Prior to the consolidation of the Han intellectual milieu, Xunzi had defined the *Annals* as "laconic" indicating that in order to understand the text a teacher is needed (thus further validating the theory of its esoteric character which will be central to the New Text and to Kang himself); Mencius, meanwhile, had stressed the importance of the *Spring and Autumn* as the real key to access the true teaching of Confucius:

> When the world declined and the Way fell into obscurity, heresies and violences again arose. There were instances of regicides and parricides. Confucius was apprehensive and composed the Spring and Autumn. Strictly speaking, this is the emperor's prerogative. That is why Confucius said, 'Those who understand me, will do so through the Spring and Autumn; those who condemn me will also do so because of the Spring and Autumn.'[3]

And again:

> In ancient times Yu controlled the Flood and brought peace to the empire; the duke of Zhou subjugated the northern and southern barbarians,

---

1 The original term, *lin* 麟, stands for a horned deer, thus explaining why the word is also translated as "mystical deer" or—as in one of the quotations presented in this chapter—"fallow-deer." However, the presence of the horn and its mythical aura make "unicorn" a more evocative translation into Western languages.
2 《哀公十四年春，西狩獲麟》 *Chunqiu, Ai* 14.1.
3 Mengzi 3B.9, in D.C. Lau (ed.), *Mencius* (Middlesex: Penguin Books, 1976), 114.

drove away wild animals and brought security to the people; Confucius completed the Spring and Autumn and struck terror into the hearts of rebellious subjects and undutiful sons.[4]

The composition of the *Annals*, then, as interpreted by Mencius, was the response by Confucius to a comprehensive crisis of civilization. Historiography (or the registration of events) was therefore conceived as a *moral* and *political* act, characterized by its possession of a "transformative power"[5] which could grant the legitimacy to rule a civilized society. It was a depository of moral teachings, omens, or occult meanings, and consequently endowed with a *religious* dimension, familiar from the ancient sacral value of historical writing seen in the first Chinese dynasties.[6] The link between divination and commentary, explicit in another classic the *Book of Changes*, was manifest even in the more apparently innocuous and objective *Annals*. A philological examination of the *Chunqiu*, moreover, seems to confirm these assumptions: its echoing of ancient divination practices under the Shang is made even clearer "by the fact that many such events recorded in the Annals, such as eclipses, fires and floods, are construed as omens or portents."[7] And what omen could be more intriguing than the appearance of a unicorn in a forest?

Turning back to the *lin*, in the esoteric traditions of Chinese Classicism towards which the New Text School would later lean, this sign began to be interpreted as an omen signalling to Confucius that he would not inherit the mandate of Heaven. The unicorn was generally considered as an image of regality. Its capture, then, communicated the approach of difficult times, in which the teachings of the past were to be forgotten, leading to the dismantlement of the Zhou moral and political system. Confucius, informed of the ominous hunt, realized that the end of his own political project was approaching, and that he was doomed to be an "uncrowned king." Consequently, he would leave his secret message to posterity in the *Annals*, which were thereby the product more of an encoder than a recorder of historical facts. As Csikszentmihalyi puts it: "When Confucius realized that he lived in an age that would not recognize

---

4 Mengzi 3B.9, in Lau, *Mencius*, 115.
5 Sarah A. Queen, *From chronicle to Canon: the hermeneutics of the Spring and Autumn, according to Tung Chung-Shu* (Cambridge: Cambridge University Press, 1996), 121.
6 Jacques Gernet argues that the single entries of texts similar to the *Annals of Lu* were presented at the ancestral temple of Zhou rulers by the *dashi*, or grand scribe, with a clearly ceremonial function. See Jacques Gernet, *A History of Chinese Civilization*, translated by J.R. Foster and C. Hartman (Cambridge: Cambridge University Press, 1982), 84.
7 John B. Henderson, *Scripture, Canon, Commentary: A comparison of Confucian and Western exegesis* (Princeton NJ: Princeton University Press, 1991), 67.

his ability to rule, he used the historical records available to him as a key, adding, deleting and changing information so that when a future ruler compared the product of his editing against original records, a blueprint for government emerged."[8]

Following this intuition, then, from the fourth to the third century BC a number of master–disciple lineages started to "transform the Spring and Autumns from a terse historical chronicle to a text embodying the highest ideal of the Confucian tradition."[9] In particular, three interpretive schools emerged in the second century BC, all using a prevalently oral form of transmission, dating back to pre-Han times and later crystallized in written texts: the Gongyang, the Guliang, and the Zuo traditions. These three philosophical lineages contested the correct interpretation of the *Annals*, so "stimulating some of the most substantial doctrinal, political, cosmological and legal debates of the Han, as they competed for imperial patronage within the new empire."[10] The Gongyang School, claiming a direct link to the Master himself through his disciple Zi Xia, who would have transmitted the secret knowledge to the founder Gongyang Gao, established itself as home to the most robustly esoteric and eschatological method of reading the *Annals*. Inspired by the Mencian view of the chronicle of Lu as a powerful political legacy, the Gongyang scholars would fascinate and inspire intellectuals for centuries, granting the *Spring and Autumn* the status of a political depository of almost cosmological width: "For restoring order in chaotic times and effecting a return to what is correct, nothing comes closer than the Spring and Autumn," they argued.[11]

It is not surprising, then, that the most influential thinker under the most energetic ruler of the Han dynasty, would use such a powerful philosophical tool in order to establish a new and durable form of legitimacy for the imperial institutions.

Dong Zhongshu 董仲舒 (195–105 BC), who dominated intellectual life at the time of Emperor Wudi 武帝 (r. 140–87 BC) and is rightly considered one of the most influential thinkers of early imperial China, crafted the so-called Han Confucianism in order to systematize the impressive quantity of texts produced during the Warring States period and create a well-defined Canon. Dong devoted much of his lifelong scholarship to the study of the *Spring and Autumn*, adopting the Gongyang approach. His view was condensed into the

---

8   Mark Czikszentmihalyi, "Confucius and the Analects in the Han," in Bryan W. Van Norden (ed.), *Confucius and the Analects: New Essays* (Oxford: Oxford University Press, 2002: 134–162.), 142.
9   Queen, *From chronicle to Canon*, 115.
10 Ibid.
11 Gongyang Commentary to Duke Ai 14.1, quoted in Queen, *From chronicle to Canon*, 122.

well-known *Chunqiu Fanlu* 春秋繁露, *A String of Pearls from the Annals*, Dong's most famous and significant work.[12] Providing a "holistic way"[13] to interpret the Classics—and at the same time using extensive cross-references between the *Annals* and the *Odes* or the *Documents*, in a sort of comprehensive and hypertextual pattern[14]—Dong valued the chronicles of Lu not just as a historical account but as a textual device for exploring the past and anticipating the future: sharing Mencius' view, Dong was convinced that Confucius had set forth his ethical precepts through the judgments collected in the *Annals*: "The ruler of the State must not fail to study the Spring and Autumn," Dong warned.[15]

The aforementioned appearance of the unicorn in the forest is commented upon in *A String of Pearls* as a symbol bequeathed by Confucius to posterity with the aim to communicate his own global civilizing mission in a safe language:

> When a *lin* was captured in a hunt in the west, Confucius said: "My way has come to an end! My way has come to an end!" Three years later he was dead. From this omen we see that the sage knows the efficacy of Heaven's mandate and that there are situations in which one cannot escape his fate.[16]

The *String of Pearls* is not just an exegesis of the *Annals*'s entries, then, but a thorough reinterpretation of the Classics in moral and cosmological terms. Through his work Dong provided both a synthesis of and a new impulse to the earlier Gongyang tradition. Its philosophical value notwithstanding, Dong's ideological architecture served mainly as the effective basis of legitimacy for the re-centralizing phase of the mid Han dynasty. According to some scholars, the Gongyang definition of Confucius as an "uncrowned king" may constitute a political third way in the debate on the identity of the Empire, standing

---

12　The *Chunqiu Fanlu* might be, as convincingly argued by Sarah Queen, a later compilation by an anonymous compiler who lived some time between the third and sixth centuries, putting together both Dong's first-hand writings and other materials not authored by him. For a summary and analysis of the various chapters composing the *Chunqiu Fanlu*, see Queen, *From chronicle to Canon*, 69–112.

13　Queen, *From Chronicle to Canon*, 123. Anne Cheng also uses the term "holistic" with regard to Dong Zhongshu's philosophical synthesis in her *History of Chinese Thought*.

14　For an application of the hypertextual form to Chinese Classics, see Moeller's innovative study of the Daodejing, Hans-George Moeller, *The Philosophy of the Daodejing* (New York NY: Columbia University Press, 2006).

15　*Chunqiu Fanlu* 6/3b.9–4a.1, quoted and translated in Queen, *From chronicle to Canon*, 122.

16　Benjamin Elman, *Classicism, Politics, and Kinship: The Ch'ang-chou School of New Text Confucianism in Late Imperial China* (Berkeley CA: University of California Press, 1990).

between the two extremes of Qin legalism on one side and the uncritical acceptance of Zhou nostalgia on the other.[17]

2　The New Text School: Philology and Politics

Dong's prophetic view of Confucius's teachings was progressively dismissed in the following centuries, simultaneous with the disintegration of the Han imperial order. Within a millennium, the holistic cosmology of Dong Zhongshu would be superseded by a new orthodoxy. Later defined as Song Neo-Confucianism,[18] the ideology crafted by Zhu Xi and his followers under the name of Dao Learning emerged as a consistently different—and more rational, we might say—approach to Classicism, in response to a new social and political context. Dismissed and discarded, the old esoteric reading of the Confucian Canon was not forgotten, however, but remained behind the curtain of Chinese orthodoxy. Silently, it rose again to prominence more than five centuries later, under the label of "New Text School," at a time when China (during the end of the eighteenth century, thus not yet impacted upon by the West) was again experimenting with deep social and political transformation. Turning once more to Reinhart Koselleck's concept of *Sattelzeit*, we might detect some "modern" forces at work at the same time, both in Europe and in China. Why they bloomed in Europe and were suffocated (or perhaps only retarded) in China might be an interesting way to approach the emergence of the New Text School in the eighteenth century. At that time, the return to the philosophical stage of the Gongyang tradition was evidently connected to the efforts of some prominent gentry lineages in the Jiangnan region—the economic core of the Empire—who were striving to reaffirm their political right to take part in the administration of China under Manchu rule.

As explained by Philip Kuhn in his study on the origins of the modern Chinese State, and most importantly in the extensive research undertaken by Benjamin Elman, the re-emergence of such a heterodox tradition in the intellectual debates of the time was not limited to its purely cultural interest (as Dong's synthesis had been before them). In their attack on the consolidated Old Text tradition, which had embodied the imperial orthodoxy since the Song redefinition of the Tradition, the New Text scholars were using philology

---

17　Queen, *From chronicle to Canon*, 185.
18　It must be remembered that "neo-Confucianism" is a considerably "free" Western translation of the philosophical tradition known in China as the School of the Principle (*Lixue*, 理学).

as a political weapon. The real concern for the Jiangnan literati was less the falsification of the Classics at the time of Wang Mang the usurper (r. 9–25 CE)—which Kang Youwei himself would strongly denounce in one of his first important works (*A Study of the Xin Forgeries* 新學偽經考 1896), thus gaining him fame as a "Chinese Luther"—than the manifestation of the gentry's disaffection with orthodoxy in general and with the Qing institutions in particular, especially after the credibility of the imperial authorities had been severely buffeted by the breaking of the Heshen scandal.[19]

Then, in a context of tension and distrust, the unicorn was spotted again. Song Xiangfeng 宋翔鳳 (1776–1860), a prominent New Text scholar, whose mother was a member of the prestigious Zhuang lineage of Changzhou, thus comments upon the catch as follows:[20]

> Why was this entry made? In order to record an extraordinary event. What was extraordinary in this? It was not an animal of the central states. Who was the one who hunted it? Someone who gathered firewood. One who gathers firewood is a man of mean position. Why does the text use the term "hunt" in this context? In order to magnify the event. Why magnify it? It was magnified on account of the capture of the *lin*. Why so? The *lin* is a benevolent animal. When there is a true king, it appears. When there is no true king, it does not appear. Someone informed Confucius saying: "There is a fallow-deer and it is horned!" Confucius said: "For whose sake has it come?" He turned his sleeve and wiped his face. His tears wet his robe. When Yan Yuan died, the master said: "Alas! Heaven has caused me this loss." When Zi Lu died, the master said: "Alas! Heaven is cutting me off!" When a *lin* was captured in a hunt in the west, Confucius said: "My way has come to an end!"[21]

The *Chunqiu weiyan kongtu* 春秋微言孔圖, *A Confucian Chart Explaining the Secrets of the Annals*, one of the Han apocrypha which had served as a

---

[19] Heshen 和珅 (1746–1799), a member of the imperial guard, was the favourite of Emperor Qianlong. During the last years of the latter's long reign, he had managed to establish an "empire-wide net of corruption" which had granted him a personal wealth surpassing the imperial coffers. On the political consequences of the scandal see Kuhn 2002: 114–115. For an evaluation of its significance in the decline of the Qing also see Pamela Kyle Crossley, *The Wobbling Pivot. China since 1800: an interpretive history* (Chichester: Wiley-Blackwell, 2010:), 36–7.

[20] See below note 24.

[21] Song Xianfeng, *Lunyu shuoyi*, 389.1b, quoted in Elman, *Classicism, Politics, and Kinship*, 209.

source of inspiration for the New Text scholars (Song Xiangfeng included), added an even more esoteric tone to the passage, which attains an almost apocalyptic pitch:

> After the *lin* was caught, Heaven rained blood which formed into writing on the main gate of the capital of Lu, and which said: 'Quickly prepare laws, for the sage Confucius will die; the Zhou will be destroyed; a comet will appear from the east. The government of the Qin will arise and will suddenly destroy the literary arts. But though the written records will then be dispersed, the teachings of Confucius will not be interrupted.'[22]

This uninterrupted secret teaching of Confucius, embodied by the unicorn coming among men to announce the approach of a political crisis, is here used as the proxy for a political vision based on virtue and wisdom, rather than on the monopoly of violence. According to what both Elman and Kuhn argue for in their conclusions, the emergence of the New Text School conceals an energetic "call to action" against the decline of Qing centralism, following the Heshen scandal. Ironically, though, we might observe some centuries later that Dong's *centralizing* cosmology was serving as a source of inspiration for a number of *centrifugal* intellectual and political forces which were increasingly striving with the Court in the name of a wider involvement of the scholar-officials both at a local and a central level in the administration of the Empire. And ironically, they would be finally used by Kang Youwei as the justification for a project of re-centralization of the collapsing monarchical institutions.

That blurred boundary between philology and philosophy (to cite again Benjamin Elman's seminal book) is characteristic of the New Text School: its advocates were imbued with a "compelling, voluntaristic vision of human responsibility for upholding the universal standards of heaven (discovered by the sages)."[23] Zhuang Cunyu[24] and his fellows, following the path indicated

---

22 Quoted in Elman, *Classicism, Politics, and Kinship*, 209–10.
23 Elman, *Classicism, Politics, and Kinship*, 146.
24 Among the many New Text scholars of late eighteenth century, Zhuang Cunyu 庄村与 (1719–1788) was possibly the most influential. His family, established in Changzhou but claiming a Northern origin stretching back to the Song, constituted one of the most powerful lineages in the area, providing an outstanding number of degree holders throughout the Qing period. After earning the *jinshi* in 1745, Cunyu moved to Beijing to serve as a member of the Grand Secretariat. In 1786 he left the capital because of his clash with the Heshen clique and made his return to Changzhou, committing the rest of his life to textual studies. Following the pioneers of the *kaozheng* tradition like Yang Sheng, Hao Jing, Yao Jiheng, or his fellow Yangzhou resident Yang Fangda, Zhuang devoted his entire life to the exegesis of the Classics. In his hands, though, the philological approach of his

by the Gongyang commentators, looked through the Classics to find a set of symbolic messages to easily convey a strong moral judgment and build a theoretical basis for political action. And those philosophical tools retrieved from esoteric Confucianism included something that would become central to Kang's thought, namely an evolutionary and linear vision of history: thus Gong Zichen 龔自珍 (1792–1841), another New Text champion whose work would deeply influence Kang, criticized the Qing's failure to respond to internal and external pressures by using the very same theory of the Three Ages by which the fate of mankind is to progress *towards* (and not move away *from*) a Golden Age. The timeline of the *Datong Shu* was ready. The Age of Great Concord, which would follow the Age of Chaos and the Age of Rising Equality, was in Gong's mind the deadline for political action. This may suggest that a linear vision of history had already emerged out of the Chinese Classical tradition, prior to any significant impact by Western theories; if so, it is to be considered as a fully indigenous philosophical mutation more than a bland importation.[25] In this light, linearity does not seem to emerge as linked necessarily to the development of the Nation, as bespoken by Kang's own anti-nationalist universalism. As we pointed out above, scholars like Philip Kuhn and Benjamin Elman have convincingly described the concrete political implications of the eighteenth- and nineteenth-century New Text speculations as expressing mainly domestic dynamics. Moreover, some recent tendencies in global and global intellectual history seem to suggest that the gradual emergence of a linear interpretation of history and its consequences in terms of political theories were part of the same global trends (historicization, identity-building processes, the emergence of modern Statism etc.), manifesting in slightly different times and with different results.[26] The Koselleckian concept of *Sattelzeit* can be expanded as a global category, as long as different paces and different "politicizations" are recognized in each specific context.

The mixture of historical linearity, philosophical heterodoxy, political activism, and even messianic tendencies—sometimes concealed, sometimes fully visible—elaborated by the New Text scholars will provide a formidable ideological platform for Kang. Certainly, the linearity proposed by the New Text scholars was not as explicit as Kang's: in their understanding, there is no

---

predecessors assumed a fully political dimension, voicing his discontent with the Court. His most significant work is the *Chunqiu zhengci*, a "correct interpretation of the Annals" which is a clear homage to the Gongyang tradition. For an extensive survey on Zhuang Cunyu's life and works, see Elman, *Classicism, Politics, and Kinship*, 92–156.

25 See Kwong, "The Rise of the linear perspective."
26 See for example Jürgen Osterhammel, *The Transformation of the World. A Global History of the Nineteenth Century*, (Princeton NJ: Princeton University Press, 2014).

assurance of eternity, for the age of Supreme Equality might easily collapse again into an age of Chaos, thus starting again the (natural) cycle of history. In Kang, however, the cyclical element gives way to a completely linear projection of change: once reached, the *datong* will be perpetually preserved. The New Text core heritage was thus shaped and more clearly directed through the—direct or indirect—contact with Western intellectual currents. Yan Fu's *Tianyan lun* 天演論, published after the first Sino-Japanese war, being the spearhead for the diffusion of knowledge of Western natural science (which was called in late Qing *gezhi xue* 格致學), especially biology and stratigraphy, played a key role in helping Kang Youwei and Liang Qichao form their linear vision of history.

The "politicization" of linearity is at play both in Kang's attempts to save China from collapse in 1898 and in the global prophecy of a peaceful future on display in the *Datong Shu*; linearity thus appears as a *fil rouge* running through his production. Whereas Zhuang Cunyu and his fellow scholars had used the Gongyang annotations as "the chief tools left from the early empire that could be used to reconstruct the Han 'meaning' of the Annals," and thereby to affirm their right to participate in imperial politics, Kang Youwei would transform those instances into a much more powerful ideological weapon, potentially disrupting the whole Confucian traditional social and political architecture. Zhuang and his followers had "left unconsidered how Gongyang Confucianism would later apply to New Text controversies that he himself only vaguely perceived."[27] In other words, "the conservative intent behind his emphasis in the late eighteenth century on the *Gongyang zhuan* to counter the deleterious effects of the Heshen era is analytically distinct from the more radical consequences of full-blown New Text Confucianism in the early nineteenth century."[28] The political appeals of the Jiangnan literati for the reopening of the *yanlu* 言路, literally the "path of speech," veiling their claim for more representation in the decision-making processes at the imperial level under the philological confrontation between New and Old Text, were substantially different from the much more radical conclusions (both in political and philosophical terms) that their vision of history and power would produce in Kang Youwei's final elaboration.

This short survey of a significant, and yet often overlooked, part of Chinese Classicism presents Kang Youwei not as the lonely creator of an unprecedented form of Confucianism emerging out of nowhere in the context of the late nineteenth century—or worse, originating from some abrupt Western shock—but

---

27   Elman, *Classicism, Politics, and Kinship*, 183.
28   *Ibid.*

as the last interpreter, albeit in his own terms autonomous and unorthodox, of a venerable tradition stretching from Mencius to Dong Zhongshu and then resumed by the New Text school of Changzhou.

A last passage remains to be examined: how did Kang become part of this philosophical lineage, given the fact that he was raised in the far south of the Empire, relatively far from the Jiangnan region? The link connecting the Changzhou lineages of the New Text and Kang, synthetically presented thereafter, is an interesting and significant piece of the complex mosaic of intellectual (and political) life in nineteenth-century China.

3 Kang in the Sea of Learning

The New Text School, woven in Changzhou and in the Jiangnan region by the Zhuang and the Liu lineage (entwined by a tradition of intermarriage) was not just a local phenomenon: it was disseminated in other parts of the Empire thanks to the usual mobility of the literati. In Guangdong, a New Text "branch" had been established by a prominent member of the Jiangnan gentry: this was Ruan Yuan 阮元 (1764–1849, *jinshi* 1789), a native of Yangzhou who had served in Guangzhou as governor general of Liangguang from 1817 to 1826. Shortly after his arrival in Guangzhou, Ruan showed his deep concern for the patronage of scholarship; his curriculum included previous service as governor of Zhejiang (where he had established the House for the Study of the Essence of the Classics, *Gujingjingshe* 詁經精舍) and in Jiangxi where, adhering to his Han-studies formation, he had sponsored the reprinting of a collection of pre-Song classical exegeses.[29] The most important point in his literary agenda resulted in the foundation of the Hall of the Sea of Learning, *Xuehaitang* 學海堂, inaugurated in 1821 in Guangzhou and soon to become the cradle of a robust tradition of Han learning in the remote south of the Empire.[30] Ruan Yuan's legacy is thus strong enough to explain Kang Youwei's early inclination toward Han learning. It must be said, though, that it was not the only interpretive tradition found in the area: before embracing Han learning, Kang, together with Jian Chaoliang, had been one of the two most famous students of Zhu Ciqi, a

---

29 Steven B. Miles, *The Sea of Learning: Mobility and Identity in Nineteenth-Century Guangzhou* (Cambridge MA: Harvard University Press, 2006), 91–2. A detailed biography of Ruan Yuan can also be found in Betty Wei, *Ruan Yuan, 1764–1849: The Life and Work of a Major Scholar-official in Nineteenth Century China Before the Opium War* (Hong Kong: Hong Kong University Press, 2006.).

30 For an analysis of the Xuehiatang curriculum and of its most notable scholars, see Miles, *The Sea of Learning*, 94–111.

scholar who had been conducting lectures on the Zhu lineage on the School of the Ritual Hill in Guangdong since 1857. Under Zhu, Kang was instructed in the typically Qing philological research method *kaozheng* 考証, using both the Han and Song interpretive traditions of the Classics until he left the school in 1879 with juvenile furor, embracing a fully Han-learning approach to the Classics (though he would later look back fondly on his years there).[31]

Steven Miles points out that Han studies were much more strongly rooted in the urban context of Guangzhou than in the rural Enclosure District where Kang's family resided: elites in a big city were probably more eager to question imperial orthodoxy than their counterparts in the countryside. With regard to this aspect, in the mutation of the New Text School from the Jiangnan lineages in the early Qing to the Hundred Days experience, Kang's reformist/utopian elaboration also manifests an interesting social pattern. As mentioned earlier, the New Text School had flourished in the eighteenth century as a reaction by the local elites to their estrangement from central political decision-making processes. Later, through Ruan Yuan's efforts, these instances would migrate to a more peripheral setting, Guangdong. There, the unorthodox interpretation of Classicism did not find a *regional* and *localist* expression—possibly claiming a sort of "federalist" disruption of the Empire. Rather, the ideological material provided by the New School was used by Kang Youwei, a member of the far-southern rural gentry, not to discuss the necessity of a strong central imperial institution, but to reform and eventually strengthen it, and to concoct a *global* identity for the Chinese people (fully expressed in the *Datong Shu*) instead of praising local sentiments.

But the *Xuehaitang* could not fully satisfy Kang's desire for innovation: although clearly influenced by the Sea of Learning and, after his experience with Zhu, personally instructed by teachers formed in that academy, Kang passed through a rebellious period of isolation and meditation in the early 1880s, after which he eventually established his own school and curriculum, offering a much more "extremist" option for young students in the area.[32] At this point Kang would finally embrace the New Text as it had been spread into Guangdong from the Jiangzi valley through Hunan by Dai Wang (1837–1873) and, most importantly for Kang's intellectual biography, by the Hunanese Wang Kaiyun 王闿運 (1833–1916). The latter was the teacher of Liao Ping 廖平 (1852–1932), whose works Kang read in 1884. The degree of Kang's indebtedness to Liao is still a matter of debate, ranging from accusations of "plagiarism"

---

31   Miles, *The Sea of Learning*, 262–3.
32   Liang Qichao, Kang's most famous pupil, had enrolled at the Xuehaitang in 1887, then moved to Kang's Thousand Tree Cottage Hall in 1891. See "Liang Qichao" in Antonio S. Cua (ed), *The Encyclopedia of Chinese Philosophy* (London: Routledge, 2003).

to the recognition of a "parallel development"—a riddle not facilitated by Kang's difficulty in acknowledging his sources or his inspirations.[33] Certainly, as pointed out by Wang Young-tsu, it is hard to interpret Kang's intellectual development within Confucianism as a pure matter of "scholarship": he was in search of a political ideology, and he found in the Gongyang tradition the most viable philosophical and hermeneutical foundation for his claims, and his conversion to the New Text School should be framed within this exigence.

The discourse on the prophetical role of Confucius, found in the Gongyang interpretation of the *Annals*, provided Kang with a philosophical (and almost religious) justification for an incisive political activism to re-legitimate an ailing Empire; he also used the "evolutionary" vision of history encoded in the esoteric Confucianism as the basis for his description of the Age of Great Concord, through a chronological road map articulated around the gradual emergence of the principles of Unity *tong* 同, and Equality *ping* 平. This teleological and optimistic view of history, reflecting Kang's "zestful outlook on life,"[34] by which the sage has the moral duty to anticipate the future in order to accelerate its advent, can be considered as a force underlying Kang's reforms and utopianism simultaneously. The connection between the two apparently diverging perspectives (Chinese monarchy and universal Republic) is to be found in Kang's philosophy of history. If change is a universal and natural mechanism (and in this sense the legacy of the *Book of Changes* is fully in play), then "doing politics" means understanding Time and helping it proceed without obstructions. A Chinese monarchical State is both the result of Time and will, in due course, be an obstacle that must be overcome in progressing toward the establishment of a wider (and better) political order. This is no philosophical contradiction, but rather a pragmatic view of political action which includes a utopian outcome.

To further clarify how the linear vision of human history presented by Kang was fully rooted in his relationship to the Classics, rather than being a Western import or a rushed reaction to sudden external threats, it is now time to present some of Kang's own writings on the issue.

4 Confucius as a Prophet: Tradition, Evolution, and Empathy

A relatively quick analysis of some texts written by Kang Youwei in the years preceding the Hundred Days reforms will shed some light on how the aforementioned philosophical legacy of the Gongyang and the New Text School was

---

33 See Wong, *Beyond Confucian China*.
34 Hsiao, *A Modern China and a New World*, 28.

used to shape the reformer's own system of thought. Apparently distant from the cosmic projection of the *Book of Great Concord*, these philosophical and philological talks—which belong to the seminal period between the establishment of Kang's school in Guangdong and the dramatic events of 1898—are on the contrary a useful indicator of the Confucian roots of the *Datong Shu*.

The first text is an extract from *A Study on Dong Zhongshu's Spring and Autumn* 春秋懂氏學, printed in 1897 by Kang's brother's publishing house together with the well-known *Confucius as a Reformer*. This work, albeit relatively unknown, plays an important role in the definition of Kang's theoretical system and contains the first articulation of his philosophy of history as the evolution of mankind through the so-called Three Ages.[35] Throughout the eight books of the *Study*, Kang crowns Dong and the Gongyang tradition as the true heir to Confucius; most importantly, he uses Dong's comments to find "an open space for the interpretation" of the Classics in his own terms.[36]

In the preface to the *Study*, here translated in its entirety, Kang makes an explicit "profession of faith" to the Gongyang tradition and pays homage to his intellectual pantheon, placing himself in continuity with the New Text scholars of Jiangnan and with their Han predecessors. Like them, he professes his intention to behave, in his words, like a "politically active sage."

> If we are not feathered, horned or clawed beasts, then we must behave according to the Way; to follow it, we must learn it. Those who don't learn the Way, may be considered as non-humans. Those who don't follow it, may be called savages. But where does the Way stem from? It comes from the Sages. And who do the Sages follow? They follow Confucius. And where is the Way of Confucius contained? In the Six Classics.
>
> The Six Classics, so beaming and beautiful, so vast and rich: how can they be synthesized? Their essence resides in the Annals. The Four Books, and the Odes, Documents, Rites and Music—which serve as the official canon—are also enclosed there. And who affirmed it? Mencius. He argued that Yu and Tang, Wen, Wu and the Duke of Zhou, and even Confucius himself, they all venerated no other book more than the Spring and Autumn.

---

35 For an in-depth analysis of the *Study*, see Li Zonggui, *Chuantong yu xiandai zhi jian* 传统与现代之间 (Beijing: Beijing Shifan Daxue Chubanshe, 2011) (English translation, *Between Tradition and Modernity: Philosophical Reflections on the Modernization of Chinese Culture*, Oxford: Chartridge Books, 2014).

36 Li, *Between tradition and modernity*, 332.

Where do the Three Commentaries on the Annals come from? They come from the Gongyang School. Who said this? Mencius. He thus lectured on the Annals: "Its clients were Duke Huan of Qi and Duke Wen of Jin,[37] it is written like a history, but its meaning is encrypted." The Zuo Commentary analyses the facts as a historical text, but it has nothing to do with the Way of Confucius; only the Gongyang Commentary did actually grasp the true meaning of the Annals. Talking about the Annals, Mencius once said: "They were made by Heaven." Now, while the Guliang Commentary does not shed light on the essence of the Annals, because it hands down the Way of Confucius but does not illuminate it, the Gongyang Commentary is the only one that clarifies the theory of the "uncrowned king": in fact, it represents the true transmission of the Annals.

The Annals contain thousands of words, their prescriptions are so numerous, their principles are so luminous, and there have been more than two hundred efforts to interpret the uncountable teachings of Confucius! Confused by so many strange and different theories, who shall we trust? According to the Wefts, Confucius said: "My books are confused, Dong will unravel them." And what was confused, was then ordered. So Sima Qian wrote: "When the Han prospered, Dong Zhongshu was the only one to shed light on the Annals." Two prominent Han scholars of the Gongyang School—Yan Pengzu[38] and Yan Anle—simply followed his studies. Liu Xiang[39] defined Dong Zhongshu as an "imperial assistant," not inferior to Yi and Lü.[40] Even Liu Xin, whose forgeries constituted a serious blow to the Gongyang tradition, defined Dong as the "leader of the Classicists." In Zhu Xi's discussion on the "great personalities following the Three Dynasties," Dong is referred to as the only "pure Classicist" able to transmit the teachings in the clearest possible way, the only one

---

37 Two of the Five Hegemons of the Spring and Autumn period.
38 Yan Pengzu is remembered for having presented the Gongyang reading of the *Annals* during a debate on the true meaning of the Classics organized by Emperor Xuan of the Han in 51 BCE. See Li, *Between tradition and modernity*, 243–44.
39 Liu Xiang 刘向 (77–76 BCE) was a government official and prolific author of the Han dynasty. Famous for his Biographies of Exemplary Women (*Lienü zhuan* 列女传) he also compiled the first catalogue of the imperial library. He was linked to the Guliang tradition.
40 Yi and Lü are mentioned as exemplary officials in the Documents. See Shu IV 3.8, in James Legge, *Li Chi: Book of Rites. An encyclopedia of ancient ceremonial usages, religious creeds, and social institutions* (New Hyde Park NY: University Books [1967], originally published in 1885).

who attained to the pre-Qin tradition: to those who intend to study the Gongyang, then, following Dong will suffice.

However, even among the Gongyang School's texts there are many strange and diverse theories, some of them so dubious that they made me suspicious in the past. But reading the String of Pearls—where you see Confucius reforming the Zhou, renewing the monarchy, and condensing the essence of the Three Dynasties as a treasure stored for people to discover it, while the Way progresses unceasingly—can we really consider Dong as foolish, and incapable of understanding? When Dong explains the *tianxia* how can we not trust him?

I highly praise Dong's study as having no equal among today's scholars, nor among the Zhou and Qin texts, for his search for the roots of the world, his understanding of the principles of yin and yang, his intuition of the origins of life, his vicinity to the source of the creations of the sages. He spread the laws, clarified the sense of life and firmly established benevolence and empathy, linking Heaven and man: nothing can match this!

The Annals are trusted as the sacred text of Classicism. And great sages like Mencius or Xunzi are the giants of Classicism, because they have grasped the roots of Confucius's teachings. Someone could say: The strange and abstruse words of Dong's String of Pearls have nothing to do with them! The knowledge of Dong does not reach that of Mencius or Xunzi! The fact, though, is that the latter have transmitted the Master's direct teachings, which is not Dong's case. As Wang Zhongren[41] said: "The knowledge of King Wen passed to Confucius; the knowledge of Confucius passed to Dong Zhongshu." Dong's theory surpasses Mengzi and Xunzi; in fact there is nothing comparable to it in the entire production of Classicists. If we examine Dong, we can give a fresh look to Master Kong's great teachings! And yet, his books have not been read in schools for a long time; they were discarded, manipulated, ruined, abandoned with no rope nor bridge to reach them.

After the emergence of the Ancient Text, and later with the establishment of the Song Confucianism, Dong's philosophy was considered as an antiquated theory, as coming from a "foreign" country, as an absurdity coming from an age of different customs and habits, whose fundamentals are now difficult to understand; two thousand years are like the

---

41 Courtesy name of Wang Chong 王充 (27–97) a prominent philosopher of the Eastern Han period, known for his rational approach to tradition, well displayed in the *Lunheng*, his major work.

Pacific Ocean, and with no vessel to sail it they are a disorienting vastness, shocking and sad as the vision of drifting sand.

Ling Shu's appearance in Jiangsu, then, was like a joyful light in darkness: he drained the river of words and unveiled their meaning.[42] Like a savage entering in a library, or a deaf man listening to Heaven again, like someone who is blessed to see a glowing jade, one cannot spend enough words of praise for his work.

Through Dong Zhongshu, the Gongyang Commentaries are explained; through the Gongyang, the Annals are explained; through the Annals, the Six Classics are explained and they reveal the roots of the Way of Confucius: what a beautiful architecture it is! Limitless and full of secret wonders, like a thousand temples one inside the other, like a palace made of scrolls, like a melody sung by the Immortals! One can study it again and again, exhausting one's own efforts, and yet one will not master it! And isn't it true that a gentleman finds his pleasure in good study and deep reflection?

This preface was written by Kang Youwei of Nanhai, on the first day of the tenth month of the 23rd year of Guangxu era, Qing dynasty, the year 2448 since the birth of Confucius.[43]

---

42 Kang refers here to Ling Shu, uncle and mentor of Liu Wenqi, prominent scholar of the New Text School in Changzhou, author of *Gongyang wenda* (Questions and Answers on the Gongyang Commentary). The Liu lineage was linked by intermarriage to the Zhuangs. See Elman, *Classicism, Politics, and Kinship*, 246. Also see above note 40.

43 *Kang Youwei zhenglunji*: 195–197. My translation. Original text: 苟非毛羽爪角之倫，有所行，必有道焉；有所效，必有教焉。無教者，謂之禽獸；無道者，謂之野人。道教何從？從聖人；聖人何從？從孔子；孔子之道何在？在六經；六經粲然深美，浩然繁博，將何統乎？　統一於春秋；詩書禮樂並立學官，統於春秋，有據乎？拘於孟子；孟子述禹、湯、文、武、周公而及孔子，不及其他書，惟尊春秋。春秋三傳何從乎？從公羊氏；有據乎？拘於孟子。孟子發春秋之學曰："其事則齊桓、晉文，其文則史，其義則丘取之矣。"左傳詳文於事，是史也，於孔子之道無於焉，惟公羊獨詳春秋之義。孟子述春秋之學曰："春秋，天子之事也。"谷梁傳不明春秋王義，傳孔子之道而不光焉。惟公羊詳素王改制之義，故春秋之傳在公羊也。春秋文成數萬，其旨數千，大義烺烺，然僅二百余，脫略甚矣，安能見孔子數千之大旨哉！又多非常異義可怪之論，意者不足傳信乎？春秋緯："孔子曰：亂我書者，董仲舒。"亂者，理也。太史公曰："漢興，唯董生明於春秋，兩漢博士公羊家嚴彭祖、顏安樂皆其后學。"　劉向稱董仲舒為王者之佐，雖伊、呂無以加，即劉歆作偽，力攻公羊，亦稱為群儒首。朱子論三代下人物，獨推董生為醇儒，其傳師說最詳，其去先秦不遠，然則欲學公羊者，舍董生安歸。雖然，公羊家多非常異義可怪之說，輒疑異之，吾昔亦疑怪之。及讀繁露，則孔子改制變周，以春秋當新王，王魯紲杞，以夏、殷、周為三統，如探家人筐篋，日道不休，董子何所樂而誕謾是，董子豈愚而不知辯是。然而董子舉以告天下則是，豈不可用心哉！吾以董子學推之，今學家說而莫不同，以董子說推之，周秦之書

The Annals of Lu, the Gongyang Commentaries, Dong Zhongshu, and the New Text School of Jiangnan are the foundations of Kang's esoteric tradition (which is the "orthodox" one, in his eyes). Their interaction with cogent political questions (legitimacy, representation, "modernity") will pave the path towards the 1898 Reforms and the *Datong Shu*.

Even more significant to the understanding of Kang's philosophical elaboration are the lectures he gave to his students in Guangdong between 1891 and 1896 in his own academy. Collected into the *Wanmu caotang kousho* 萬木草堂口說, *Instructions from the Hall of the Thousand Trees Cottage*, these lessons, albeit sketchy and sometimes chaotic as students' transcriptions can be, convey Kang's view of Chinese tradition as it was being elaborated in the years prior to his active involvement in Beijing politics. The following text, in particular, is eloquently entitled "Confucius as a Reformer": in this lecture, Kang anticipates and summarizes the content of his major book, published with the same title one year later.

> The Six Classics were all compiled by Confucius. Odes, Documents, Rites, and Music were produced when he was young. The Book of Changes and the Annals, in his late years.
>
> The Annals transmit human facts, while the Book of Changes introduces the Way of Heaven, therefore the Invariable Mean must be commented upon on these premises. The Six Classics are enlightened by the Annals.
>
> Xunzi taught the Guliang Commentary, while Mencius transmitted the Gongyang. Gongming Yi was the pupil of Zi Xia and must have

---

而無不同。若其探本天元，著達陰陽，明人物生生之始，推聖人制作之源，揚綱紀，白性命，本仁誼，貫天人，本數末度，莫不兼運。信乎明於春秋為群儒宗也。然大賢如孟、荀，為孔門龍象，求得孔子立制之本，如繁露之微言，奧義不可得焉。董生道不高於孟、荀，何以能此？然則是皆孔子口說之所傳，而非董子之為之也。善乎王仲任之言曰："文王之文，傳於孔子；孔子之文，傳於仲舒。"故所發言軼荀超孟，實為儒學群書之所無。若微董生，安從復窺孔子之大道哉！顧是書久誦於學官，闕奪百出，如臨絕壑崩崖，無組索，無鐵梁，惟有廢然而返。又自古學變后，今為宋儒之學，視董生舊說，如游異國，語言不解，風俗服食宮室皆殊絕，或不求其本而妄議之，故二千年來遂如泛太平洋而無輪艦，適瀚海而無鄉導，徒爾爾向若而驚，望流沙而嘆，人從幾絕。近惟得江都凌氏曙為空谷足音，似人而喜，然緣文疏以，如野人入冊府，聾者之聽鈞天，駭瑋麗，不能贊一辭也。況於條舉以告人哉！不量竅啟，數宗廟百官之美，因董子以通公羊，因公羊以通春秋，因春秋以通六經，而窺孔子之道本，昧昧思之，如圖建章之宮，寫霓裳之曲，豈不涯哉！庶俾學者亦竭其鑽仰止愚雲爾。好學深思之君子，其亦樂道之歟？孔子生二千四百十八年，為有清光緒二十三年十月朔日，南海康有為廣復記。

been a contemporary of Zi Si, since he often quotes King Wen. For example, in the Gongyang we can read: "What is the name of the ruler? It is King Wen."

Gongming Yi was the grandmaster of the Gongyang tradition. Gongming stands for Gongyang, because—as stated by the Dictionary of Names in the Explanation of the Six Classics—"*ming*, *meng* and *yang* are homophones." In *Mozi*, the Gongmeng is mentioned: it stands for Gongyang. Lord Gongyang was a contemporary of Mozi and instructed him in the great principles, that's why Mozi is so close to his doctrines; Mencius held Gongyang's words in such great esteem that he defined the Annals as "made by a Son of Heaven." All the paths lead to the Gongyang, then. […] Confucian reformism is rooted in Heaven. The Original Principle is where the *qi* begins. The Original governs Heaven, Heaven governs the Prince, the Prince governs the people. Master Zeng said: "The sky does not have two suns, the people do not have two kings, the mourner does not have two worries." Mengzi's teachings were established in the One, too. Xunzi's theories were also established in the One, therefore Li Si—who was his disciple—served Qin and made the great unification possible. The Way of Earth and Heaven originates from the One; the Way of the living beings originates from the Two. The Book of Changes speaks of life, and for life to appear, Two is a necessary precondition; in this regard, the Book of Changes talks extensively of yin and yang. The Annals speak of politics, politics are governed by the One; in this regard the Annals magnify universal rule.[44]

[…] The Prince and the Sage are the foundations of a good government. […] The Analects address Confucian virtues, but they do not speak of reforms. Confucius's reforms, though, can be found in the Six Classics. The Book of Changes is considered as having been written by the Three Sages, by Yu or by King Wen, but actually it was Confucius's work. All the Six Classics are Confucius's work, in fact. Even the *Lun Heng* acknowledges that the Documents were compiled by Confucius. The *Zhuangzi* affirms that Confucius translated the Twelve Classics and presented them to Laozi: in fact he is talking about the Six Classics and the Six Wefts. Much of Confucius' verbal teaching is contained in the Wefts. […]

44　The term "magnification of universal rule" (大一统) was widely used by Dong Zhonghsu and He Xiu in their interpretation of the *Annals* and was later elaborated by the Song scholar Ouyang Xiu. See Elman, *Classicism, Politics, and Kinship*, 154.

Why are the Guliang and the Gongyang commentaries so different? Because Confucius transmitted many instructions and not each one of them was accurately transcribed. [...]

Any tradition can only come out from Confucius. [...] Look from the eight directions and the four sides and then you will always see the centre; look from any place at any time and then you will see Confucius. [...] Confucius's internal institutions are based on the respect for the father; Confucius's external institutions are based on the well-field system. [...] Before the Annals, ministers were appointed by the ruler; two thousand years later, they are elected: this is Confucius's institutional model. [...] Confucius wrote the Wefts, Liu Xin wrote the Omens; later, people criticized both works together [as if they were the same thing], and that was a big mistake.[45] The Lords of Yansheng[46] should wear once more their noble attire, and enjoy a high consultative authority. [...]

Mencius said: "The Three Dynasties lost the world as they lost benevolence." And again: "When the memory of the Kings faded, the Odes were forgotten; when the Odes where forgotten, then the Annals were compiled." We can say that after the Zhou were forgotten, Confucius continued their tradition through the Annals. [...]

Classicism (*Ru*) is the name of the tradition specially crafted by Confucius.[47] His verbal transmissions were transcribed in the Analects. However, although we define Classicism as a "tradition," among its members there are scholars big and small, refined and vulgar, expert and stupid, pedantic, limited: that's why there is a difference between a gentleman and a petty man. [...]

As stated by the *Huainanzi*, "the Shang transformed the Xia, the Zhou transformed the Shang and the Annals transformed the Zhou." The rites of the three dynasties were different, but the Annals synthesized them. [...] The whole meaning of the Annals is stored in an oral transmission;

---

45 Liu Xin, the presumed author of the Old Text forgeries during the Wang Mang era (8–25), compiled a collection of Auguries, *Chenwei* 谶纬, based on the Wefts. In Kang's opinion this caused the lack of credibility suffered by the Confucian Apocrypha in the following centuries.

46 This is the title assigned to the descendants of Confucius.

47 This passage is interesting with regard to the question of the translation of *ru* 儒: the original term which we render as "Confucianism" should be better translated as "Classicism." The Western translation, though, seems a perfect fit for Kang's interpretation, given the centrality of the Master in his own view of Classicism (which will be developed in a well-defined religion based on the cult of Confucius).

this oral transmission is better known as Gongyang School, and the Gongyang School is better known under the name of Dong Zhongshu.[48]

In sum: according to Kang Youwei—as well as to his predecessors—Confucius was not a mere compiler but a prophet, endowed with a far-reaching *political* mission, which may be synthesized as the removal of those obstacles preventing Time flowing *naturally* toward the construction of a global order based on equality, and in which the establishment of common-oriented institutions will mark the return of the government to the *public* sphere. The *Annals of Lu*, accordingly, are not the plain registration of past events, archived and selected with strictly moral purposes, but rather an esoteric message based on a progressive and evolutionary vision of history.

In Book Two of the aforementioned *Study on Dong Zhongshu's Spring and Autumn*, Kang sets out in full detail an interpretation of human history as proceeding from the chaos generated by selfish instincts to the joyful experience of global peace and commonality: "The first stage is marked by political chaos and social anomie, the second stage is characterized by the reestablishment of legitimate political order, and the third stage emerges when the world as

---

48 *Wanmu caotang koushuo*, 25–31. My translation. Original text: 六經皆孔子所作。詩、書、禮、樂、少年所作。易、春秋、晚年所作。春秋專言人事，易兼言天道，所以中庸必講本諸身。六經以春秋為至貴。荀子傳穀梁，孟子傳公羊。公明儀既子夏弟子，與子思同時，屢稱引文王。公羊：王者孰謂？ 謂文王也。公明儀的為公羊大師。公明高既公羊高，經傳釋詞引釋名：名、孟、羊皆同音。墨子有公孟篇，既公羊。公羊與墨子同時，其教大明，故墨子攻之甚至，而孟子甚尊其言，謂：春秋，天子之事。條條與公羊相通。[...] 孔子改制之學，皆本於天。元，氣之始，故以元統天，以天統君，以君統人。曾自言：天無二月，民無二王，喪無二主。故孟子言定於一。荀子亦發揮定於一，所以李斯為荀子弟子，相奏而大一統。天地之道出於一，生生之道出於二。易言生也，生必二而后生，故易多言陰陽。春秋言治，治統於一，故春秋大一統也。[...] 君，師，治之本。 [...] 論語說孔子德性，改制則未言。孔子改制，見諸六經。易以為三聖，或謂禹，或謂文王，實孔子作。六經皆孔子作。論衡亦知書經為孔子作。庄子天雲篇：孔子繙十二經，以見老子。既六經、六緯。孔子口說多在緯。 [...] 穀梁、公羊何以不同？孔子口說甚多，各不備錄也。[...] 諸教皆不能出孔學之外。[...] 合八方四面，然后見中央。合中外古今，然後見孔子。[...]孔子內制始父子，外制井田。[...] 孔子作緯，劉歆作讖，后人攻讖並緯，大繆。衍聖公請復明衣冠，高宗嚴旨申飭。[...] 孟子謂：三代之失天下也，以不仁。又謂：王者之跡息，而詩亡；詩亡，然後春秋作。可知東遷后已當周王，而孔子怡春秋繼周也。[...] 儒為孔子特創教名，孔子且口自述之，著於論語。但儒為教名，雖為儒教中人，而或為大儒，或為小儒；或為雅儒，或為俗儒；或為通儒，或為愚儒、迂儒、陋儒。此君子、小人之別也。[...] 淮南子：殷變夏，周變殷，春秋變周。三代之禮不同以春秋為一代。[...] 春秋之意，全在口說。口說莫如公羊，公羊莫如懂子。

a whole experiences great harmony."[49] This linear vision of human evolution was elaborated by Kang on the basis of Dong Zhongshu and He Xiu's reading of the *Annals*, of course, but also, and more overtly, through another piece of the Confucian Canon, the *Record of the Rites* (*Liji* 禮記). In this regard, in another of his lessons at the Thousand Trees Cottage, Kang discusses the *Liyun* 禮運, the chapter of the *Rites* in which Confucius described the Three Ages in full detail, and which is generally credited for providing the clearest definition of *datong*.

> The compiler of the *Liyun* was Zi You. Zi Si was a disciple of Zi You, not of Mencius. Beside Yanzi,[50] Zi You was the most important of all Confucius' pupils. [...] Xunzi developed Zi Xia's studies, while Mencius developed Zi You's. When the Master talked about rites, he was referring to the Age of Comfort, not to the Age of Concord. When the world is a "family," there is much to say about rites and less about empathy; when the world is a "community," there is much to say about empathy and less about rites. Since Mencius says much about empathy and less about rites, he is focusing on the Age of Concord. Since Xunzi says much about rites and less about empathy, he is focusing on the Age of Comfort. [...] For Confucius, people's life is based on *two* while people's government is contained in *one*. Two is the number of life, and that's why men and women form couples. One is the number of government, and that's why there can be only one monarch.[51]

This short passage presents two more aspects that are worth noticing in addition to the references to the Age of Comfort and the Age of Concord, and which underlie the same evolutionary pattern that will be fully developed in the *Datong Shu*.

First: the valourizing of "unity" (the One) as the pivotal element for the attainment of stability and peace, both on a local level (figuring as the strengthening of monarchy as an institutional form better suited to represent "unity" than a fragmented republic) and on a global one (as the one-world government

---

49 Quoted in Li, *Between tradition and modernity*, 337.
50 One of the disciples of Confucius.
51 *Wanmu caotang koushuo*: 45–46. My translation. Original text: 著禮運者，子游。子思出於子游，非出於曾子。顏子之外，子游第一。[...] 荀子發揮子夏之學，孟子發揮子游之學。夫子之言禮，專論小康，不論大同。天下為家，言禮多而仁少。天下為公，言仁多而言禮少。孟子多言仁，少言禮，大同也。荀子多言禮，少言仁，小康也。[...]孔子勝任本於二，治人統於一。生於二，故立夫婦。統於一，故獨有一君。

that will follow the demise of diverse nations), which is a clear tribute to the Confucian-Legalist political synthesis.[52]

Second: the focus on *empathy* as the characteristic value of the Age of Concord, compared to the attention to ritualism which belongs, according to Kang's view, to the previous Age of Rising Equality. Attributing empathy to the Age of Concord, a stage which is *subsequent* and not *opposite* to the Age of Rising Equality (this pattern of an organic evolution across stages, so different from the Hegelian and Marxist view of historical evolution based on an equation between change and conflict, should not be overlooked), Kang tries to harmonize the strict face of Confucianism (that of the often severe respect for etiquette, constantly used by imperial and local institutions to exert their control over individuals) with his own utopian vision of a world with no boundaries nor hierarchies among individuals. Abandoning the rites in favour of a universal sense of brotherhood—as prescribed by the *Datong Shu*—then, is not betraying the Confucian roots but rather advancing along the line drawn by the Master himself and transmitted through his most secret teachings. The course of evolution of the New Text premises into the uncharted territories of a Utopia of brotherly love is thus charted.

Another excerpt from Kang's early production, in this case a short essay explicitly entitled *On the Word "Empathy"* 講仁字, and included in *Master Nanhai's Annotations* (南海師承記)—a collection published together with the *Instructions from the Hall of Thousand-Trees Cottage*—sheds more light on the author's elaborations on the key Confucian virtue and on the relation to his utopianism.

> The teaching of Confucius has its main purpose in the establishment of *ren*, empathy, as we can see in this quotation from the Analects: "Be established in empathy." The Annals of Master Lü also underline how Confucius had empathy in great esteem. Laozi inaugurated another kind of theory which did not encourage empathy: in the *Daodejing* it is said that "Heaven has no mercy and considers the myriad of creatures as straw dogs, so the Sage has no mercy and considers human beings as straw dogs." Such a teaching is clearly in opposition to Confucius. Therefore, we can divide the entire course of Chinese thought between those teachings which focus on empathy and those which do not. Confucius values empathy, therefore considering the power of virtue as superior to

---

52   On this, see Yuri Pines, *The Everlasting Empire: The political culture of ancient China and its imperial legacy* (Princeton NJ: Princeton University Press, 2012).

punishments; Laozi praises cynicism, therefore his followers Han Feizi and Shenzi considered punishments as superior to virtue.

Mencius said: "Being human means being empathic," and this is a very straightforward explanation. "Dwell in empathy," it is said; and if we take out from the character for "dwell" 依 the radical "man," then we have the character for "wear" 衣: empathy is like a garment from which at no point in your life can you divest yourself.

Dong Zhongshu gave the most essential interpretation of empathy. And the Buddhist saying "to cut your own flesh to feed the eagles," or to "kill yourself to feed a tiger," can be seen as depicting the extreme consequences of empathy as the ideal of "equality" among all the living beings. This is close to Mozi. Throughout ancient and modern literature there is not a single text without a mention of *ren*. In Song times, though, people regarded empathy as an undefined word, therefore in their books a lot is said about *righteousness*, but much less about empathy. If we examine the first encounters between China and foreign countries, wars and killings invariably succeeded; but when the Sages emerged, they spread their teachings and wars and killings diminished: we can say that such was the effect of empathy. If we want to understand the future, we can see it as a progression towards empathy. Thanks to growing equality there will be no conflicts and when the world will be unified, empathy will reach its zenith. A man with an arid heart cannot feel empathy, that's why Zhang Nanxuan[53] defined aridity as the greatest evil. Since the teaching of Laozi is all about *endurance*, then endurance cannot be considered as "empathic." Confucius called empathy "the Heart of Heaven," which from Spring brings life; Laozi, on the other side, said that the World feels no empathy, which from Winter starts to kill. Yet giving and taking life is the natural course of the world. According to some Western research, for every 100 people, 96 are being born while four are being killed. Life far outnumbers death, and Confucianism triumphs over Laozi's view of the universe! Every religion affirms that in those that kill a human being, love for their own kind is extinguished. For Buddhists, each of the six levels of samsara [defining every living creature] must be preserved, which is impossible because even the most empathic of men cannot avoid killing some creature of another species. Empathy has its demarcation line and its different degrees through which it can be applied. Any discourse on humanity starts from this point. The highest form of empathy corresponds to filial piety. As Confucius said: "Such is filial piety: rooted in

---

53 Zhang Nanxuan 張南軒 (1113–1180) was a Neo-Confucian scholar.

empathy!" And Mencius said: "The Way of Yao and Shun is now called filial piety." For those who have learned it, it means *recompensing the parents*. The *Book of Documents* reads: "The Lord established virtue by which everything is recompensed." And which human relationship can be more based on reciprocity than the parental one? According to the *Book of the Odes* "a clear sky is not better than the virtue of reciprocity." Extending our paternal tie from *our* father to *all* the fathers, and extending our maternal tie to all her relatives, respecting them with no exception: that is how a village is born; paternity is a natural tendency, it cannot be rationally explained. Brothers can have the same features but different souls and that may cause problems, but in the end their sense of brotherhood will prevail. Families can be on bad terms for two reasons: for opinions or for money. Each member of a family has to make some concessions, abandoning petty resentments in the name of a major relation, when it is possible. If we look at the difference between good and bad people, we see that those who feel trust and pity are fully aware of their humanity. Those who lack trust are weak, those who lack pity are mean: endowed with such a nature, they should not be taken into consideration. There are magnanimous and uncorrupted persons, but there has never been a stingy person who was not corrupted. The principles of trust and pity make the emergence of a civilization based on common interest possible: there, fields are cultivated, storehouses are kept, and study is promoted. Today, the Suzhou Academy follows those principles of "common interest" and its pupils are purely empathic and present a paternal attitude, they could share three boats full of ale with Shi Manqing.[54] The strength of foreign countries resides in their empathic force, whereas China, now the world of selfishness, has reached her utmost weakness.[55]

---

54   Shi Manqing 石曼卿 (994–1041), a Song poet famous for his habit of getting drunk with guests while composing poems.

55   *Wanmu caotang koushuo*: 189–190. My translation. Original text: 孔子之教，其宗旨在仁，故論語有'依於仁'一條。呂氏春秋言孔子貴仁。自老子始倡不仁之學，故其道德經中，天地不仁，以萬物為芻狗；聖人不仁，以百姓為芻狗。其教旨與孔子大相反。故向來中國教旨隻仁與不仁而已。孔教尚仁，故貴德賤刑。老子主不仁，故后學申、韓之徒貴刑賤仁。孟子謂：人者，仁也。此解最直捷通達。'依於仁'，聖人下一'依'字，有如衣服一般，終身不可舍。董子發仁最精。佛教所謂割肉食鷹，殺身食虎，仁之極，所謂平等者，此也。然而近於墨氏矣。通古今之書，不外講一仁字。宋人看仁字猶未透，以其書多言義，少言仁也。考中國外國之始，無不爭奪相殺漸久，聖人出而教化之，而爭奪漸少，所謂仁也。究其后，亦歸於仁。平等無爭，而天下一統矣，仁之極也。凡人有鄙吝之心者便是不仁，故張南軒以鄙吝為大惡。為老子之學者全是能忍，能忍便是不仁。孔子謂仁為天心，從春生起；老子言天地不仁，

The reference in this extract to the Buddhist ideal of an impassionate compassion, leading to self-sacrifice for the benefit of the world, bears witnesses to Kang's deep affinity with Mahayana, as well as to his syncretic attitude. *Empathy* is one of the key words of Kang's political utopia, then, as will be the case for his contemporary Tan Sitong, who not coincidentally will entitle his own Utopia *Renxue* 仁學, or *A Study on Empathy*. The issue of the Buddhist traces within Kang's utopianism will be further discussed in the next chapter.

Another short essay, also included in *Master Nanhai's Annotations* and entitled *On the Gongyang Commentary and the System of Dynastic Succession*, usefully underlines the importance of *ren* in the emergence of any form of civilization.

> Foreign countries did value human sacrifices, which then appeared to be in contrast with the Way of humanity. They also considered their masters as speaking on behalf of spirits, which was an idea of the ancient shamanic culture. Then the importance of human beings was finally considered: Confucius defined human beings as "children of the universe," putting empathy at the centre of his doctrine and establishing a theory in which regality was not an external value.[56]

These two last extracts show how the fulfilment of human nature (and the establishment of a correct form of civilization) is in Kang's view strictly linked to the progressive enlargement of the concept of empathy, moving from one's closest relatives (father and mother) to a much wider community. When the

---

從冬殺起。生殺亦天地自然之理，西人考之，一百分中，生人直九十四分，死人直六分，生人遠多於殺人，孔教則勝於老子矣。凡諸教皆殺人者，死愛同類也。倘謂六度輪回，一切皆保護，則其勢不能，故極仁之人不能不殺異類。既有仁而界限出焉，差等立焉，此其勢也。人間之義，皆從此出。仁之最大者莫如孝弟，故有子曰：孝弟也者，其為仁之本歟。孟子曰：堯、舜之道，孝弟而已矣。夫足額這所以報父母也。書言：太上有立德，其次重報施。凡人類應酬，無不重報，況父母乎？故詩雲：故報之德昊天罔極。若夫推父之義以至於諸父，推母之義以至於諸男，無不要孝敬，是以莊生雲：父子天性也，不可解於心。兄弟之難處者，以刑氣同而魂魄異也，大約總要兄弟恰恰為主。家庭不睦有二：一曰意見，二錢財。家庭之間全要委曲，充小嫌而全大論，方可。欲觀人之善惡，觀其任恤便知其人矣。其不仁者便弱，其不恤者便佞，具此氣質，其餘不足觀矣。有闊大而不貪，未有吝嗇而不貪。仁恤之義，范文正公能開之，義田、養倉、義學是也。今蘇州學宮是范文正公故宅，其子純仁猶有父風，能以三船麥分與石曼卿。外國之強全在能仁，中國一自私自利之天下，故弱至今日。

56 *Ibid*: 194–195. My translation. Original text: 外國無不重祭祀，蓋祭祀乃人道所不可廢。外國祭師能通鬼神之語，既太古巫之義也。凡向來主祭之人甚重，如孔子號乾坤之子，孔子之義以仁為主，故有王者無外之義。

principle of *ren* is expanded to the entire human species, Kang expects, the *datong* will be attained.

In summary, Kang's lectures and his philological elaborations are an interesting testimony to his personal commitment to the redefinition and reorganization of Chinese Classicism. More importantly, they are necessary to frame Kang's utopianism in its proper context. With its roots firmly planted in the long-lasting debate on the Classics, Kang's elaboration on *datong* appears as a mainly Chinese cultural product, interacting with—and not simply spurred by—Western influences. More will be said on this in Chapter 3.

5   Reform and Utopia: Two Stages, One History

If the "long nineteenth century" can be correctly considered as an age of historicization—a time when "the arts, philosophy and sciences were now studied as they took shape over the course of time" and when even religions, or quasi-religious traditions, were hardly able to "escape historicization"[57]—then the confrontation between Old and New Text scholars among the Chinese Classicists might be interpreted as the Chinese version (built upon Chinese foundations, and accelerated by wider external forces) of a wider *global* intellectual wave. As already anticipated, it might even be useful as a means of relating the European Saddle-period to the Chinese situation.

As Jürgen Osterhammel puts it: "The basic options regarding the problems of the age were everywhere the same, in a spectrum that went from militant rejection of the new and alien to large-scale adaptation to what were considered the dominant forces of the contemporary world. More interesting than the extremes are the many intermediate solutions, which cannot be grasped through a simple counterposition of 'tradition' and 'modernity'."[58] Kang's reinterpretation of Confucianism may appear to belong to such an "interesting" and intermediate category, then, in which the boundaries between local and foreign, traditional and modern seem to be blurred. The progressive vision of history acting as the philosophical framework of the *Datong Shu* was retrieved from the Confucian Canon, then, and certainly not from any "social Darwinist" influence coming from Western texts. Kang's thought was undoubtedly rooted in Chinese tradition; but rather than being a simple local reaction to the challenges of Western modernity, it may be defined as the last major effort to reorganize the Central Tradition (as Zurcker effectively translates *Ru* 儒) in the

---

57   Osterhammel, *The Transformation of the World*, 897–898.
58   Ibid., 900.

face of new threats, Western intrusion *included* (but not alone). In sum, the continuity of Kang's philosophy with the New Text tradition demonstrates that internal Chinese dynamics (both local and central) were at play long before the so-called Western shock, and were subsequently merged into the later confrontation with—and importation of—foreign concepts and theories.

From this perspective, then, some of the accusations that Kang bears responsibility for undermining the credibility of Confucianism—through his denunciation of Han forgeries before 1911, and his staunch conservatism afterwards—appear not entirely convincing. It has been asserted that "It was but a short distance from questioning the authenticity of ancient history to denying the validity of Confucianism."[59] Yet this claim seems ungenerous, given the fact that Kang was simply the last in a very long line of inquirers striving to define the real nature of Classicism and to put it to political use. Moreover, the re-emergence of Confucianism in contemporary China—even as a sort of publicly sponsored "national religion" in addition to its more typical function as a State ideology—seems to contradict Hsiao Kung-chuan's argument concerning the "burial" of Confucianism which ostensibly took place in late imperial times. The significance of Kang's Classicism is fully understandable only outside the typical categories of conservative or revolutionary, and more generally beyond the simple schema of China versus the West which was forged as a means to grasp the late Qing period. His effort counted for something more than just "filling old bottles with new wine,"[60] trying to operate a change within tradition. His endeavour is much better framed within a wider global context where traditions were reshaped to respond to political and social agitations. It is therefore fascinating to imagine whether, should the West not have collided with China, Kang's reflections would have nonetheless taken a very similar path, and whether the New Text political claims would have been extended to their extreme conclusions without any external threat posed to Chinese sovereignty. But such is not the scope of this book.

This brief survey of Kang's earlier philosophy—viewed from the vantage point of his later utopianism—shows beyond any doubt that the *Datong Shu* cannot be considered as a unique specimen in Kang's production, nor as a fancy appendix to it. It was not a final detour from a more rational political

---

59 Hsiao, *A Modern China and a New World*, 130.
60 Feng Youlan, *A History of Chinese Philosophy* (Princeton NJ: Princeton University Press, 1953) vol. 2, 720.

path,[61] nor the culmination of a "second phase" of his thought.[62] Instead, it must be considered as fully embedded in Kang's earliest reflections on the meaning of tradition and on the trajectory of human history and mundane institutions. These early cues had simply been waiting to be taken to their ultimate conclusion.

The unicorn's appearance, as an omen of the necessity for a rectification of politics, accompanies Kang's thought from its inception up to the final elaborated stage, as he tried to give the original Confucian universalism a newer and wider mode of expression.

Hsiao Kung-chuan—whose study on Kang's philosophy is still the most authoritative source for any research on this thinker—observes that the *Datong Shu*'s description of how single nations will unite to form a single world government curiously proceeds according to the three stages of progress conceived by the Gongyang School; this being "one of the few places in the book where Kang, unintentionally perhaps, showed his intellectual ties with Confucianism."[63] In fact, it appears more plausible that Kang had *intentionally* linked his entire *Book of Great Concord* to the rest of his production, right from the title itself. In this sense, his ideal of history as a progression toward *datong* marks the apex of a Universal Reform encoded by Confucius in the most secret recesses of his legacy.

---

61   This has been the view adopted for decades by many Communist scholars intending to draw a clear line separating Kang's reformism and his indecisive utopianism. For more on this aspect, see Chapter 7, below.
62   Roger Darrobers, for example, defines the *Datong Shu* "*un cas à part*" in Kang's production. Roger Darrobers, "Du confucianisme reformé à l'utopie universelle." (*Études chinoises*, XIX/1–2, 2000, 15–65), 16.
63   Hsiao, *A Modern China and a New World*, 461.

CHAPTER 2

Indra's Net
Buddhism and the Hidden Face of Kang's Confucianism

1   The Age of Empathy

Having briefly sketched the main source of Kang's philosophical and conceptual framework in the New Text Confucianism, we now move to analysing some excerpts from the *Datong Shu* in order to shed light on some of its *leitmotifs*. The following translation is an extract from Part One of the book:

> Kang says: I am a man, how could I tolerate to escape men without sharing their suffering? I was born in a family from the love of two persons and we have an obligation toward them. If I left them, leaving my family, I would be so deceitful, so despicable! I was born in a country, I love its culture and I was trained in it, and I have a duty as a citizen. If I fled from my country and abandon it when it is experiencing a crisis and its culture is menaced by destruction, I should be blamed for such a lack of responsibility. I was born in this world, and I consider all the human beings of every country in the world to be my "different" brothers. We care for those we know. So I took the philosophical essence of every culture—from ancient India, Greece, Persia and Rome to modern England, France, Germany and America—and I sipped it, I couched and I dreamed; with the sages, masters, scholars and great individuals of this world I stood hand in hand, couch by couch, sleeve by sleeve, sharing our meals and propagating their love. Day by day I enjoyed and used the diverse beauty of architectures, clothes and foods, vehicles, artefacts, teachings, arts and music coming from all over the world, thereby stimulating my senses and elevating my spirit. If someone progresses, then I progress with him; if someone degenerates, then I degenerate with him, if someone rejoices then I rejoice with him, if someone suffers then I suffer with him: it really is [a force] all-penetrating like electricity and all-encompassing like *qi*. And we can extend this to every living being in this world: savages, trees and plants, fishes and insects, birds and beasts, those born from the womb or in the water, from an egg or from a metamorphosis, all of them, in their infinite appearances, I consider as my reflections, I am penetrated by their awareness, I am absorbed by their love, how could I be indifferent? I enjoy their beautiful colours, I am happy for their brimming

delight; but when their colour is pallid, and their fate is tragic, I feel pallor and sadness right in the middle of my heart. Shall I escape from the vastity of this Earth? Shall I sacrifice myself to Brahman, purifying my soul in a snowy cave? And yet if everybody left his family to be a hermit, in a few decades the whole of human civilization would revert to a planet inhabited by plants, trees, birds and beasts: how could I tolerate this? Mars, Saturn, Uranus, Jupiter, Neptune, they all host some living beings. But I cannot connect with them, distances are obscure: I wish to love them but they are too far away. Interstellar vastnesses, the uncountable star clusters, galaxies and nebulae, they are all manifestations of Heaven, I saw them with my interior eye, I experienced them while traveling with my spirit. In their countries their inhabitants' happiness for rites and arts, as well as their conflicts and wars, spread vastly and limitless. They are people generated by Heaven, and although I have not yet been able to see them, if they have a form and an intellect, then they are not different from the people of my planet. In my celestial wanderings, I saw the happiest worlds, I saw the most suffering worlds; when they were happy I rejoiced, when they suffered, I tried to help. Since I am a creature of all Heavens, how could I abandon the world and the universe, abandoning my species and escaping relations to enjoy a solitary happiness? Those whose self-awareness is small, they also have a small heart; those whose self-awareness is vast, they also have a vast loving heart.[1]

---

1 *Datong Shu*: 4–5. My translation. Original text: 康子曰：吾既為人，吾將忍心而逃人，不共其憂患焉？生於一家，受人之鞠育而后有其生，則有家人之荷擔。若逃之而出其家，其自為則巧矣，其負恩則何忍矣！生於一國，受一國之文明而后有其知，則有國民之責任。若逃之而棄其國，其國亡種滅而文明隨之墮壞，其責任亦太甚矣。生於大地，則大地萬國之人類皆吾同胞之異體之也。既與有知，則與有親。凡印度、希臘、波斯、羅馬及近世英、法、德、美之先哲之精英，吾已嚽之飲之，胙之枕之，魂夢通之；於今萬國之元老、碩儒、名士、美人，亦多握手接芮、聯袂分羹而致其親愛矣。凡大地萬國之宮室、服食、舟車、什器、政教、樂之飛奇偉麗者，日受而用之，以刺觸其心目，感蕩其魂氣。其進化耶則相於共進，退化耶則相與共退，其樂耶相與共其樂，其苦耶相與共其苦，誠如電之無不相通矣，如氣之無不相周矣。乃至大地之生番、野人、草木、介魚、昆蟲、鳥獸，凡胎生、濕生、卵生、化生之萬形千匯，亦皆與我耳目相接，魂知相通，愛磁相攝，而吾何能忍然！彼其色相好，吾樂之；生趣盎，吾怡之；其色相憔悴，生趣慘悽，吾亦有憔悴慘悽動於中焉。莽莽大地，吾又將焉逃於其外？將為婆羅門之舍身雪窟中以煉精魂，然人人齊家舍身，則全地文明不數十年而復為狉榛草木鳥獸之世界，吾更何忍出此也！火星、土星、木星、天王、海王諸星之生物耶，莽不與接，杳冥為期，吾欲仁之，遠無所施。恆星之大，星團、星雲、星氣之多，諸天之表，目本相見，神嘗與游。其國士女、禮樂、文章之樂與兵戎戰伐之爭，浩浩無涯。為天為人，雖吾所未能覯，而苟有物類有知識者，即與吾地吾人無異情焉。吾為天游，想像一極

Kang's peculiar classical "esotericism," introduced in the previous chapter, appears here as a bridge connecting Confucianism to other religious and philosophical currents. Empathy—the pivotal virtue of *ren*—assumes a Buddhist nuance and transcends any discourse on "civilization," thus becoming a truly global value. The old ideal of benevolence is finally directed toward mankind in its entirety, while the political claim for a "common" society assumes a worldwide dimension and the pursuit of happiness overcomes any form of social or ethnic division. The venerable dichotomy separating an inner imperial space from the outer one in the traditional political cosmology is overcome, as there are no more "barbarians" to civilize in the Age of Supreme Equality, when *tianxia* will become a geographical unit encompassing the whole planet.

Kang's philosophy of history has as its engine a certain view of empathy: by opening his text with a detailed focus on the progressive eradication of all those boundaries which cause humans to suffer, the author explicitly presents his debt to a Buddhist mindset. Kang himself said to his student that "Sages put empathy at the centre, and so did Buddhism: 'He who can feel compassion' is one of the names of Buddha."[2]

2 Huayan Heritage and Mahayana Revival

In fact, Kang's lifelong fascination with Mahayana Buddhism was no secret; and, as will be argued, should not be considered surprising for a "Confucianist." He himself described his familiarity with meditation techniques in his autobiography, as part of his interest in one of the most important Buddhist schools that flourished in China: the *Huayan Zong* 華嚴宗, the Doctrine of the Garland.[3] Inspired by a view of human existence as an inter-connected infinity, in which any single being shares the same nature of Buddha, the masters of the Huayan tradition developed a peculiar approach to Buddhist thinking.

樂之世界，想像一極苦之世界，樂者吾樂者，苦者吾救之。吾為諸天之一物，無寧能舍世界天界、絕類逃倫而獨樂哉！其覺知少者，其愛心亦少；其覺知大者，其仁心亦大。

[2] "圣人以仁为主，既佛家亦是。能仁者，佛号也。" Quoted in Wei Yixia 魏义霞, "Foxue: Kang Youwei zhexue de zhuyao laiyuan 佛学：康有为哲学的主要来源." (*Zhexue fenxi* 2, 2 2011: 75–83), 77.

[3] Established in the Tang period by thinkers such as Du Shun (557–640) and Fa Zang (643–712), the Huayan School derived its name from the *Gandavyuha Sutra*, or Garland Sutra, a major Mahayana text focusing on the description of the Infinity of Buddhahood. The best work on this tradition is still Garma C.C. Chang, *The Buddhist teaching of totality: The philosophy of Hwa Yen Buddhism* (London: London University Press, 1971), in which the Huayan is presented as "the crown of all Buddhist teachings."

Their account was centred on the reduction of worldly multiplicity through an approach defined as "totalistic": namely, they elaborated an ideal of a "round totality of Buddhahood" in which there is "not even room for contradiction" and where the "inconsistencies all become harmonious."[4] As in the Hindu myth of Indra's net—a structure encompassing any (apparent) diversity within a higher form of unity—individuals are *connected* and *exalted* through their Buddhahood rather than *destroyed* or *annihilated* as pure illusions. By this token, the Huayan vision of the world is naturally directed toward syncretism and comparison: it is not surprising, then, that Kang would be sympathetic to this doctrine, drawing inspiration from the "universal connection" theory of the Huayan for sustaining his world-oriented reflections.

The syncretic approach adopted by Kang also resonated with the teachings of another Buddhist School, the *Tiantai* 天台宗. As Chun-fang Yu has argued with regard to Late Ming Buddhism, both Tiantai and Huayan, "in their comprehensive, architectonic approach toward the entire corpus of Buddhist teaching, as evidenced by their 'classification of Buddhist doctrine' (*banjiao* 班教), were in their own way syncretic systems of thought," providing "theoretical rationales for the sectarian synthesis of later periods."[5] For example, the Tiantai concept of *yixin* 一心, "one mind," by which the simultaneous adoption of different paths for reaching enlightenment is justified, originally responded to the general syncretic necessity of a complex setting such as early imperial China. This effort at reducing diversity and fragmentation to the One principle, interpreting phenomena as its refractions, is strikingly reminiscent of the esoteric Confucian view of historical progression as summarized in the previous chapter and used by Kang as the general scheme of the *Datong Shu*: historical progression follows a universal pattern, whose manifestations are restricted by spatial and human contingencies. The difference, though, lies in Kang's explicitly political use of this intuition and, more importantly, in its temporal linearity: whereas the Buddhist interpretation of the relationship between the One and the Many is synchronous and atemporal, Kang presents it as the progressive unfolding of a historical mechanism, requiring human action to be unveiled. These differences notwithstanding, it is not surprising that the "Confucian reformer" Kang would later confess in his *nianpu* to have found the ultimate inspiration for the composition of his Utopia while sitting in a "deep state of meditation," as the pattern of past and future history—up to that

---

4 Chang, *The Buddhist teaching*, ix.
5 Yu Junfang, *The renewal of Buddhism in China. Chu-hung and the late Ming synthesis* (New York NY: Columbia University Press, 1981), 224.

moment elaborated only theoretically—became fully visible to his mind. The experience happened in 1878, when Kang was twenty:

> While sitting in meditation, I suddenly saw that the ten thousand creatures of Heaven and Earth and I were all of the same substance. I received the light and I attained sagehood, and such a happiness made me laugh. Then I suddenly thought of the sufferings of living beings, and such a sadness made me cry.[6]

This meditative technique is also mentioned in chapter one of the *Datong Shu*, where Kang confesses to having experienced both the happiest and the unhappiest worlds in his "astral journeys," aiming to increase his empathic attitude. In that same excerpt, there is another clear example of Kang's affinity with the Huayan worldview, when the author hints at the existence of other inhabited worlds out in the vast universe, each one with its own historical path, naturally proceeding from chaos to unity. As pointed out by Garma Chang, for Huayan thinkers "human history has no unique significance; there are numerous histories of other sentient beings of equal significance in other universes," and at the same time, "history is imbued with great significance because it is a necessary process for the realization of Perfection for all human beings."[7] The long march to Supreme Equality and the Buddhist aspiration to Buddhahood seem to merge together in Kang's concept of *datong*, forming an indistinguishably historical *and* spiritual attainment available not just to the entire world, but potentially to the whole universe.

This may appear surprising if we consider Confucianism, or more generally Classicism or *Ruism*, as something different—or even antithetical—to Buddhist metaphysics. However, Kang's intellectual experience proves such a view to be wrong. To Kang's eyes, his experience with Huayan and Chan Buddhism and his participation in the "manufacturing" of an innovative reading of the Classics are part of the *same* philosophical construction. The principle of *datong* also works in internal terms, as a way of harmonizing different threads into a philosophical concord. Kang's theoretical approach is marked by the aspiration for Unity and it consequently appears as a syncretic model in which different traditions (Confucianism, Buddhism, Western contributions)

---

6 Quoted in Thompson, *Ta-tung shu*, 3. Note the similarity with the Huayan meditative process, described by Garma C.C. Chang as the connection of individuals to "a vast Ocean-mirror in which the infinite dramas in the universe are spontaneously and simultaneously reflected" in a "kaleidoscope of multi-dimensional, mutual projections and interpenetrations." Chang, *The Buddhist teaching*, x.

7 Ibid., xiv.

are inextricably linked, merged, and mixed. Confucianism (or Classicism), as reshaped by Kang in his philosophy, is not conceived as a boundary drawn to separate the "truth" from the falsity of other traditions; rather, it is a pattern, a grid through which every historical or philosophical experience can be arranged. A small example will suffice: while lecturing his students at the *Wanmu* school on Confucian cosmology, Kang dedicates one short passage to the five agents, noting that they correspond to the four elements of Buddhism (佛氏地、水、火、风，即儒家之五行).[8]

Kang is not the first Confucian—nor the last—to adopt a syncretic attitude, of course. More generally, we might say that a deep, albeit often obscure, influence of Buddhism can be detected among Classicists from late Ming onward. In other words, the Sinicization of Buddhism which took place during the late Ming and is clearly visible in late Qing philosophers like Kang, rather than being the product of a time of decline when the splendour of the Tang had already faded away, appears as a complex and fertile process of syncretic adaptation. Syncretism is a "creative enterprise" by which "ideas in one tradition become developed as a result of the stimulation supplied by compatible ideas from other traditions,"[9] and such a definition seems to fit perfectly with Kang's own creative process. The syncretism fully exposed in the *Datong Shu* is equally at work in Tan Sitong's *Renxue*, just to mention a text sharing the utopian nature of Kang's Great Concord.[10] Moreover, Kang's connection to the milieu of late imperial Buddhist reformers is an undeniable fact. Recent studies on the Mahayana renaissance of the late Qing have focused on a number of figures active in the reorganization of Buddhism in a "modern" sense. Some of them—and not the minor ones—were actually part of Kang's *entourage*, knew him, and even cooperated with him. Such is the case of Yang Wenhui 楊文會 (1837–1911), the well-known founder of the Jingling Sutra Publishing House, or the even more famous Taixu 太虛 (1890–1947), the reformer monk who explicitly mentioned Kang as one of his sources of inspiration for his project of an institutionalized and reorganized Buddhism.[11] Buddhist reformers surely studied Kang's attempt at structuring Confucianism as a "modern" Church

---

8   Kang Youwei, *Wanmu caotang koushuo*, 46.
9   Yu, *The renewal of Buddhism*, 101.
10 On Tan Sitong and a summary of his *Renxue*, see Charlotte Furth "Intellectual Change: From the Reform Movement to the May Fourth Movement, 1895–1920," in Ou-Fan Lee and Merle Goldman (eds), *An Intellectual History of Modern China* (Cambridge: Cambridge University Press, 2002, 13–96), esp. 18–25.
11 For a complete survey of late Qing and early Republican Buddhism "modernism" and its leading figures, see John Makeham (ed), *Transforming Consciousness: Yogacara Thought in Modern China* (Oxford: Oxford University Press 2014).

from 1898 onward, and they certainly shared his interest in Christianity as a model for a politically active and organized religion: not coincidentally, both Kang and Yang Wenhui had great esteem for Timothy Richard (1845–1919), the British missionary who inspired the former with his translated essays on reformism, and helped the latter in the translation of the *Awakening of Faith*, a central piece of the Buddhist revival in modern China.[12]

Although discarded by Lawrence Thompson as a minor influence in the creative process behind the *Datong Shu* and in Kang's philosophical elaboration in general,[13] and although defined by Hsiao Kung-chuan as a possibly "disturbing element from a strictly philosophical point of view,"[14] Buddhist contributions clearly cannot be hastily dismissed as uninfluential in Kang's elaborations. Rather, as underlined by some contemporary Chinese scholars, a "Buddhist flavour" is "undeniably present in Kang's philosophy" as part of his general "debt to Chinese traditional thought,"[15] and his genuine concern for the "reasons of suffering" (*kudi* 苦諦) represents a "clear Buddhist inspiration."[16] In a recent paper, Wei Yixia even affirms that "without taking Buddhist influences into consideration, one cannot understand Kang's philosophy nor fully appreciate his praise for Confucianism."[17] Kang himself often cites Buddhism as one of his sources of inspiration, coupling it with Classicism (*Ru*) as if they were part of the same structure; see for example this passage, where he describes the creative process behind his *Principles of Mankind*, the precursor of *Datong Shu*:

> Mingling the obscure indications of the Classics, investigating the esoteric meanings of Classicism and Buddhism, examining the new theories in China and the West, exploring to the limits the subtle transformations of Heaven and Man, I assembled any teaching, I surveyed the world, analysed the past and the present and tried to foresee the future.[18]

---

12   See Vincent Goossaert and David Palmer, *The Religious Question in Modern China* (Chicago: University of Chicago Press, 2010), chapters 1–2.
13   "It is quite obvious that K'ang is not really indebted to Buddhism for anything more than the emphasis on the fact of suffering." Thompson, *Ta-tung shu*.
14   Hsiao, *A Modern China and a New World*, 152.
15   Wang Bin 汪斌, "Kang Youwei sixiangzhong de foxue qingjie 康有为思想中的佛学情结." (*Heilongjiang shizhi*, 10, 2008, 8–9), 8.
16   Fan Chaole 樊朝乐, "Kang Youwei 'Datong Shu' de kuleguan 康有为《大同书》的苦乐观." (*Chongqing keji xueyuan xuebao*, 4, 2012, 31–32), 31.
17   Wei Yixia, "Foxue", 83.
18   Kang Youwei, *Kang Nanhai zibian nianpu*, quoted in Wang Bin, "Kang Youwei sixiangzhong de foxue", 8. My translation. Original text: 合經子之奧旨，探儒佛之微旨，參中西之新理，窮天人之賾變，搜合諸教，批析大地，剖析今古，窮察后來。

The following is Liang Qichao's brief description of his master's philosophy:

> His philosophy is a philosophy of universal love. His philosophy is a philosophy of happiness. His philosophy is a philosophy of evolution. His philosophy is a philosophy of socialism.[19]

According to Wei, any point of this very concise synthesis of Kang's thought can be linked to the Mahayana: the love for mankind as a whole, the pursuit of happiness and the "communism" of the Age of Concord are all manifestations of a universalist thinking, of course; but Kang's view on evolution, although mainly derived from the Classics and namely from the *Yijing*, was also developed under the influence of the Buddhist ideal of *samsara*.[20] Such a position, albeit providing an interesting insight into the subject of this chapter, might appear equally extremist in its opposition to that of Thompson and Hsiao: and it is surely risky, in reacting to those who deny any noticeable Buddhist element in Kang, to instead interpret the *whole* of Kang's philosophy in Buddhist terms.

But the question might be easily resolved once we define, as already said, the Buddhist elements or nuances (mainly deriving from a Huayan / Tiantai form of Buddhism) as an inextricable part of Kang's own Confucianism. Let us take, for example, the pivotal concept of *ren*, benevolence, empathy. The word itself, as is well known, is part of the Confucian Canon. Although the Master himself never fully clarified its meaning in the *Analects*, it was Mencius who stressed its "loving" energy. In the Song period, Zhu Xi and the Cheng brothers would start a new round of debates on the nature of *ren*, fitting it into their general view of a cosmos governed by a principle (*li* 理). Cheng Hao in particular interpreted it as a life-giving force, connecting the myriad things, but without stressing its character of a subjective act of love or compassion. Cheng Yi would be even more specific, connecting *ren* to human nature (*xing* 性) and separating it from love, which is assigned to the realm of emotions (*qing* 情).[21] Even Zhu Xi, credited for adjusting Cheng's theories and coining a definition of *ren* as the "principle of love," did not view empathy as based "on the assumption of the unity of all things" nor does his view "emphasize only the universalistic extension" of its loving quality.[22] Kang—who, as a late-imperial Confucianist was

---

19 Liang Qichao, *Nanhai Kang xiansheng zhuan* 南海康先生傳 pp. 488–489, quoted in Wei Yixia, "Foxue", 75.
20 Wei Yixia, "Foxue", 79–82.
21 Chan, *The Buddhist teaching*, 215–216.
22 Ibid., 221.

more than familiar with Song and Ming Neo-Confucianism—will nonetheless give his own personal interpretation of *ren*, extending it to a universal level, thus transcending Zhu Xi's account with an undeniable Buddhist nuance.

However, Kang's approach to Buddhism is twofold. If on the one hand he considers some Buddhist theories and images as part of his broader vision of history, man, and the world, on the other hand, he is not shy in criticizing Buddhism as a devotional religion. Its clergy, he writes, "entices people with the promise of Paradise" exactly "as Christian priests do."[23] These harsh critiques clarify Kang's view of religion in general. While valuing the social importance of religious identities as a powerful political tool in the process of State-building (as his own proposal for the establishment of a National Confucian Church in 1898 clearly proves, as well as his interest in the role of Catholicism in the Italian unification, as it appears from his diaries),[24] Kang is no admirer of religious institutions thriving on people's credulity, and nor does he share the ideas of asceticism or "extraneity to the world" conveyed by some spiritual traditions (as demonstrated by his criticism of hermits presented in the quoted extract from the *Datong Shu*). We might say that Kang makes a clear-cut distinction between *religious organizations*—which are subject to the rules of Time, and evolve accordingly, serving the cause of further unification towards the Great Concord before dissolving—and *individual practices* of self-perfecting, which are non-confessional and necessary to become a Sage and to help the world reach *datong*. Even though its real weight in Kang's *Weltanschauung* is still a matter of discussion, then, the role of Buddhism in the philosophical process leading to the *Datong Shu*—and especially in the universalization of Confucian empathy—cannot be denied nor dismissed.

3   Reincarnation and Politics

Another extract from Part One of the *Datong Shu* (specifically, from the section dedicated to the survey of the different causes of human suffering) will be useful to further investigate Kang's relationship with Buddhism. Thompson—who was rather sceptical about this issue, as said—did not translate it, summarizing the whole section and providing only the titles of the subchapters dealing with the pain of wandering in *samsara*. The first is rendered by Thompson as "On the sufferings due to being born in the different stages of existence"; but

---

23   Kang Youwei, *Wanmu caotang koushuo*, 195.
24   More on this in the next chapter.

we might better translate it as "On the sufferings due to reincarnation," since Kang uses the very specific term *toutai* 投胎, which undeniably belongs to a Buddhist lexicon.[25] Here, the author addresses the "primeval cause" of suffering, which lies in the disparity of human conditions. After the establishment of the first hierarchical forms and the rise of civilization, mankind was arranged in a pyramidal structure, Kang says: the few at the top, the many below. Since the majority of the global population has always been part of the latter, it is not surprising that the world is a sea of suffering. The Buddhist view that even if "we accidentally reincarnate in different bodies" we are all made of the same substance, is here fully conveyed by the author's words. However, such a "spiritual" ideal can provide no relief unless a "political" program of the eradication of differences is carried out, the author underlines. Again, a "meditative," spiritual, and individual premise does not lead to the praise of a hermit's life but rather to a classic Confucian call to public action by the sage, echoing Wang Yangming's principle of "unity of thought and action."

> Primitives, having just differentiated from beasts, roaming and wandering considered the Earth as a single country and presented no differences between them, eating blood, wearing no clothes, living in caves or dwelling in trees. When the Sages appeared, and culture gradually spread, they started to build homes and palaces, to wear clothes and prepare food, to develop rites, music, books, and vehicles; at the top they established a king, at the bottom they put captives and slaves; poor people became beggars, while the rich learned how to break the rules; males were honoured and women oppressed, humans were valued and monkeys were despised; noble and humble families were considered as different species; nomads and literati were considered as the opposite stages of human intelligence; prestige was arranged in different levels and social differences were thus established. Alas, what a fate! This brought a difference in incarnations. Someone incarnates in a prince, and when he grows up he becomes an emperor, owns an entire country, and is venerated as a heavenly ruler, arbitrarily dispensing life and death, deciding punishments and rewards, agitating winds and thunders with his breath, moulding hills and mountains with his pace, causing wars and cracking bones in one moment of anger, making the whole world rejoice in one moment of happiness.

---

25 Since *toutai* literally indicates the act of a soul entering a body, I translate it both as "reincarnation" and as "incarnation," depending on the context. However, it is an undeniably Buddhist presence in Kang's book.

Someone else instead unhappily incarnates in a slave, and he knows that from birth to death he will always be a slave, serving others with his own body while he can't rest, hearing insults while he can't reply; even if he is gifted with the wisdom of a sage he won't be able to serve as an official, even if he sacrifices his life for a good cause he won't be honoured, even if he serves well he will not be considered as a member of society and his posterity will be for ever in servitude. But social hierarchies can only be theorized in terms of virtue and talent: worthy people can occupy high positions, people of lower quality can occupy lower positions; so, with nine virtues one becomes a ruler, with three virtues one becomes a householder: Heaven manufactures people's brilliancy, this is a general principle. [...] Now, these mixtures of body and virtue are called men: as Confucius said, men cannot make men, only Heaven can. The Master said: any thing cannot be generated without yang, without yin, and without Heaven; only when the three are put together, life appears. That's why it is said that "a mother can have a child, also Heaven can have a child." We are all sons of Heaven, we are all brothers, but we accidentally incarnate in different bodies; our body is eventually thrown away, the value of our life is like that of an ant, our existence is as light as a feather, but we cannot spread our wings and fly away, perpetually driven down to this world; and even the wisdom of the sages cannot liberate us, the universe itself cannot feel compassion for us, our parents themselves cannot save us. In the world there's so much sorrow and the accident of reincarnation really is the ultimate cause of suffering; how does it come about that Heaven has established this earth and yet cannot shake it and save us? If we look to the world in its entirety: birds and beasts are so numerous that we can't count them. And women, they are half of the living population. Poor families, nomads, servants, they all account for 70 or 80% of the male population, whereas those who incarnate as kings, millionaires, or noble and wealthy families are very few throughout the world. Alas! How does it come about that empathic people, capable of compassion, are so few and have to face the immeasurable calamity of uncountable people suffering all together, without finding a way to save them? Maybe there is no way? This has been the disgrace of benevolent sages and philosophers for thousands and thousands of years.[26]

---

26   Kang Youwei, *Datong Shu*, 10, 12–13. My translation. Original text: 太古之野人，甫離獸身，狉狉榛榛，全地如一而無等差，茹血，衣皮，穴處，巢居。自聖智日出，文明日舒，宮室，服食，禮樂，書車；上立帝王，下設虜奴；貧為乞丐，富為陶朱；尊男卑女，貴人賤狙；華族寒門，別若烏魚；蠻獠都上，絕

Another intriguing example of Kang's Buddhist influences and references is provided in the last part of the *Datong Shu*, where the marvellous scientific and technological progress that will increasingly improve people's life in the age of Concord is described.[27] In the following passage, in particular, the author foresees this evolution in terms of nutritional habits: "universal vegetarianism" will triumph, as the natural outcome of empathy (*ren*) will expand to every living creature.

> In the age of Concord, new technologies will be provided day by day in order to substitute meat products in the name of "similarity" [between animals and men] until eating birds or mammals will be banned, as the principle of empathy will progress to its maximum. Mammals are the most similar to human beings and they will be the first whose consumption will be prohibited; then birds' consumption will be banned and finally it will extend to fishes. Crustaceans are the most distant from men and the less intelligent, therefore it will be still possible to eat them, but finally, when it will appear that they have intelligence and feelings too, their consumption will be prohibited as well. [...] Brahmanism and Buddhism were the first religions to issue the prohibition of killing other beings, and it really was a proof of the utmost empathy. But in a world where countries still fought one another and men still ate their similar, how could people possibly conceive of loving birds and beasts?[28]

出智愚；燦然列極，天淵之殊。嗚呼命哉！投胎之異也。一為王子之胎，長即為帝王矣，富有國土，貴極天帝，生殺任意，開賞從心，呼吸動風雷，舉動壓山岳，一怒之戰，百萬骨枯，一喜之賞，普天歡動。不幸而為奴虜之胎，一出世即永為奴虜矣，終身執役而不得息所人鞭撻而不敢報，雖有聖哲而不得仕，雖死節烈而不得贈位，雖為義僕而不顧人列，子子孫孫世襲為隸。夫貴賤之宜，隻論才德，大賢受大位，小賢受小位，故九德為帝，三德有家，天工人亮，乃公裡也。[...] 凡此體膚才智，等是人也，孔子所謂人非人能為，天所生也。孔子又曰：夫物，非陽不生，非陰不生，非天不生，三合然后生。故謂之"母之子也可，天之子也可"。同是天子，實為同胞，而乃偶誤投胎終身擲棄，生賤螻蟻，命輕鴻毛，不能奮飛，永分淪落，雖有仁聖不能拯拔，雖有天地不能哀憐，雖有父母不能愛助。天下固多因苦，而投胎之誤，實為苦惱之萬原，是豈天造地設而無可振救歟？而普觀天地，禽獸之多，固無可言。即論女身，實居生民之半，而寒門窮子，邊蠻奴隸，又佔男子十分之七八，而為帝王、巨富、華族、高門之胎者，舉世無幾也。嗚呼！悲惱之仁人，若之何為茲少數，而坐令無涯多數之人物同罹無量之厄滅，而不思所以振救之歟？得非數千年聖哲仁人之大恥歟！

27 See below, Chapter 3.
28 Kang Youwei, *Datong Shu*, 320. My translation. Original text: 大同之世新制日出，則有能代肉品之精華而大益相同者，至是，則可不食鳥獸之肉而至仁成矣。獸與人同本而至親，首戒食之，次漸戒食鳥，次漸戒食魚焉。虫魚與人最疏，

Albeit seldom visible in Kang's major political works, then, the Buddhist influence is nevertheless an important element in his philosophical elaborations. The concern for human suffering, and the eradication of any social boundary as the only way to overcome it, forms a significant part of the author's account of the meaning of life and the final destination of history, reinforcing the universal dimension of his Confucianism.

In the *Datong Shu* this mixture of Classicism, esoteric Confucianism, and Buddhist concerns is displayed in its full richness. Then, in Kang's last years, the meditative element becomes predominant: if a "second phase" can be defined in Kang's speculations, it is not in the *Datong Shu* itself—which is intertwined with his political thought and activism, as will be repeatedly pointed out throughout this book—but rather in the spiritual shift occurring in the final phase of his life, when Kang announces that the Great Concord is not the last stage of human evolution. Beyond the "end of history" lies a sort of *individual* fourth stage, he says. And when history ends, men will start to pursue immortality: "After the Great Concord there will first be the knowledge of immortality; after that, there will be the knowledge of Buddhahood; after them, there will be the knowledge of astral journeys.[29] I will write another book on the subject."[30] Salvation lies outside of history, Kang eventually announces. The fascinating collection of essays and lectures dedicated to the so-called "celestial wanderings" (astral journeys) are both the coronation and the overcoming of the *Datong Shu* itself. Finally subscribing to Buddhist idealism and setting up a new school in Shanghai (established in 1926) where he instructed his disciples in meditative techniques, "having relinquished the role of social reformer, [Kang] now assumed the role of a heaven-roaming prophet."[31] Denounced as patent "escapism,"[32] Kang's final journey *outside* history seems to reflect his disappointment. Again, rather than yield to a contradiction, Kang rather shifts his attention to the highest level of individual evolution, which can only be attained at the end of a solitary journey beyond any category of time and space. Armed with this assumption, Kang seems to abandon his optimist view on historical evolution, embracing the very same

---

又最愚，故在可食之列，然以有知而痛苦也，故終戒之。 [...] 婆羅門及佛法首創戒殺，實為至仁，但國爭未了，人猶相食，何能逾級而愛及鳥獸？

29 I have translated *tianyou* 天游 as "astral journeys" instead of "roaming to Heaven" in order to get closer to a Western esoteric lexicon.

30 Kang Youwei, *Datong Shu* quoted in Hsiao, *A Modern China and a New World*, 171, here translated with modifications.

31 Hsiao, *A Modern China and a New World*, 175.

32 *Ibid.*

"hermitic" approach to life he so harshly criticized in his Utopia. As he would write four years before his death, on February 26, 1923, "I'm an old man, who has rendered no useful service to the country and found no place on earth to bury his sorrows, [and can] manage now only to make excursions into the heavens."[33]

[33] *Ibid.*, 173.

CHAPTER 3

State and Science
The Weight of the West

1   Models of Unity: Western Examples and Universal Patterns

It is now time to examine how Kang's vision of human destiny—in which a heterodox and progressive interpretation of Confucianism is blended with a Buddhist sense of salvation as a universal task—is articulated by the philosopher within the political reality of his time. In other words, after surveying the classical roots of Kang's concept of *datong*, the elements deriving from the specific time and circumstance in which he *used* the concept, and the specific political challenges for which he elaborated it, have to be assessed. And this is where the West enters the stage.

As we have already remarked, the *Book of Great Concord* is not solely a Utopia: the prophecy of the world of tomorrow is just a part of the text, whereas a great deal of space is devoted to observations of the path unfolding *to* that world, from primeval times to the present. In other words, in his work Kang focuses on the past and the present of mankind as much as he does on its future.

The drift towards unity prophesied by Confucius is presented by Kang as an implacable universal mechanism beating the time of mankind's evolution, stretching from the constitution of smaller units at the dawn of civilization to the establishment of the one-world government in the Age of Concord.

This interpretation of human history is not restricted to the *Datong Shu*, but emerges throughout his entire production, as a pattern structuring and connecting his lifetime's endeavour. Kang's universalism is not just a "potential" universalism, as in classical Confucianism, but a real attempt at talking about the globe in its entirety. Belonging in this sense to the "modern" age, Kang acknowledges the existence of the wider world: his speculation is not limited to China. On the contrary, we can say that although the foundations of his philosophy of history and of change are inherently Chinese, they were set in motion and amalgamated through his (mainly indirect) contact with the West. Since his first journey to Hong Kong in 1878, Kang had been impressed by the material side of European progress, as reflected in the buildings (or in the social organization) of the British possession. The same impression was confirmed in 1882, as he passed through the foreign concessions in Shanghai. His subsequent encounter with the textual materials provided by missionaries or by the Jiangnan Arsenal enriched his view through a clearer understanding of progress in its more visible aspects. And, as will be argued later, it decisively shaped his Confucianism. At the cost of being too simplistic, we could define Kang's effort as an attempt to move from an imperial dimension to a global one, presenting the "nationalist" stage as one passage in a grander process. It is no surprise, then, that his utopian gaze roams the entire planet—with a coincidence between the imperial concept of *tianxia* (all-under-heaven, or "universe") and *shijie* (the modern concept translating a more scientific and geographically accurate understanding of the "world")—as he is eager to learn and use examples from the other continents to reinforce and justify his theories. To Kang's eyes, China unquestionably needs to learn from other countries (but also from her past) and must become a strong State, as his personal involvement in the 1898 reforms demonstrates. But a strong State is not the final goal (in Hegelian terms): defying any essentialist view of "cultures" and "traditions," Kang paints a universal fresco in which the strengthening of States is just a step toward perpetual peace. This explains Kang's interest in foreign examples of State-building, and more specifically of State-building following processes of unification: they serve at once as a model for internal reforms in the Chinese context and as a demonstration of the progression from chaos to ever wider forms of political order as the natural direction of history.

One example of Kang's keen attention to processes of unification can be found in his European travel diaries, written in 1904 and published one year later with the title *Ouzhou shiyiguo youji* 歐洲十一國游記, *A Travel Journal from Eleven European Countries*. Here, the author describes his tour through the European continent in the years following his 1898 exile, mainly focusing on France, Germany, and Italy.[1]

The Italian journal is particularly interesting in this regard. The following extract presents a summary of Italy's struggle for unification, providing a useful reminder of how Kang's vision of historical progression was used as a "universal compass" applicable to every geographical and cultural context (with some interesting hints of a comparative history, as well).

> Italy emerged from the fall of Rome, when the Germanic general Alaricus seized the city with his army. Attila of the Huns invaded it with 700 thousand men. It was as calamitous as when Liu Yuan and Shi Le destroyed the Jin dynasty. Subsequently, Italy was subordinate to the Germanic general Ataulf until Theodoric and the Ostrogoths defeated him. The borders

---

[1] The most complete account in a Western language of Kang's journeys is still Lo Jung-Pang (ed), *K'ang Yu-wei: A biography and a symposium* (Tucson AR: The University of Arizona Press, 1967).

of his kingdom were the Danube at the North and Spain at the West. They wore their swords on leather belts, and yet could use Latin, speaking a mixed language from which Italian derived. Similarly, Fu Jian of the Former Qin and Murong Chui fought a long battle for the control of the Central Plains, and they could use Chinese language. When the Eastern Roman Empire was founded claiming only partial sovereignty over the former Empire, it was like the establishment of the Southern dynasties in China. In 520 CE the ruler of Eastern Roman Empire Justinian promoted a new code and pacified Carthage and North Africa, taking control of the Vandal kingdom, seizing the Ostrogoths and reconquering Italy. It was as when Liu Yu of the Liu Song pacified the Qin and the Jin and recovered Henan. [*Kang then proceeds with an extensive survey of the history of the partitions of Italy and its subjugation to a number of foreign powers*]

Through the last millennium, conflicts in Italy were not few, it was divided in many smaller countries although it was ideally united by the pope. While the rest of the European countries were experiencing feudalism, the free cities of Italy were able to flourish and protect themselves. Otherwise, where independence was not possible, the authority was exerted by external powers such as Germany, France, or Spain; alternatively, in other parts of Italy autonomy was preserved in kingdoms or feuds: in the North, the Kingdom of Sardinia, Venice, Lombardy, Modena, and Parma; in the South, Rome, Tuscany, and Naples. Three centuries ago, Venice and Lombardy became subject to the Austrian kingdom as other smaller units which were since then ruled by Vienna. When Napoleon defeated Austria, he obtained Northern Italy and in the 60th year of Qianlong era [1796] he was crowned King of Italy in Milan. The event was commemorated with an arch of triumph in Milan, which I have visited. Then, he enthroned one of his generals as king of Naples. When Napoleon was defeated, the Council of Vienna revived the previous territorial asset and all the small units in northern Italy went back to Austrian rule. However, many Italians started to suffer this oppression, aspiring to unification as a reaction against Austria. On the 28th year of Daoguang, a new revolution occurred in France, therefore inspiring Lombardy and Venice to rebel against Austria. In Rome people revolted against the Pope, as well; at the same time Albert King of Sardinia, who advocated the rule of law and independence, gained the support of all the Northern states which had all turned away from Austria. The following year France moved her armies to Rome and reinstalled the Pope. Intimidated, the other States did not react. King Emmanuel II of Sardinia alone promulgated a constitution and therefore conquered the minds and hearts of the people.

STATE AND SCIENCE   59

In the third year of Xianfeng, Cavour became Prime Minister and fought Austria making an alliance with England and France: he won and took Lombardy. Consequently, Venice, Parma and Modena, Tuscany and Lazio joined the Kingdom of Sardinia, with Naples and Sicily left as the only resistant. In the 10th year of Xianfeng, they were rapidly annihilated by Garibaldi's armies and annexed to the Kingdom of Sardinia. The following year, when I was three years old, the Italian Parliament was inaugurated and Emmanuel was proclaimed King of Italy, thus concluding the process of Italian unification.

Only Rome and Venice were left out, the first under the Pope, the latter under Austria. In the 5th year of Tongzhi, when I was eight, in the war between Prussia and Austria, the Italians supported Prussia in its victory, gaining Venice as a reward. Then, in the 9th year of Tongzhi, when I was already twelve, a war between Prussia and France erupted: the French army abandoned Rome and the King of Italy deprived the Pope of his power and moved the capital to Rome, thus accomplishing what is today's Italy, which everybody recognizes as a personal success of Cavour. So many wars and disorders resulted in a poor country. After two thousand years things have changed and perhaps its people have ceased to suffer.[2]

---

2   Kang Youwei, *Ouzhou shiyiguo youji*, 168–171. My translation. Original text: 意大利自羅馬解紐，日耳曼大將阿拉烈，以重兵屠羅馬。匈牙利之祖曷提拉，擁七十萬眾以蹂踐。此如劉淵、石勒之广晉，慘禍同焉。其后意大利隸於日耳曼大將阿道塞，而帖何他力與峨特广之。其國境北自丹牛波河，西底西班牙境。衣皮帶劍，而能用羅馬文化，言語雜糅，於是意大利語出焉。此為苻堅、慕容垂爭長中原之世，亦能用中國文化者也。時東羅馬偏安，猶南朝矣，何其似那。及西五百二十年，東羅馬英主如斯底年興，即制定法律者也，乃平定迦太基及非洲復汪德羅國，降峨特狄，恢復意大利。此猶劉裕之平秦齊、復河南矣。[...]　意大利千年以來，戰爭無窮，中分為數小國，而以教皇為正統。蓋當時歐洲各國，封建盛行，故意大利自有都市，亦得保全其間，以延綿千載。或不能自立，而隸屬於強國如日耳曼、法國、西班牙，而自治之國體尚存焉，或則仍為封侯也。其北部之國五，曰薩諦尼亞、斐呢上、倫巴多、摩丹拿、巴爾馬。其南部之國，曰羅馬、塔土加裡、奈波裡。三百年來，倫巴多、斐呢上隸為澳國地，餘各小邦，皆制於澳。當拿破命盛時，勝澳，得意大利之北部，以乾隆六十年，於美蘭戴倫巴多王冠，而為意王。今其紀功牌坊在美蘭，吾嘗見之。又使其將王奈波裡焉。及拿破命敗，維也納會議歸舊地，意諸小國復歸於澳。而意人多慎其壓制，欲合為一國以拒澳。道光二十八年，法革命再起，倫巴多、斐呢上起而抗澳。羅馬民惡教皇而放之，薩諦尼亞王阿爾培主民政而自立，北部個邦從之，皆背澳矣。逾年，法人以兵戍羅馬，復教皇位。個邦畏之，不敢動。惟諦迪尼亞王伊曼奴核第二，先立憲政，人心皆歸之。咸豐三年，加富爾為相，結英法以戰澳，破之，得倫巴多地。於是斐呢上國、巴爾馬國、摩丹拿國，多士加納國，拉丁阿那國個小邦歸薩諦尼，惟奈波裡、西西裡未定。咸豐十年，加裡波的起義兵徇滅，而歸之於薩諦尼王。於是咸豐十一年，我生之四歲，意大利

This narrative pattern adopted in his Italian diary is multiplied extensively by Kang throughout the *Datong Shu*, where the history of the whole world is interpreted through the ideological lens of a progressive evolution from division to unity.

In Part Five of the *Datong Shu*, where Kang praises the "abolition of nations" as a necessary step toward Concord, the "global teleological" approach to history (with a strong comparative component) again plays a major role.[3] The dynamics underlying historical progress are conceived as "universal" categories, as already said; thus, European or American developments are by no means considered by the author as peculiar to some specific cultural or geographical sphere and therefore "alien" to a Chinese context. Rather, they are interpreted as facets of a collective game in which China was often an outstanding participant (and can still be, Kang implies). The following extract is a clear example of this view: mingling references to imperial and pre-imperial Chinese history with a wide set of Western case studies, Kang attempts to describe in detail the different typologies of political unification (and, by reflection, of "political modernity," according to his view) that mark the course of human history.

> Now, in order to achieve the Great Concord, it is first necessary to get rid of the armies, then to unite countries through a comprehensive alliance and finally to have a common assembly in charge: following this sequence, the day of Great Concord will finally come. There are three typologies of alliance among countries: the one by which each country enjoys an equal status in the alliance; the ones called federations, by which single countries manage internal affairs while delegating greater issues to a common government; the ones by which even the names of former countries are erased until they are transformed into prefectures subject to a common government. These three kinds of union can be enforced naturally according to the times, but they can never be pushed forward through the use of force.
>
> **Alliances** occur among equal countries, like those of Jin and Chu in the Spring and Autumn period; they are characterized by a reciprocal recognition of authority, by an agreement on disarmament and by the

---

開國會，推伊曼奴核為意大利王，而意國統一之業成。惟羅馬尚屬教皇，斐呢土尚屬澳。同治五年，我生之九歲，普澳之戰，意人助普而勝，得斐呢土。及同治九年，我生之十三歲矣，普法之戰，法兵去羅馬，意王收教皇之權，遂入都羅馬，遂為今之意大利國，皆賢相加富爾之力也。以爭亂如此，故窮弱。二千年來之變，其民酷矣耗哉。

3   In the Zhonghua edition it is presented as Part Two. Together with a significant portion of Part One, it was published in 1913 on *Bu Ren*.

fact that the countries participating in it are all relatively small.[4] Other examples of this kind include the League of the Greek *poleis*, the Treaty of Vienna in modern Europe, and the alliance between Russia and France or that between Germany, Austria, and Italy.

They do not imply a central administration, as sovereignty still resides in each country, but the members use envoys and embassies to arrange decisions and they consider signed treaties as binding, as it happened recently in Holland with the international conference on disarmament.[5] So, in this kind of alliance, sovereignty dwells in the participant countries, each of them pursuing its own interests; at the same time, none is so strong as to assume control, none menaces the others nor feels threatened by them: disarming one day and quarrelling the next, this is not plausible. In conclusion, since each country is independent and there is no hegemonic power, national armies are dismantled, and this balanced alliance among equals is the first step toward the establishment of a common assembly, making this kind of union characteristic of the Age of Chaos.

Federations, in which members manage internal affairs whereas issues of greater importance are delegated to a superior governmental structure, are similar to the institutions of the Three Dynasties of Xia, Shang, and Zhou or to the supremacy of Duke Huan of Qi and Duke Wen of Jin, or to the present-day German Empire. It must be said that the hegemony of Huan and Qi was not very solid, though. The Three Dynasties and modern Germany, on the contrary, were able to create a consistent structure. Both had a king at their apex and, although their political systems were different, both were able to act as strong powers. Germany, for example, albeit a federation, has a different number of representatives for any state: while Prussia can count on 17 representatives, a much bigger state like Bavaria has only 6, Saxony and Württemberg have 4, Hesse and Baden have 3, Mecklenburg-Schwerin has 2 and the other 17 states and free cities have 1 each. The prime minister of Prussia, moreover, acts as prime minister of Germany by virtue of his state's power. Issues related

---

4 The comparison between inter-state dynamics in the Spring and Autumn period and similar inter-national intercourses in Early modern Europe (or in the contemporary world) has been constantly gaining ground in the last decades, especially in China, proving to be a flourishing field of study. See for example Victoria Tin-bor Hui, *War and State Formation in Ancient China and Early Modern Europe* (Cambridge: Cambridge University Press, 2005).

5 Kang here refers to the First Hague Convention of 1899, where international negotiations on disarmament, law of wars, and war crimes took place. A Second Hague Convention was held in 1907; the Third, planned for 1914, never took place following the outbreak of WWI.

to the army and the navy, to postal services and railways, are all under the authority of the Empire, but the federal government, regardless of its power, cannot interfere into the internal policies of the single states. After the federation is constituted, a common assembly is empowered and a federal government is established, which is superior to the single states, although it cannot address their internal affairs; at the same time, a federal army and a federal law are enforced to quell single states; there are many other cases similar to the German one, but they emerged from a common decision and do not have an emperor. This kind of federation is the institutional system proper to the Age of Rising Equality.

Examples of **Unions** in which pre-existing countries are erased and transformed into provinces subject to a new common government, are the United States of America and Switzerland. Once the common government is established, state boundaries are progressively dismantled and local rulers are disempowered. Gradually, the territory is unified, until each state becomes a province administered by a common government whose officials are selected by representatives elected by the people. Each province establishes its small government structure, as it happens in the United States or in Switzerland. At that time, with no more nations nor kings, people will trust each other and will be equals, and the world will be a commonweal: that is what is called Great Concord. This form of union is the institutional system of the Age of Supreme Equality.[6]

---

6 Kang Youwei, *Datong Shu*, 221–222. My translation. Original text: 今欲至大同，先自弭兵會倡之，次以聯盟締之，繼以公議會導之，次第以赴，蓋有必至大同之一日焉。夫聯合邦國之體有三：有各國平等聯盟之體；有各聯邦自行內治，而大政統一於大政府之體；有削除邦國之號域，各建自由州郡而統一於公政府之體。凡此三體，皆因時勢之自然以為推遷，而不能一時強合者也。各國平等聯盟者，如春秋之晉、楚，權力相等，訂盟弭兵，而諸小國從之。若希臘各國之盟，近世歐洲維也納后諸約，及俄、法之同盟，德、奧、意之同盟是也。是其政體並無中央政府，主權各在其國，但遣使訂約，以約章為范圍，既各有其私利，並無一強有力者制之，忽尋忽寒，今日弭兵而明日開釁，最不可恃者也。然既各國並立，無一大力以制之，則謀弭各國之兵爭，亦必自平等聯盟立公議會之制始矣，此聯合據亂世之制也。各聯邦自理內治，而大政統一於大政府之體，若三代之夏、商、周，春秋之齊桓、晉文，今之德國是也。然桓、文之霸權，體未堅固。若三代之與德國，則統一之體甚堅固矣。但三代及德國皆有帝王，雖治體不同，而皆以強力為之。如德國聯邦治體，雖並許各國舉議員，而普魯士得佔十七人，其余大國，若巴威略則舉六人，薩遜、瓦敦堡則舉四人，黑雪、巴敦則舉三人，滅克林布休林則舉二人，其余十七國及自主市府各舉一人。而普魯士相為德意志大宰相，遂有大權。其余海陸軍、郵政、鐵道皆歸德意志帝國統之，則大政府極有權力，但不及內治耳。聯合之后，公議會積有權力，則設公政府，立各國之上，雖不干預各國內治，而有公兵公律以彈壓各國，則亦類於德國聯邦之制矣，但皆出於公舉，無帝王耳。此聯合升平世之制

By virtue of Kang's impressively "modern" global sensibility, in which Confucian universalism meets Hegelian teleology, Western and Chinese elements appear in this passage as pieces of the same mosaic, composing a world history *sui generis*. This diffuse presence of foreign elements in Kang's book (as in many of his later works) has led some scholars to the conclusion that the *Datong Shu*, as a whole, is first and foremost the product of Kang's impact with the outer world, serving the author as a sort of "universalist escape" from the sad state of his declining country after the failure of 1898. Such an approach is misleading, though, as it would be to consider Kang's evolutionary vision of history as solely inspired by social Darwinism rather than by Chinese Classicism itself—an assumption criticized earlier in Chapter 1—or as interpreting his material approach to human progress as somehow influenced by Marxism—as will be argued later in Chapters 5 and 6.

Of course, Western elements are abundant throughout the book, as the excerpts presented throughout this chapter demonstrate. And, yes, especially when dealing with scientific accomplishments or institutional models, they witness Kang's eager review of foreign "success stories" before and after 1898. His essays on the good models of Peter the Great and the Meiji Emperor,[7] or on the "bad model" of dismembered Poland, all of them written in the year of the failed reforms, also reflect this interest in the outer world as a repository of examples—or as a mirror for government, to borrow a traditional term. This is further evidence of how the main ideological foundation of the *Datong Shu* was laid down long before Kang's exile, stemming from mainly Chinese ideological and political concerns. In this sense, we could say that foreign references serve Kang as handholds for his own "domestic" theories.

As a historian *and* a political thinker, Kang Youwei devoted much of his scholarship, both before and after his foreign journeys, to a comparative study of the world. Some of his most interesting historical works were composed in parallel to the final draft of the *Datong Shu*, to which they certainly supplied an impressive amount of materials. The previously cited references to

---

也。削除邦國號域，各建自主州郡而統一於公政府者，若美國、瑞士之制是也。公政府既立，國界日除，君名日去。漸而大地合一，諸國改為州郡，而統於全地公政府，由公民公舉議員及行官以統之。各地設小政府，略如美、瑞。於是時，無邦國，無帝王，人人相親，人人平等，天下為公，是謂大同。此聯合太平世也。

7 Meiji Japan was used by Kang as a blueprint for political reforms in his *Riben bianzheng kao* 日本變政考, *Survey of the Political Reforms in Japan*, presented to Emperor Guangxu in 1898 in the form of an annotated chronology enriched with hortatory comments. The "ghost" of Poland, as the daunting example of a failed State, was used by Kang in another essay written in 1898, *Bolan fenmei ji* 波蘭分滅紀, *Account of the Dismemberment of Poland*.

German history, for example, became the main subject of an essay written in 1906, *Deguo bianzhi ji* 德國變政記, *Account of Political Reforms in Germany*, a remarkable document of "intercultural history" in which Germany is considered by the author as belonging to the same category (*tonglei* 同類) as China, and therefore serving—according to a traditional Confucian approach to historiography—as a "mirror for reform."[8] It appears clear, then, that the references to ancient Greece, pre-modern Poland, or modern Germany serve only as examples of "local" elaborations of the very same universal patterns determining what Kang calls "progress." In other words, the *Datong Shu*'s vision of "modernity" is more easily placed into a global perspective, rather than in a plain "China-vs-West" scheme or that of "tradition-vs-revolution." Kang's universalism also prevents us from considering his use of Chinese philosophical tools on the one hand and the observation of Western habits on the other as a nod to the famous prescription by Zhang Zhidong to "use the West as a utility and China as the essence" (*zhong wei ti, xi wei yong* 中為體，西為用).[9] In Kang's case, a completely different philosophical approach seems to be at work. As Charlotte Furth argued while comparing Kang Youwei with Tan Sitong, Yan Fu, and Liang Qichao, "the complex intellectual relations between these four may be represented by seeing Kang and Tan as drawing most deeply upon native roots for their philosophical synthesis, by contrast with the Western inspired Social Darwinism of Yan Fu and Liang Qichao"; consequently, we see "Kang and Tan tending to internationalism, reminiscent of the *tianxia* ideal of a Sinocentric cosmos, to utopianism as they projected the canonical golden age on to the future, and to faith in the Confucian ideal of *ren* (goodness) as a cosmic-moral principle," while Yan and Liang "appear encouraged by their Social Darwinist orientation to take more nationalistic, pragmatic and secular perspectives."[10] One of the major contributions of *Datong Shu*, Furth goes on, is to "present the idea of evolution integrated into a cosmology which linked the process of evolutionary unfolding with social change," recognizing on one side "the transvaluation of social values which the new stage of world history portended," but on the other "remaining confident that Confucian

---

8   For a detailed analysis of Kang's essay on Germany, with some interesting considerations on the author's historiographical methodology as well, see Roland Felber, "The Use of Analogy by Kang Youwei in Writings on European History." (*Oriens Extremus*, 40, 1, 1997, 64–77).

9   Zhang Zhidong 張之洞 (1837–1909), governor-general of Huguang, Liangguang, and Liangjiang, and member of the Great Council, was among the strongest advocates of the military and technological modernization of China.

10 Furth, "Intellectual Change", 19.

spiritual truth would continue to be the metaphysical source of the pattern of change."[11]

There is no Western superiority *per se* in Kang's view, but only the awareness that the West is at that moment in a more advanced stage (as had happened to China many times in centuries past, as Kang points out while revamping memories of the most glorious ages of the Empire). From this perspective, Kang does not use Western (and Asian, or African) examples as samples of *cultural diversities*. In this sense, Kang Youwei distanced himself from the majority of his contemporaries interested in "modernity," both in and outside China, refusing any discussion over the "cultural diversities" lying behind a sort of doomed backwardness to which the non-Western world would have been subject. Therefore, Kang does not intend to eradicate Chinese traditional culture in the name of a suddenly discovered and "alien" modernity, nor does his project imply the adaptation of China to foreign values as an uncritical rejection of tradition. And, differently from more recent advocates of the "rediscovery of Confucianism" in contemporary China—as will become clear in the last part of this book—he does not imagine Chinese traditional culture as a possible corrective force to the flaws of Western democracy and liberalism. Kang's familiarity with imperial universalism prevents him from implying a sort of separation between a Chinese essence and a Western superstructure, as in Zhang Zhidong's approach. The descriptions of foreign institutional systems and of foreign countries' scientific development represent a universal *material* superstructure emerging over an equally universal *ideal* structure in which Chinese elements are shaped by currents that we may easily define "global." The only difference is in their appearance in time. These "chronological discrepancies" will find a natural resolution with the end of history: utopia becomes the only possible solution to the questions of modernity.

In summary, then, "Kang's impassioned plea for China to follow the course of material civilization was merely a 'necessary step to universal peace' or 'the utopia of all nations'," and he "repeatedly cautioned that the happy destiny must be reached step by step, one should never leap forward"; so "while Kang's patriotic calls for national survival through material learning sound highly nationalistic, the material civilization is in itself universalistic."[12]

Although, in Kang's universal vision, China and the rest of the world do not represent different historical courses, they nonetheless temporarily find themselves in different stages within the same historical flux. Rejecting the

---

11   Ibid.
12   Wong Young-tsu 汪榮祖, "The Search for Material Civilization: Kang Youwei's Journey to the West." (*Taiwan Journal of East Asian Studies*, 5, 1, 2008, 33–59).

interpretation of Kang's philosophy as the result of a forced "Westernization" does not mean that the author was not aware of the superiority of the West *at that time*. On the contrary, as underscored through the previously presented extracts and as evidenced by Kang's historical production as a whole, he considered many Western countries (and Meiji Japan as well) as more advanced in their progression towards Concord than his own country. Swedish Sinologist Goran Malmqvist has even linked Kang's *datong* utopia with the author's experience of Sweden's early welfare state, for example.[13]

Generally speaking, it emerges from Kang's writings that there are two aspects in which the West and Japan must be considered as more successful than China, and therefore can be used as a mirror for comparison: State-building and scientific development. The existence of a strong and solid administrative machine (albeit on a still "limited" national rather than universal scale, as required by the Age of Comfort, preceding the Age of Concord), and secondly the subsequent full-fledged technological and scientific capacities of a well-functioning government, are in Kang's eyes two symbols of a history of success in which China is still lagging behind. As he made clear in his "Chang'an speeches" of 1923, in order to build a peaceful (*he*, 和) country, "commonality" (*gong*, 共) is needed. And this "commonality" is not just achieved through political structures and through the choice of a "public-oriented" (*gong*, 公) regime type. It is also materially visible through the achievements of the state capacity in the form of connecting infrastructures as railways, telephones, or banks.[14] State (or "state capacity") and Science (its technological achievements, including their value in terms of community-building), then, are two parameters that can serve to lead China out of its crises, as demonstrated by Kang's political writings; and they are, consequently, two central topics in the narration of the world of tomorrow in the *Datong Shu*. It is towards these two elements that our attention will be now turned.

2   Rethinking the State: Imperial Legacies and Global Challenges

The universal drift towards Unity described in the *Datong Shu*, and central to Kang's whole political production, can be summarized as the strengthening of

---

13   See *Datong: The Great Society*, a documentary by Evans Chan produced in 2011 (Hong Kong).

14   For a detailed analysis of the Chang'an speeches, with a special attention to the political and material aspects of "commonality," see Zhang Yongle 章永乐, "Bu neng gong ze bu neng he: wanqi Kang Youwei de guojia jiangoulun yu zhengtilun 不能共则不能和：晚期康有为的国家建构论与政体论." (*Sixiang zhenxian*, 42, 6, 2016, 55–63).

State authorities so that they emerge from a chaotic context; their progressive assimilation through alliances of various kinds; and finally their confluence into a global government. Even in the last and most utopian phase of history, a governing structure will be needed, as Kang affirms in detail throughout his book. In fact, an even more efficient political order will be necessary, since the administrative capacities of the one-world government in terms of planning and managing the lives of its citizens will have to be considerably superior (and not inferior, nor shallower, as in other anarchist utopias of the time) to those of more ancient political forms. Without doubt, "Statism," as the theorization of a strong central structure of government—be it the Chinese Empire struggling for survival or the global government of a future Utopia—is a central feature of Kang's thought.

Modern Statism, as theorized and implemented in the West throughout the "long nineteenth century," can be defined in terms of increased efficiency in the "greater control of state apparatuses over their own population"[15] thanks to the widespread "emergence of new technologies of local and central governance."[16] More precisely, as Osterhammel defines it, "in the history of the organization of political power, the nineteenth century represents a transitional stage of differentiation and renewed simplification," by which the "main developmental tendencies of the State" can be sketched as follows: "construction of militarized industrial states with new capacities for empire building"; "invention of the modern state bureaucracy based on principles of generality and rational efficiency"; "systematic expansion of powers to extract taxes form society"; "redefinition of the state as a provider of public goods"; "development of the constitutional role of law and a new idea of the citizen, involving a legitimate claim to the protection of private interests and a say in political life"; and "rise of the political type 'dictatorship' as a formalization of clientelist relations and/or the exercise of technocratic rule by acclamation."[17]

Such a tendency was certainly visible in the West at the time when Kang was striving to help his ailing country out of decline. However, we cannot consider the theorization of the State's functions and capacity as a European peculiarity. On the contrary, to quote Jacques Gernet, "the functioning of China's institutions manifests a type of rational organization which was not achieved in the West until the modern era, in other words fairly recently."[18] Following a

---

15 Osterhammel, *The Transformation of the World*, 909.
16 Ibid.
17 Ibid., 573–574.
18 Jacques Gernet, "Introduction," in Stuart Schram (ed.), *The Scope of State Power in China* (London: Soas, 1985, xxvii–xxxiv), xxviii.

suggestion by Karl Bünger, it must also be pointed out, though, that the presence in imperial China of the main institutions which characterize the "modern State" in Europe "does not mean that this occurred in an identical sequence of phases, nor that there were not basic peculiarities of the Chinese state, just as there is a great variety of institutional forms among the European nations."[19]

Again, as we have already had cause to note with regard to other issues, Kang's interest in the efficiency of the Chinese State cannot *in itself* be considered as a banal imitation process following the observation of Western institutional models and theoretical assumptions, but rather constitutes a critical response to the ongoing crisis of the Chinese institutions, and to the crumbling concept of "political order" which had manifested in the final years of Qianlong's rule and was rooted in the long-standing question of the underrepresentation of the local elites at a central level (as the discussion on the emergence of New Text School in Chapter 1 also demonstrated). To borrow Peter Zarrow's words, the reform movement of the 1890s, to which Kang was central, "was partly, but only partly, about building up the 'wealth and power' of the Chinese state. It was fundamentally about redefining the State."[20]

Kang strove to redefine the State with his feet well grounded in the aspiration for a revival and reinforcement of the classical "long-standing links between the sage-king ideal and the image of the populace as the foundation of the state (*minben*) in Mencius."[21] Thus to Kang's eyes the emperor embodies the venerable Confucian principle of *gong*, or commonality, by which the ruler and the ruled are kept together. The gap between the diverse components of a given society can be therefore bridged only by a good State, conceived as a "shared destiny" more than a mere administrative body. The recurring use of the locution *weigong* 為公 (meaning "becoming public" or "common") in the tables describing the attainment of *datong*, reveals much about Kang's image of a perfect State and his connection to traditional elaborations in this regard (and to the *Book of Rites* in particular). Much has been written on the Confucian ideal of *gong* and the issue will be addressed later in Chapter 6 when dealing with the roots of Kang's debated "socialism." This kind of State promoted by Kang clearly implied a renewed concept of sovereignty and a new set of institutional bodies. And those terms were not coincidentally imported from Japan: *zhuquan* (sovereignty, or supreme power) 主權 from the Japanese *shuken*, *guoti* (state structure), 國體 from *kokutai*, and *zhengti* (institutional

---

19   Karl Bünger, "The Chinese State Between Yesterday and Tomorrow," in Stuart Schram (ed.), *The Scope of State Power in China*, (London: Soas, 1985, xiii–xxvi), xv.
20   Zarrow, *After Empire*, 54.
21   Ibid.

STATE AND SCIENCE 69

structure) 政體 from *seitai*, the latter widely used by political thinkers such as Katō Hiroyuki 加藤弘之 (1836–1916), who was in turn deeply influenced by German theories of the state and by social Darwinism.[22]

While those of Kang's works that were drafted for an explicit political use—such as the essay on Meiji Japan or *Confucius as a Reformer*—express this ideal of the State with a well-defined focus on late-nineteenth-century China, in the *Datong Shu* the aspiration to a *common* polity is directly transferred up to a global dimension. There is no difference in the philosophical assumption underlying the two blueprints (one for China, the other for the entire world), so it would be difficult to charge Kang with "duplicity." This coherence is made visible through Kang's constant and coherent rejection of any "national" discourse based on the reinforcement of ethnic or divisive boundaries, as discussed in the next chapter.

Another extract from Kang's Italian diary will further clarify his interpretation of *gong* and his view on the scope of the State in the fulfilment of a public and common duty: in this case, the preservation of historical and artistic legacies carried out in that southern European country is praised as a *public-minded* policy of the sort lacking in China.

> There is another noteworthy aspect for which Rome has to be praised. The two-thousand-year-old ruins of imperial palaces and temples have been preserved until today in huge quantity, their spoiled walls standing and facing each other. People of all kind, soldiers and bandits, have repeatedly plundered them and yet nobody dared to destroy them. Today, cultured persons understand the importance of carefully protecting them, appraising them and taking them as an example. No one would ever take a brick away from them, or bury them under new buildings: on the contrary, their public preservation is considered as a national resource.
>
> In today's world tourists can visit them, admiring such a legacy with their own eyes, and drawing pictures as a souvenir before leaving.
>
> On the contrary, in our country the Epang Palace in Xi'an was burned by Xiang Yu[23] and the fire lasted three months. Again, the rebuilt palace was burned down during the Red Eyebrows revolt. The barracks of Qigao, twenty-six *zhang* tall, were destroyed by emperor Wudi of Zhou. The beautiful Spring Watching Palace of Chen Houzhu, its height measuring dozens of *zhang*, adorned with gold and pearls, was destroyed when the

---

22 Ibid., 98.
23 Xiang Yu (232–202 BC), the warlord who led the revolt against Qin Shi Huangdi, then defeated by his ally Liu Bang, founder of the Han dynasty.

Sui annihilated Chen. And there are so many similar stories. Therefore, in our country there are very few buildings which are older than five hundred years. In my Guangdong, for example, the mansions of wealthy families like the Pan, the Lu, the Wu, the Ye, were surrounded by parks and gardens, beautiful and refined, bringing prestige to China: I visited them all in my youth. Take the Purple Residence, the Wu's palace with eighteen halls: its gates, its windows, its columns, and its parkways were all so fanciful, they had no equal. However, last year the Wu family suddenly decided to use that space to open a new avenue; following similar events, all the great mansions of Guangdong have now disappeared. When they want to renovate their houses, rich families do not care about the huge expenses and build new structures, exquisite and secluded, decorated and fashionable, realized with ingenious craftmanship.

But take for example the temples of Nara and Nikko in Japan: visitors leave offerings, and so they receive millions each year. And those beautiful artefacts can be used by posterity to enhance their progress: "why cannot we make even more beautiful things?" they think. But if you ignore the treasure that these legacies represent for the masses, and wipe them away overnight, then how will people's efforts in any field ever surpass those neglected examples from the past? With all our beautiful Chinese millenary buildings gone, in the future nobody will ever be able to transmit their techniques. The acting puppets of Song Yanshi, the *menniao* of Gong Shu and Mo Di, the seismograph of Zhang Heng, the wheelbarrows of Zhuge Liang, the steamboat of Southern Qi's Zu Chongzhi, the hidden doors in the library of emperor Yangdi of the Sui, the traveling cities of the Xianbei, the clocks of Emperor Shundi of the Yuan: all these accomplishments could not be preserved for posterity, and that's what makes the West so advanced in its technology today. As it can no more honour its heroes, our country does not understand the importance of preserving its heritage, and this is a great failure. When you ignore how to honour your heroes, when you ignore how to preserve your past, then you behave exactly like the barbarians, and that's what's unfortunately happening to our people. You can have thousand-year-old artefacts and then you wipe them away in two minutes, this is an enormous waste. You can have a thousand-year-old culture, and yet have no solid evidence to witness it. Westerners cannot read our old books, and since they have Rome in highest esteem, they say that we don't have a culture![24]

---

24 Kang Youwei, *Ouzhou shiyiguo youji*, 115–116. My translation. Original text: 惟羅馬亦有可敬者。二千年之頹宮古廟，至今猶存者無數。危牆壞壁，都中相望。而都

What makes this passage interesting is Kang's concept of "commonality," which historically works exactly as his concept of "unification": it is a universal philosophical parameter apt to judge whether an institutional system is well-functioning or not, anywhere and anytime. Indeed, this is another "universalist" element safeguarding his philosophy from the contradiction between the concern for the strengthening of the Empire on the one hand and his utopian internationalism on the other.

Furthermore, the role of the State in a relatively minor issue such as the preservation of the relics from the past is, in Kang's view, a crucial point in terms of the "public service" offered to its citizens, but also to citizens from all over the world: rather than being a mere instrument in the definition of the cultural and artistic boundaries of some "national identity": Kang deems history and its legacies as important not from an ethnic point of view but, more pragmatically, as the preservation of a mirror through which mankind, no matter *where* in the world, can learn something and speed up its march towards *Datong*. A Confucian traditional sense for history as a moral guide is at play here, as Kang once more confronts the arguments of Chinese nationalists (and of nationalists in general).

It is noticeable how Statism and internationalism—in other words, national concerns and cosmopolitan aspirations—as two of the main intellectual and political trends emerging between the nineteenth and twentieth century, are

人累經萬劫，爭亂盜賊，經二千年，乃無有毀者。今都人士皆知愛護，皆知嘆美，皆知效法，無有取其一磚，拾其一泥者，而公保守之，以為國榮。令大地過客，皆得游觀，生其嘆慕，睹其實跡，拓影而去，足以為憑。

而我國阿房之宮，燒於項羽，大火三月。未央、建章之宮，燒於赤眉之亂。仙掌金人，為魏明帝於鄴，已而入於河北。齊高氏之營，高二十六丈者，周武帝則毀之。陳后主結綺臨春之宮，高數十丈，盛飾珠寶，隋滅陳則毀之。餘皆類是。故吾國絕少五百年前之宮室。即如粵巨富，著潘、盧、伍、葉者，其居近者，十八鋪伍紫垣宅，一門一窗一欄一楹木，皆別花式，無有同者。而前年伍家不振，忽改為卷，遂使全粵巨宅，無一存者。夫以諸巨富者之講求土木，不惜費。其玲瓏窈窕，花樣新奇，皆幾經匠心，乃創新構。若如日本之日光廟及奈良廟，游者收費，歲入數十萬。而所存美術精品，后人得由此益加改良進步，則其美術豈不更精焉？乃不知為公眾之寶，而一旦掃除，后人再欲講求，亦不過僅全其域，談何容易勝之乎？故中國數千年美術精技，一出旋廢，后人或且不能再傳其法。若宋偃師之演劇木人，公輸、墨翟之天上鬥鳥，張衡之地動儀，諸葛之木牛流馬，南齊祖沖之之輪船，隋煬之圖書開門掩門，開帳垂帳之金人，宇文愷之行城，元順帝之鐘表，皆不能傳於后，至使歐美今以工藝盛強於地球。此則伍國人不知崇敬英雄，不知保存古物之大罪也。然不知崇敬英雄，不知保存古物，則真野蠻人之行，而我國人乃不幸有之。則雖有千萬文明之具，而為二者之掃除，亦可耗然盡亦。雖有文史流傳，而無實形指睹。西人不能讀我古書也，宜西人之尊稱羅馬，而輕我無文，亦固然哉！

both detectable as major influences in Kang's production, indeed suggesting that their interaction in the long nineteenth century is far more complex that their superficially conflicting appearance may suggest.[25]

This is what Mark Mazower had to say about internationalism, that fundamental feature of modern history, in his impressive reconstruction of the ideal of a "world political order":

> Sometime between the 1770s and the 1830s, it became possible, against the backdrop of the French Revolution and the Concert of Europe, to imagine an alternative international politics, one that acknowledged the diversity of peoples, beliefs and forms of government and showed their reconciliation under the banner of civilization. This was new. And [...] we should see internationalism in the context of a fast-changing society's ravenous appetite for ideas about the future in general.[26]

Under this light, the detailed descriptions included in Part Five and Seven of the *Book of Great Concord*, through which the institutional models of the Age of Concord are explained, form a coherent picture in which the ideal of world democracy on one side coexists with the theorization of the capillary capacity of control of territory and individuals by a one-world administration on the other. In regard to his internationalist aspirations, Kang's description of the gradual realization of a global polity is not so different from the thought of Saint-Simon and his disciples.[27] Again, as Mazower points out: "Saint-Simonians valued the coming together of men in 'associations' as the best way of overcoming the enmities of the past; moreover, they imagined this process occurring not merely within streets, villages or towns, but in a series of concentric circles the largest of which would ultimately envelope the globe and encompass all mankind."[28] Consciously or unconsciously, Kang was building both his political project and his Utopia over a progressively global extension of nineteenth-century Statism (the same Statism he had used in the Hundred Days program) infused with twentieth-century internationalism (witnessed by

---

25   For a redefinition of this interaction in a Chinese context, see Rebecca Karl, *Staging the World: Chinese Nationalism at the Turn of the Twentieth Century* (Durham NC: Duke University Press, 2002).

26   Mark Mazower, *Governing the World. The History of an Idea*. (London: Penguin Press, 2012), 24.

27   Claude Henri de Rouvroy, comte de Saint-Simon (1760–1825), French philosopher, considered as one of the "founding fathers" of modern socialism. His industrialist theories influenced liberals like Mills, anarchists like Proudhon, and communists like Marx and Engels themselves. See Alan Ryan, *On Politics: A History of Political Thought, From Herodotus to the Present* (New York NY: Liveright, 2012), 647–651.

28   Mazower, *Governing the World*, 97.

his enthusiasm for the proclamation of the League of Nations in 1919, for example). We could therefore define Kang's utopianism as the gradual expansion of his nineteenth-century statist concerns to a more universal twentieth-century dimension, concluded by the flourishing of a global State "democratically" supervising every aspect of the life of its citizens—from health promotion to industrial production.

The debate on Kang's ideals of "socialism" and "democracy" will be addressed in the following chapters, but his interest in scientific progress will be examined now as another mark of the Western references in the *Datong Shu*.

3 Embracing Science: the Universal Language of Progress

Kang's overseas journeys did not alter the fundamentals of his thought, as we know. Certainly, though, they provided him with the opportunity to enrich his set of "examples" used in expressing his own view of historical development and his political prescriptions for strengthening China: his world tour further developed his ability to judge each nation's positioning along the advancement toward the end of history using universal parameters such as the State and Science. We could also define his measuring tools from a merely philosophical point of view, as indicators of the degree of *tong* 同 and *gong* 公 (unification and commonality) and of the level of "material culture" (which Kang defines as the level of *le* 樂, or satisfaction, of each individual) attained by any community of people. Kang's own concept of "modernization," as already noted, aims to be objective, and pragmatically based on the results provided by the optimization of social, individual, and natural forces provided by more and more effective forms of group organization. Therefore, Western countries are often mentioned and admired for their scientific and technological accomplishments, which are—in Kang's opinion—the logical outcome of the empowerment of their central administrations. Similarly to what has already been said about the State, then, Science—as a manifestation of the former's capacities—functions for Kang as an unmistakable parameter defining the universal process of "advancement." This approach resonates with what disciples of Saint-Simon like Père L'Enfantin—whose internationalism was not coincidentally based on the aspiration for "unity between East and West"—or August Comte—whose three-stage vision of history moved from a Theological to a Scientific Age[29]—had been preaching in the mid nineteenth century, for

---

29 The systematic application of a scientific approach to matters of public administration was praised as the only way to peace and prosperity by Comte in his *Plan of Scientific Studies Necessary for the Reorganization of Society*, 1822.

example. The Saint-Simonian "concept of the engineer as laborer for mankind, the technician as harmonizer of people," and a "quasi-evolutionary rationale for the principle of international organization, connecting life's origin in small, simple biological microorganisms along a great chain of beings to its ultimate flowering in complex social international structures" had modelled a sort of "early form of technocracy" based on an "almost mystical faith in the perfectibility of man."[30] Constituting the core of nineteenth-century Western utopianism, science was soon to become a sort of "universal unifier," overcoming any cultural or political boundary.[31] The optimism of monumental projects, which may sound familiar from Kang's dream of Great Concord, such as the diffusion of Esperanto as a world language, or the Union of International Associations envisioned by the Belgian diplomat Paul Otlet (to be hosted in Brussels in a magnificent World City, whose project was drafted by the rising star Le Corbusier),[32] faded away with the eruption of World War I. The idea of scientific progress as a universal path, though, remained alive throughout the twentieth century, fundamentally influencing every aspect of social and cultural life; if anything, it could be said that the faith in the future was indeed reinforced after the tragedy of the war, as it converged in socialist technocratic ideals on the one side, and on the myth of scientific progress in Western liberal democracies on the other.

Turning back to Kang, it is of no surprise that the visible stress on the importance of material development in the *Datong Shu* (infrastructure, institutional mechanisms, or public health policies) was sincerely admired by some of its Marxist commentators throughout the twentieth century, as a (partly misunderstood) proof of Kang's "socialist materialism." In the 1950s, philosopher Li Zehou 李泽厚 would stress Kang's attention to "material culture" in an effort at linking the Confucian reformer to Marxist theories: "The author, depicting the difficulties that block human progress, tends to use the material culture of advanced Western countries as a basis for comparison," Li would write, to pick out just one example.[33] Notwithstanding his admirable efforts, Kang's ostensible Marxism remains more in Li Zehou's mind than in Kang's, as the roots of

---

30   Mazower, *Governing the World*, 98.
31   A fascinating account of European scientific utopianism in the nineteenth century can be found in John Tresch, *The Romantic Machine: Utopian Science and Technology after Napoleon* (Chicago IL: University of Chicago Press, 2012).
32   Kang himself devoted a relevant section of the *Datong Shu* to the progression towards a common universal language, interestingly echoing the many previous attempts at unifying communication among men, among which Zamenhof's was but the most successful. On Otlet and his ideas of a World Union, see Mazower, *Governing the World*, 104–109.
33   Li Zehou 李泽厚, "Lun Kang Youwei de Datong Shu 论康有为的大同书." (*Wenshizhe*, 1955). Included in *Zhongguo jindai sixiangshi lun* 中国近代思想史论 (Beijing: Renmin chubanshe, 1979), 133–134. More on this in Chapter 7.

Kang's utopianism are more Confucian than Marxist (or generally "Western"). Instead of tracing a direct connection between the two philosophers, then, it might be easier to consider Kang and Marx as both directly or indirectly influenced by Saint-Simonian optimism, and by a generic nineteenth-century utopian tone and a "modern" view of historical linearity, rather than *explicitly* linked by some form of ideological relationship. In fact, it might be said that "Kang largely reached his material interpretation of history on his own," especially after the extensive world-tour of 1904–1905 made him understand the enormous gap between the West and Qing China; certainly, his philosophical elaborations were not triggered by the encounter with some form of Marxist materialism—which on the contrary he often had cause to criticize as too centred around a conflictual vision of history, unacceptable to someone like Kang who praised global peace, and who had formed his own view of history on the organicistic, correlative, and natural philosophy of the *Yijng*.[34]

With regard to scientific development, Part Eight is by far the most "visionary" section of the *Datong Shu*, and probably the most utopian in purely literary terms. Here, in a lively and fascinating manner, Kang describes the marvellous results of the technological triumph which will mark the Age of Concord, putting an end to millennia of suffering and lack of commodities. This section opens with a neat philosophical premise, clarifying once more the roots of Kang's materialism. Without mentioning any Marxist paradigm such as class struggle, Kang appeals to natural philosophy: men are *naturally* brought to the full satisfaction of their needs. As culture advances, so does the refinement of people's "needs" and the goals of "material culture." If some similarity with a Western thinker is to be identified, Jeremy Bentham here seems a much better candidate than Karl Marx.[35]

> At the beginning of human civilization, people suffered from hunger and searched for herbs and fruits or birds and beasts to feed themselves; when they could not find such things they were worried, but when they got them and could eat abundantly, then they were satisfied. People suffered from the physical consequences of storms and rains, climbing on trees to find shelter and weaving hemp to make clothes; when they could not find such things they were worried, but when they got them and could find repair, then they were satisfied. People were harmed by insects, snakes and wild animals, and they used stilt dwellings and caves to defend themselves; when they could not find such places, they were worried, when they got them and could dwell there, then they were satisfied.

---

34   Wong, "The Search for Material Civilization", 47.
35   For an analysis of Bentham's utilitarianism see Ryan, *On Politics*, 695–728.

People suffered from the impossibility to fulfill their love desires, looking for a male or female partner to embrace; when they could not find a partner they were worried, when they got it they were satisfied. Then the sages came, took over and carried forward: eating became a matter of culinary art, concoction and harmonization of flavours; only then could it be satisfying. Clothing became a matter of refined materials, accessories, colours and rules of elegance, hats and sandals: only then could it be satisfying. Dwelling became a matter of halls and palaces, gardens and pavilions, sculptures, and paintings, with the insertion of birds and flowers: only then could it be satisfying. The desire for a partner became a matter of beauty and intelligence, of "white face and dark eyes," of perfumes and hairdressing, of coloured clothes and feathered garments, of clear voice and gentle movements: only then could it be satisfying. What made people satisfied, was considered as straightening out, enhancing, inspiring, and elating one's soul and body. When one could not attain these satisfying things, that was considered as hurting the spirit, causing gloom and melancholia. As the ideal of satisfaction progressed indefinitely, so did the concept of suffering, since the two are interconnected and the constant aspiration at fulfilling one's desires and avoiding suffering is called "progress."

Sages created new instruments to accomplish their mission and to let the people evolve, they created a new understanding of the world, supplementing it to govern people, draining all their capabilities to set up a system based on education and ritual. All the sages, everywhere and in any way, have acted following no other principle than the ideal of helping people to attain joy and avoid suffering. The possibility of letting individuals increase happiness and decrease suffering is called progress, and it is moved by virtue. When individuals cannot increase their happiness, and suffering consequently expands, that is called regression and it is ruled by evil. The arts and talents of every sage in the world can be fitted into one of these two categories. However, the sage considers happiness and suffering as coming in cycles and engendering one another, and only after having looked at their single fractions can he finally define what is progress and what is regression. The sage considers happiness and suffering as manifesting themselves according to time and space, and only after having assessed the weight of these categories can he decide what is to take and what is to discard.[36]

---

36 Kang Youwei, *Datong Shu*, 317–318. My translation. Original text: 當生民之初，以機為苦，則求草木之實，鳥獸之肉以果腹焉，不得肉實則憂，得而食之、飽之、

STATE AND SCIENCE   77

This simple but effective explication of the material essence of human progress, serves Kang as an introduction to the description of the "material" attainments of the Age of Concord. In a world where no private property is allowed, wealth and progress will be for everyone to enjoy. Kang's fascination with scientific progress is on full display in this final part of the *Datong Shu*, where the world of tomorrow envisioned by the Confucian philosopher takes shape before the reader's eyes. Flying houses, high-speed trains, and stunning megalopolises converge to transform the last part of this philosophical and political essay into the most classic example of utopian literature.

> In the age of Great Concord, everyone will live in a public facility, with no need to build his own house, since out of every working unit there will be a guest-house. Those guest-houses will be so vast that they will lodge hundreds of rooms arranged to accommodate everyone with no difference between poor and rich. At the ground floor, it will be decorated with pearls and jades, bright and varicoloured, embellished by flowers, butterflies, and fishes. At the top, rising up to the sky, it will be covered with a glazing and multicoloured roof made of glass, its windows surrounded by the clouds, its towers made of pearl, its pavilions built from jade and jasper in eerie and uncanny shapes, not easy to describe. In addition, there will be also moving houses, winged cabins, seagoing ships, and flying vessels. There will be moving houses, because all the roads will be railroads and they will be run by trains. The biggest trains will be tens of meters high and hundreds of meters long, like the great palaces of today; they will be run by electricity, reaching everywhere. So, in order to reach everywhere

---

飲之則樂。以風雨霧露之犯肌體為苦，則披草樹、織麻葛以蔽體焉，不得則憂，得而服之則樂。以蟲蛇猛獸為苦，則檜巢土窟以避之，不得則憂，得而居之則樂。以不得人欲為苦，則求妃匹，擁男女，不得則憂，得之則樂。后有智者踵事增華，食則為之烹飪、炮炙，調和，則益樂；服則為之衣絲、加採、無色、六章、衣裳、冠履，則益樂；居則為之堂室、樓閣、園囿、雕牆、畫棟，雜以花鳥，則益樂；欲則為之美男、妙女、粉白、黛綠薰香、刮鬢、霓裳、羽衣、清歌、妙舞，則益樂。益樂者，於人之神魂體魄尤適尤宜，發揚、開解、歡欣、快暢者也。其不得是樂者則以為苦，神結體傷，鬱鬱不揚者矣。其樂之益近無量，其苦之益覺亦無量，二者交覺而日益思為求樂免苦之計，是為進化。聖人者，制器尚象，開物成務，利用前民，載成天地之道，擁相天地之宜以左右民，竭其耳目心思焉，制為禮樂政教焉。盡諸聖之千方萬術，皆以為人謀免苦求樂之具而已矣，無他道矣。能令生人樂益加樂、苦益少苦者，是進化者也，其道善。其於生人樂無所加而苦尤甚者，是退化者也，其道不善。盡諸聖之才智方術，可以二者斷之。雖然，聖法之為苦樂也，循環而相生，則視其分數以為進退焉。聖法之為苦樂也，因時而異境，則權其輕重以為去留焉。

traveling over these vast railways, house-wagons will be built. The long-standing problem caused by space-stealing buildings, which obstruct the landscape, will be overcome. [...] Flying houses and flying vessels will be built as light as balloons, getting always bigger, the small ones measuring thirty meters and the biggest ones extending to three hundred. Traveling in the air, supplied with food, its guests will see the little world beneath them: cities will look like ant-hills and its inhabitants will look like ants, mountain peaks will look like waves, seas and rivers will resemble spots of oil, and they will fly lightly as if becoming immortals without having feathers. Yet these machines will be used only for tourism, not as permanent residences. Therefore, all these vehicles—moving on rails or flying in the sky—will host big guest-houses, each room with one or two floors, and they will look like as if hundreds of thousands of cells in a honeycomb will be used as rented apartments. So, in the world of Concord, people will not build their own private homes: no matter how rich or noble or old, everyone will be living in guest-houses. Occasionally sages with a leading role, or extremely wealthy people, will build their own moving house, traveling freely from the mountains to the seas, without a permanent residence. In the world of Concord, people will appreciate traveling and will not enjoy residing in the same place for a long time. For this the old world, where people needed to be within hearing distance from each other, like dogs or chickens and grew old without ever leaving, will be a subject of mockery: trees have no intelligence, and they don't move. Herds are more intelligent than trees, so they can move but can't go too far away. And then you have the great *peng* and the yellow swan, who can move for thousands of *li*. In the old age, people who died where they were born behaved like trees, in the middle age people travelled like cattle, and finally in the age of equality they will be like the *peng* and the swan. The buildings of public facilities, guest houses, and private homes will follow precise hygienic requirements and will necessitate a medical license. During summer, public facilities and hotels will be refreshed by special machineries: water-supplied air conditioners; in winter, when the weather is freezing, hot air will be diffused without using stoves so that the temperature will constantly be suitable for well-being. [...]

In the age of Great Concord automatized ships will sail over the seas and automatized vehicles will rail over the continents. Today we already have automobiles, but they will not need a great effort to be driven, ingeniously increasing the speed. Compared to the speed of today's cars, they will be hundreds of times faster and they will carry thousands of people, moved by electricity or using new substances, light and fast like the wind.

Everyone will have a car, thus being able to travel hundreds of kilometres in the wink of an eye. As for animal-powered carts, which are now used to transport goods to close places, they will be useless once electric cars will be introduced. Boats, large and small, will be moved by electricity not by vapour, and a single person will be able to pilot it braving the waves for thousands of *li*, their rapidity incomparably superior to our ships. Their structure will be amazing, and the biggest ones will even accommodate gardens and pavilions, aquariums and aviaries, flowers, theatres and libraries and any kind of entertainment, so that many people will chose to use them as their floating homes. So, in the age of Concord the first residences will be over the mountain peaks, then they will be built over the seas and finally in the sky. In the age of Concord there will be only public residences and hotels, not private dwellings. [...]

There will be no more servants, replaced by machines which will act like animals and deliver food, too. Every dwelling will have its own telephone which will be used to order food: it will be delivered through flying devices or it will be sent on elevators directly to the dining table [...]. In the age of Concord, foods will be picked daily, extracting their essence and throwing away the discard; thanks to new devices, all kind of food will be prepared in a liquid form, like a potion. When drinking it, the nutritive essence will not be dispersed, greatly benefiting the body since liquids are very easily absorbed: therefore, the amount of food will grow day by day together with the health of the people. Those juices will be prepared with vapour and their flavour will be mood-raising, like Indian hemp for example: they do not harm the body, they are just euphorising. At that time, then, food will be prepared only by essences, water and fruit, and people will enjoy a long life.[37]

---

37 Kang Youwei, *Datong Shu*, 318–320. My translation. Original text: 大同之世，人人皆居於公所，不須建室，其公室外則有大旅店焉。當時旅店之大，有百千萬之室，備作數等，以待客之有貧富者。其下室亦復珠璣金碧，光採陸離，花草蟲魚點綴幽雅。若其上室，則騰天架空，吞雲吸氣，無色晶璃，雲窗霧檻，見闕珠宮，玉樓瑤殿，詭形殊式，不可形容。而行、飛室、海舶、飛船，四者為上矣。行室者，道路皆造大軌，足行大車。車之廣大可數丈，長可百數十丈，高可數丈，如今之大廈精室，然以電氣駛之，處處可通。蓋遍地皆於長驅鐵路外造此行室之大軌，以所行室之遷游也。蓋室屋之滯礙，在凝而不動，既無以吸天空之清氣，又無以就山水之佳景，偶能擇得。[...] 飛室、飛船者，氣球之制既精，則日推日大，可為小室、小船十數丈者，再推廣則為百數十丈。游行空中，備攜食品，從容眺詠，俯視下界，都會如垤，人民如蟻，山峰如涌波，江海若凝膏，飄飄乎不羽化而登仙焉。然是但供游行，不能常住者也。凡茲行室、飛船，一切大旅店咸備，其餘五步一樓，十步一閣蜂房水渦，幾千萬落，大小高下，拱交繡錯而聽人之租之。故太平之世，人

The concern for hygiene and health is pivotal in Kang's definition of "progress," as the following extract demonstrates, also from the final part of the book. In this sense, Kang seems to prefigure some of the trends of the twentieth century, from the generous efforts to vanquish murderous diseases on the one side, to the more disturbing authoritarian policies implemented by regimes in Europe and Asia on the other.

This medicalization of society envisioned by Kang also echoes the New Life movement implemented by Chiang Kai-shek in nationalist China, through which Confucianism will assume a sinister Orwellian nuance, and also the much more tragic policies of Nazism or Stalinism, by which the human body would become de-humanized and transformed into an instrument of State control. At this point, the dreamlike internationalist atmosphere of Kang's Utopia inadvertently becomes the dark dystopia of twentieth-century totalitarianism. Indeed, the *Book of Great Concord*, through its own richness and complexity, resonates with the complexity of its times, when the same concepts (State, participation, citizenship, progress) interact and coalesce to form different, and often opposing, historical pictures.

> In the age of Concord, everyone will enjoy a daily medical check up, so that if a disease is detected, he will be immediately hospitalized. Any

無建私宅者，雖大富貴逸老，皆居旅店而已。間或智士創新領賞，財富巨盛，亦隻自創行室，放浪於山巔水涯，而無有為坐屋者矣。蓋太平之世，人好行游，不樂常住，其於古世百裡雞狗相聞而老死不相往來，最有智愚之反也。夫草木至愚者，故系而不動。羊豕之愚勝於草木，能動而不致遠者也。若夫大鵬黃鵠，一舉千裡。古世老死不出鄉者如草木，中世游行如羊豕，太平世則如大鵬黃鵠矣。凡公所、客店、私屋制造形式，皆以合於衛生為宜，必經醫生許可。凡公所、客店，夏時置置機器，激水生風，涼氣砭骨，冬時皆通熱電，不置火爐，暖氣襲人，令氣候皆得養生之宜焉。[...]大同之世，水有自行舟，陸有自行之車。今自行之車已盛矣，異日必有坐臥從容，攜挾品物不須費力，大加速率之妙。其速率比於今者或伯千倍焉，其可增坐人數者或十百焉，或借電力，或煉新質，飄飄如御風焉。人人挾一自行車，幾可無遠不屆瞬息百數十裡。自非遠途，鐵道或隻以載重焉。其牛馬之車，但資近地載物之用，且新電車以載物，並牛馬亦無所用之。大小舟皆電運，不假水火，一人司之，破浪千裡，其疾捷亦有千百倍於今者。其鋪設偉麗，其大舟上並設林亭、魚鳥、花木、歌舞、圖書，備極娛樂，故人亦多舟居以泛宅浮家焉。故大同之始居山頂，其中居水中，其后居空中。[...]大同之世無奴仆，一切皆以機器代之，以機器為鳥獸之形而傳遞飲食之器。私室則各有電話，傳之公廚，即可飛遞。或於食桌下為機，自廚輸運至於桌中，穿窿忽上，安於桌面，則機復合，扶桌之機，即復開合運送去來。[...]大同之世。飲食日精，漸取精華而棄糟粕，當有新制，令食品皆作精汁，如藥水焉。取精汁之時，凡血精皆不走漏，以備養生，以其流質鎖流至易，故食日多而體日健。其水皆用蒸氣者，其精汁多合樂魂之品，似印度麻及酒，而於人體無損，惟加醉樂。故其時食品各種精汁汽水生果而已，故人愈壽。

farming, tending or fishing workplace, any mine or factory, any shop or hotel will have its medical supervising unit with a determined number of doctors for any member. Also, every food product will be checked by a doctor before being put into commerce. Equally, every aspect of human life—the architectural style of buildings, the measure of clothes, the suitable characteristics of streets, green spaces, toilets, baths and kitchens, the working procedures—will all be checked and evaluated by medical staff before being implemented. Those who suffer of smallpox or other infecting diseases will be immediately put in quarantine and healed with wondrous medicines. Thus, the whole world will necessarily be a neat place and diseases will be stamped out: a single untidy place is sufficient to let some illness burst; so, in the Age of Supreme Equality there will be no illness whatsoever. At that time, people will enjoy moving, there will be no depression, bodies will be strong and healthy, medical controls will be meticulous and elaborate: in the Age of Supreme Equality there will be no disease. The only extant diseases will be those caused by external factors, since illnesses caused by internal factors will have disappeared. [...]. A single drug will suffice to cure them. In the Age of Concord, then, there will be hospitals but they will be mainly empty: those who are hospitalized will soon die because if they are there, it means that their *qi* is exhausted and there is no cure. If they are suffering, doctors will examine their pulse and if they conclude that they are helpless, their *qi* will be artificially exhausted through electricity in order to spare them the atrocious pain of dying. In conclusion, when the Great Concord is established, the greatest power will not rest in common people but in doctors. As in the Age of Chaos, when killing people was highly regarded, the greatest power rested in the armies, so in the age of Equality, when giving life will be highly regarded, the greatest power—according to the spirit of the time—will rest in doctors. Enjoying the highest authority, doctors will consequently be numerous, medical schools will be the most selective, they will be supported by new instruments and their powers will be so much increased that their surgeries will resemble divine works, to a degree that is unconceivable to us. Day by day, care for life will become so refined, foods and clothes will become so excellent, longevity will increase so much, to such an unconceivable degree, that people will live to the age of 100 or 200, finally attaining lives of 1000 years.[38]

---

38 Kang Youwei, *Datong Shu*, 323–324. My translation. Original text: 大同之世，每人日有醫生來視一次，若有疾則入醫院。故所有農牧漁場、礦工作廠、商店旅館，處處皆有醫生主焉，以其人數多寡為醫生之數。凡飲食之品，皆經醫生驗視

Following the future results in the promotion of health then, an increase in longevity will finally bring mankind to its next stage, outside of the "ordinary" historical evolution. That's where science will transcend into a revival of ancient alchemical and meditative practices, and that is the exact point where Kang shifts his attention to the more esoteric side of human evolution, as pointed out in the last pages of the previous chapter. At the end of history, the distant past of the Daoist alchemist and the farthest future of medical culture will meet, Kang announces. In this fascinating prophecy, tradition and modernity will be finally reconciled at the end of times:

> At that time, people will widely debate on longevity and the study of immortality will flourish. Therefore, the ancient Chinese knowledge of the Baopuzi,[39] of Zhen Bai,[40] of the cinnabar pills, of alchemy and the creation of *qi*, of the nutrition of the vital principle and the practice of trance, of the separation from the corpse and the conscious reincarnation, will serve as a beacon to the world.[41]

而后出。及夫宮室之式，衣服之度，道路、林野、溷廁、庖浴之宜，工作之事，一切人事皆經醫生考核許可，而后得為之。其有疫痘熏傳之症，則各地早防之，亦必有妙藥掃除之。蓋必全地治淨而后疫無從起，有一地不治則疫可生焉，故太平之世無疫。太平之世，人皆樂遊，無有憂慮，體極強壯，醫視詳密，故太平世無疾。其有疾也，則外感者耳，必無內傷內因肺癆傳之疾矣。[...] 其外感者，則可一藥而愈。故太平之世，雖有病院而幾無人，其病者則將死者也，然皆氣盡而盡，莫不考終焉。若其氣盡，呻吟太苦，眾醫脈之，上醫脈之，則以電氣盡之，俾其免臨死呻吟之奇苦焉。故大同之世，人無有權，惟醫權最大。蓋亂世以殺人為主，故兵權最大；平世以生人為主，故醫權最大，時義然也。醫權最大，醫士亦最多，醫學亦最精，加有新器助之，又鼓歷之，故其時醫術神明，不可思議。養生日精，服食日妙，人壽日長，不可思議，蓋可由一二百歲而漸至千數百歲焉。

39 Written by the Jin dynasty scholar Ge Hong 葛洪 (283–343), the Baopuzi 抱朴子 is one of the most interesting among the early works on practical Daoism. Its "internal chapters" address esoteric topics such as the pursuit of physical immortality (*xian* 仙), alchemy, and demonology.

40 Zhen Bai, real name Tao Hongjing 陶弘景 (456–536) was a famous doctor and alchemist of the Southern Liang dynasty. His major works include *Annotations on the Classic of Herbals* (本草經注), a detailed *materia medica* of herbal drugs.

41 Kang Youwei, *Datong Shu*, 324. My translation. Original text: 于时人皆为长生之论，神仙之学大盛，于是中国抱朴、贞白、凡丸之事，炼煞、制气、养精、出神、尸解、胎变之旧学，乃大光于天下。

PART 2

Threads

CHAPTER 4

Nation
Defending Universalism from the Builders of Borders

1   Dreaming of a World with No Nations

As pointed out earlier, in Part Five of the *Datong Shu* Kang unfolds his view of the historical process leading through the Three Ages, from division towards unity, drawing on examples taken from the five continents. Here, the same concept is presented in a more general way:

> The *Book of Changes* reads: "Heaven created primitives, who spontaneously built feudal systems; but that brought no peace." So, in the primitive world there were many states, but strong states and weak states coexisted, big ones and small ones fought each other, day by day making war and bringing misery to the people: how unpeaceful! These difficulties were thus established by the universe. Alas, how perilous! Straits rooted in the past, thousands of sages could not alleviate them. Individuals united to form family clans, clans coalesced into tribes, tribes coalesced to form feudal states, and feudal states coalesced to form a single nation. These agglomerations from the small to the big always came through uncountable wars, always were attained by spreading uncountable grief to the people, finally forming the actual powers of the world: this has been a process taking place through the millennia over the ten thousand countries of the world. The progression by which men proceed from division to union, the principle by which the world proceeds from separation to openness—this is how Heaven naturally conducts human affairs.[1]

Similarly, in Part Two, dealing with the "abolition of racial boundaries," Kang addresses mankind's natural tendency towards the establishment of

---

1   Kang Youwei, *Datong Shu*, 202. My translation. Original text: 易曰："天造草昧，宜建侯而不寧。" 蓋草昧之世，諸國並立，則強弱相並，大小相爭，日役兵戈，塗炭生民，最不寧哉！故屯難之生，即繼於乾坤既定之后。吁嗟危哉！其險之在前，此則萬聖經營所無可如何者也。夫自由人民而成家族，積家族吞並而成部落，積部落吞並而成邦國，積邦國吞並而成一統大國。丹此吞小為大，皆由無量戰爭而來，塗炭無量人民而至，然后成今日大地之國勢，此皆輪千年來萬國已然之事。人民由分散而合聚之序，大地由隔塞而開辟之理，天運人事之自然也。

"protective boundaries," from the household, to the clan, to the nation.[2] This innate need for self-defence is considered as an obstacle on the way to the Great Unity. And among all these "identity borders," Kang argues, racial ones are the most dangerous and the most difficult to root out.

> There is a common saying: "One world, one country." But the existence of small boundaries is a damnation to the establishment of one great boundary. The more small boundaries are established, the greater are the calamities for the world. Having family boundaries to protect individuals, having national boundaries to protect the people—this makes the attainment of Great Unity and Supreme Peace a difficult task.
>
> In our China, for example, there are the boundaries of provinces, prefectures, departments, districts, sections, villages, clans, and families; and each one of us has developed his sense of membership to his province, his department, his district, his section, his village, his clan, his family, as well as his hostility to other provinces, other departments, other districts, other sections, other villages, other clans, other families. So, although the fulfilment of human happiness is to be attained through the Great Unity, mankind has, from the beginning, pursued self-protection through many divisions and barriers, and it was unavoidable. Now, once we abolish family boundaries and national boundaries, there still remains one enormous boundary obstructing the way to Great Unity and Supreme Peace: the racial boundary, which also is the most difficult one to abolish.[3]

Ethnic communities are thus described as being closer to the Age of Chaos than to the Age of Rising Peace. A similar procession is clearly set out in one of the many tables strewn throughout the *Datong Shu*, serving as another summary of Kang's vision of the progress of history toward Equality. In this one, again from Part Two, specific attention is devoted to the issue of "racial diversity," but in a way that has spurred an interesting debate on Kang's position, oscillating from praise of his "universalism" to denunciations of his "racism."

---

2   In the Shanghai Zhonghua edition it is edited as Part Four.
3   Kang Youwei, *Datong Shu*, 72. My translation. Original text: 認知恆言曰"天下國家"。丹有小界者，皆最妨害大界者也。小界之立愈多，則進於大界之害愈大。故有家界以保人，有國界以保民,而於大同太平之發達愈難。若吾中國，省，府，州，縣，局，鄉，姓，房之界既立，而私其某省，某府，某州，某縣，某局，某鄉，某姓，某房以仇敵異省，異府，異州，異縣，異局，異鄉，異姓，異房者至矣。故人道以大同為至樂，而人道之始則異多分異為自保，皆無如何之勢也。今各家界去矣，國界去矣，而尚有一非常大界以妨害大同太平之道者，則種族之界其最難者也。

TABLE 1   人類平等進化表[a] (Progression to mankind's equality)

據亂世	Age of Chaos
人類多分級。	Mankind is extremely divided.
有帝，有王，有君長，有言去君為叛逆。	There are emperors, kings, princes; those who claim the abolition of monarchs are considered to be rebels.
以世爵、貴族執政，有去各分爵級者，以為謬論。	Noblemen and aristocrats exert power; the idea of overcoming class and grade distinctions is considered as heresy.
有爵，有官，殊異於平民。	There are noblemen and functionaries, both separated from common people.
有天子、諸侯、卿、大夫、士。	There is the Son of Heaven, then princes and dukes, ministers, high officials and literati.
有皇族，機貴而執權。	At the top of aristocracy, there is an imperial lineage which exerts power.
有天僧，為法王，法師，法官。	There is a Grand Priest, acting as King of the Dharma, Master of the Dharma and Judge of the Dharma.
族分貴賤多級，仕宦有限制，賤族或不得仕宦。	Social classes are numerous; access to official positions is limited; low people are excluded.
族分貴賤，職業各有限制，不相同。	The population is divided among noblemen and low people, the system of working classes is rigid and no passage from one category to another is allowed.
女子依於其夫，為其夫之私屬，不得為平人。	Women are their husbands' property and respond to them; they are not valued as equal [to men].
一夫多妻，以男為主，一切聽男子所為。	A husband can have more than one wife and exerts his masculine authority: Whatever he says, he must be obeyed.
族分貴賤，多級，各不同婚姻。	Population is divided into many classes and inter-class marriage is not allowed.
種有黃、白、棕、黑貴賤之殊。	The existing races are the following ones: yellow, white, brown, and black, from the highest to the lowest.

TABLE 1   人類平等進化表 (Progression to mankind's equality) (cont.)

黃、白、棕、黑之體格、長短、強弱、美惡迴殊。	Yellows, whites, browns, and blacks present clear differences of physique, stature, strength, and beauty.
白、黃、棕、黑之種不同婚姻。	Yellows, whites, browns, and blacks cannot marry [someone of another race].
主國與屬部人貴賤迴殊。有買賣奴婢。	Citizens and rulers are strictly separated. There are slaves and servants.

升平世	Age of the Rising Peace
人類少級。	Mankind is less layered.
無帝王、君長，改為民主統領，有言立帝王、君長者為叛逆。	There are no emperors and kings, nor princes; democratic leadership has emerged. Those who claim their will to establish a dynasty are fought as rebels.
無貴族執政，雖間存世爵、華族，不過空名，無政權，與齊民等。	Power is not exerted by aristocrats; noblemen and members of high families, albeit still surviving, are considered as equals—they only keep their titles, without exerting any authority.
無爵，有官，少異於平民，而罷官復為民。	There is no nobility; there are only functionaries slightly differing from common people; when they cease from their duty, they return to being common citizens.
官級稍少。有統領、大夫、士三等。	The grades of government officials are less numerous, reduced to three: the president, high officials, and functionaries.
皇族雖未廢而僅有空名，不執權。	The imperial family has not been abolished yet. However, it enjoys a merely nominal prestige, without exerting any real power.
削法王，猶為法師、法官、議員。	There is no Grand Priest anymore; however, the roles of Master of the Dharma and King of the Dharma still exist, albeit filled by an official.

TABLE 1   人類平等進化表 (Progression to mankind's equality) (cont.)

雖有貴賤之族而漸平等，皆得仕宦。	Class differences still exist, and full equality has not been attained yet; however, every citizen can become a public official.
雖有貴賤之族，而職業無限，得相同。	The population is still divided between noblemen and common people; however, the system of working classes is not rigid and moving from one class to another is permitted.
女子雖不為夫之私屬而無獨立權，不得為公民、官吏，仍依於其夫。	Women are no longer their husband's property; however, they are not yet fully autonomous, they cannot exercise their rights as citizens nor can they be public officials. They are still dependent on their husbands.
一夫一妻，仍以男為主而妻從之。	Each husband can have only one wife. He still exerts his masculine authority, though, and his spouse has to obey him.
族雖有貴賤而少級，婚姻漸通。	The population is divided into classes, but to a lesser extent. Inter-class marriage is permitted.
棕、黑之種漸少，或化為黃，隻有黃、白，略有貴賤而不甚殊異。	Blacks and browns have gradually decreased, or they have merged into the yellow race; there are only yellows and whites, although not so strictly separated.
棕、黑之種漸少，或化為黃，隻有黃、白，略有智愚而不甚懸絕。	Browns and blacks have gradually decreased, or they have merged into the yellow race, and there are only yellows and whites: they still present differences—although not in an extreme fashion—in terms of intelligence
棕、黑之種漸少，或化為黃，隻有黃、白，雖有長短、強弱、美惡而不甚懸絕。	Browns and blacks have gradually decreased, or they have merged into the yellow race; there are only yellows and whites: they still present differences—although not in an extreme fashion—in terms of physique, stature, strength, and beauty.

TABLE 1   人類平等進化表 (Progression to mankind's equality) (*cont.*)

棕、黑之種漸少，各種互通婚姻。	Browns and blacks have gradually decreased, and interracial marriage is allowed.
主國與屬部人民漸平等，不殊貴賤。放免奴婢為良人，隻有雇仆。	The people and the rulers are progressively considered to be equal, not separate classes. Slavery is abolished, and servants are retributed.

太平世	Age of Supreme Peace
人類齊同無級。	Mankind, devoid of divisions, attains unity.
無帝王、君長，亦無統領，但有民舉議員以為行政，罷還復為民，有言立統領者以為叛逆。	There are no emperors, kings nor leaders, only representatives of the people taking care of public affairs; once their appointment has ceased, they return to being common citizens; those who proclaim their intention to become leaders are fought as rebels.
無貴族、賤族之別，人人平等，世爵盡廢，有言立貴族、世爵者，以為叛逆。	There are no aristocrats separated from commoners: persons are all equals, nobility has been abolished and those who proclaim their intention to establish a clan or a house are fought as rebels.
民舉為司事之人，滿任復為民，不名為官。	Those who act as representatives, once their appointment has ceased, return to being common citizens and they do not retain the qualification of "functionaries."
官級極少。隻有大夫、士二等。	The grades of government officials are few. There are only two of them—high officials and functionaries.
無皇族。	There is no imperial lineage.
無大僧。	There is no Supreme Priest.
無貴賤之族，皆為平民。	There are no classes—citizens are equal.

TABLE 1　人類平等進化表 (Progression to mankind's equality) (cont.)

無貴賤之族，職業平等，各視其才。	There is no aristocracy and there are no low people; professions are all considered as having the same dignity and everybody follows their talent.
女子有獨立權，一切與男子無異。	Women are autonomous, fully equal to men.
男女平等，各有獨立，以情好相合而立和約，有期限，不名夫婦。貴賤之族，婚姻交通皆平等。	Men and women are equal and free. Those who share reciprocal love can sign a fixed-term contract of partnership, which is not a "wedding." Inter-class marriage is allowed.
黃、白交合化而為一，無有貴賤。	Yellows and whites mingle to form one race, with no discrimination.
諸種合一，並無智愚。	All races have unified, with no differences in intellect.
諸種體格合一，皆長，皆強，皆美，平等不甚殊。	All racial types have unified; therefore, there are no differences of stature, strength, and beauty.
諸種合一無異，互通婚姻。	All races have unified and interracial partnerships are free.
無主國屬部，人民平等。	There is no such thing as a "governing class"—people are equal.
人民平等，無奴婢，亦無雇仆。	Since people are equal, there are no slaves nor retributed servants.

a　Kang Youwei, *Datong Shu*, 79–80.

Taken to its extreme consequences, this quest for *gong* can lead to results which appear very distant from a classic liberal understanding of what a democracy is. The racial policies contained in the translated table undoubtedly constitute a significant example of such a different orientation. To our eyes it is a rather sinister anticipation of the nineteenth-century theories of "final solutions" with regard to racial differences. Again, as will be argued concerning democracy in the next chapter, Kang's ideal of unity as the abolition of diversity might assume a much less desirable flavour for those who consider differences to be an enrichment rather than a brake to humanity's humanity's progression towards a better future. In Kang's eyes, though, the idea of universal racial assimilation, causing the extinction of "less-developed" human ethnic groups, might have been a positive historical outcome, signifying the abolition of one of the most heinous boundaries separating individuals, as his public stance against anti-Manchuism, to be discussed shortly, clearly demonstrates.

In summary, these passages witness Kang's anti-nationalist commitment from a philosophical point of view: where the "nation" was defined on racial premises, Kang decided to stand against it. And since Chinese nationalism, as it was emerging at the turn of the century, was largely based on such an ethnic bias, the Great Concord anti-nationalist utopia accounts for Kang's position in the years of the Revolution: though not directly related to the events preceding and following 1911, these extracts shed significant light on Kang's firm stance against "racial nationalism" in general, and his anti-Manchuism in particular, as presented in his political (and public) writings. The background of Kang's philosophical aspiration toward *gong* and *tong* as weaved in the *Datong Shu* can hardly be neglected, for example, when analysing the essays he wrote to express his concerns about the rejection of Confucian universalism in favour of a narrower "nationalist" approach.

2   Empire versus Nation: Clashing Identities in Late Qing China

Kang's battle against the conservative wing of the Court during the Summer of 1898 was not in vain, despite the coup by Cixi and his ensuing exile. Over the next decade, after the foundation of the *Baohuanghui*, Kang would travel extensively, visiting dozens of countries on three continents, collecting funds from overseas Chinese communities, and writing a considerable amount of essays, articles, and letters through which he was able to take part in his country's intellectual and political debate, even from the "outer world." The aforementioned travel journals and historical essays are just a small part of his daily production in those years. And the transformation of Chinese traditional autocracy into a constitutional monarchy on the British (or Japanese) model, remained his political aim throughout his life. Among Chinese intellectuals, however, more radical ideas such as republicanism and ethnic nationalism were rapidly spreading. When the Xinhai Revolution broke out in 1911, Kang denounced its limitations and its dangers in a series of ten essays, written a few weeks after the Wuchang Uprising and published in 1913 under the title *Jiuwanglun* 救亡論 (Saving the Country). Although Guangxu had died in 1908, Kang was still devoted to the preservation of the Empire. But China had changed. In less than a decade, even while the Nationalist Republic was ironically claiming for itself the same borders as the former Qing Empire, Kang's stern defence of a multi-ethnic monarchy radically transformed his public image. If in 1898 he was a "spectacular reformer," after 1911 he became an example of "downright reactionism": such, in 1933, was the ultimate judgment given by Hu Shi 胡適 (1891–1962) on Kang's anti-revolutionary commitment.[4]

In May 1903 the Shanghai-based nationalist newspaper *Subao* 苏報 ("The Jiangsu Journal") published long excerpts from *The Revolutionary Army* 革命軍,[5] a twenty-thousand-character pamphlet written by Zou Rong 鄒容 (1885–1905), an eighteen-year-old student from Sichuan. "Ah! Our Han race, isn't that the race which can make our motherland strong? ... Is it not the great race of a great people? Alas! The Han race, although made up of so many, has become merely the slaves of another race ... The Han are nothing but the loyal and submissive slaves of the Manchus."[6] This short quotation displays the sentiment pervading the whole text clearly enough. Zou was born in 1885, more than two centuries after the dramatic fall of the Ming dynasty and the conquest of the Celestial Empire by the foreign House of Qing. His hatred for the alien rulers who came from the northeast, then, was nothing but the "revival" of an extinct historical sentiment. Yet in his pamphlet Zou bore eloquent witness to how rapidly the new anti-Manchuism was spreading throughout China at the beginning of the twentieth century, providing a common identity and a common goal to a diverse opposition to the Court.[7]

---

4 Quoted in Hsiao, *A Modern China and a New World*, 538.
5 The full text is translated and commented upon in John Lust, *The Revolutionary Army: A Chinese Nationalist Tract of 1903* (Paris: Mouton, 1968).
6 Quoted in William T. Rowe, *China's Last Empire. The Great Qing* (Cambridge MA: Harvard University Press, 2009), 268.
7 Prasenjit Duara, *Rescuing History from the Nation. Questioning narratives of Modern China* (Chicago IL: University of Chicago Press, 1995), 144–146.

In a new global context inspired by social-Darwinist values[8] and informed by "blood-heredity and race nationalism," a significant number of Chinese political and intellectual activists were responding to the apparently endless chain of humiliations and defeats inflicted on their country in the past decades by creating a modern ethnic nationalism, drawing inspiration from what had happened in the West a century earlier. It was not a passive adaptation of foreign schemes, though, but an active process based on local sources of inspiration: Chinese reformers in the 1890s—as pointed out by Frank Dikötter—were "active agents who participated in the invention of their identities."[9]

The Great Qing 大清 that had been ruling China since 1644 was, as summarized by William T. Rowe, "something qualitatively different from the successive Chinese or alien conquest dynasties that had preceded it." It was, like the Ottoman, Tsarist, and Habsburg Empires (all of which not coincidentally met their demises in the same decade, defeated by the surge of modern nationalism), a "multinational, universal empire" which had "with astonishing success expanded the geographic scope of China and incorporated non-Han peoples such as Mongols, Jurchens, Tibetans, Inner Asian Muslims, and others into a new kind of transcendent political entity."[10] Qing emperors were consequently "simultaneous" rulers, moving in and talking to multiple cultural frames (again, a pattern similar to the one used by Ottoman sultans[11] and even by the Habsburgs' "double monarchs").[12]

Since nationalism needs well-defined borders and identities (as well as enemies) in order to consolidate itself, such a formally universal, multi-ethnic and multicultural pre-modern empire, ruled by an "alien" dynasty, unsurprisingly became the main target of the advocates of modernity. At the beginning of the twentieth century, the Manchu dynasty came increasingly to be viewed as a burden menacing China's struggle for survival.

The crisis of the late Qing Empire, then, especially after the humiliating defeat in the war with Japan over Korea (1895), was perceived as the irreversible crisis

---

8   Thomas Huxley's *Evolution and Ethics* was translated by Yan Fu 严复 (1854–1921) in 1898 and published under the title *Tianyan lun* 天演论; Herbert Spencer's *The Study of Sociology* was published in the same year as Zou Rong's pamphlet (1903), again translated by Yan Fu.

9   Frank Dikötter (ed), *The Construction of Racial Identities in China and Japan* (London: Hurst, 1997), 13.

10 Rowe, *China's Last Empire*, 284.

11 The Ottoman rulership relied on the so-called "five fingers of the Sultan" (Turks, Arabs, Jews, Greeks, and Armenians), not so different from the Qing's motto "five races under one union."

12 Pamela Kyle Crossley, *A Translucent Mirror: History and Identity in Qing Imperial History* (Oakland CA: University of California Press, 1999), 11–12.

of an *entire* model of governance, at the same time both too strict and too loose to compete with the strong, solid, and self-proclaimed "democratic" nation-states which were rising in the West (and in the East, as the Meiji Empire had shown in 1895 to a traumatized Chinese public). With the Manchus embodying what was perceived as a failed institutional organization, any anti-government activity was naturally anti-Manchuist.[13] Statist concerns—which, as noted in the previous chapter, were central to Kang's thought too—rapidly turned into the rejection of the whole imperial structure as modelled by the Qing: if China had to become a nation among nations, consolidating a racial identity was the easiest way to succeed, as European history clearly showed, according to the nationalists' interpretation. Additionally, Western science—through taxonomy, ethnography, biology, and social Darwinism—had exported to China its "science of race," making *zhongzi* 種子 (race) one of the keywords in late Qing public debate beginning in the late 1890s.[14] Ethnic rhetoric thus became an indispensable propaganda item in the last years of Qing control over China. The shadow of "barbarian rule," which had apparently been cleared from the minds of the Chinese people during the "golden age" of the eighteenth century, was once more manifesting itself. Science, the "great unifier," and so pivotal in Kang's optimistic vision of history, could indeed prove a useful ally in building new boundaries, not just abolishing them.

An interesting aspect of that search for an "exclusive identity" is that Han nationalists had in a sense been helped by the Manchus themselves: although the Manchus had voluntarily adopted Chinese habits and institutions before crushing the short-lived Shun dynasty and conquering Beijing, at the same time they had shaped for themselves a well-defined self-identity in order to keep some form of pre-eminence among the diverse peoples who comprised the Empire, shaping their own "nationalism" in the seventeenth century.[15] Even the name "Manchu" (in Manchu, *manju*, transcribed in Chinese as *Manzhou* 滿洲) was adopted officially as late as 1635 by Hong Taiji 皇太極 (1592–1643), the founder of the Great Qing, who at the same time forbade the previous ethnonym, Jurchen. Primarily, this was a political decision: forming a "new people" with their own language, dress code, and habits, in order to establish a new

---

13 Kauko Laitinen, *Chinese Nationalism in the Late Qing dynasty: Zhang Binglin as an Anti-Manchu Propagandist*, Scandinavian Institute of Asian Studies, Monograph Series, 57 (Copenhagen: Nordic Institute of Asian Studies; London: Curzon Press, 1990), 1.
14 Zarrow, *After Empire*, 150–160.
15 On the construction of the "myth" of Manchu origins, see Mark C. Elliot, *The Manchu Way. The Eight Banners and Ethnic Identity in Late Imperial China* (Stanford CA: Stanford University Press, 2001), 42–45 and Crossley, *A Translucent Mirror*.

dynasty (which was actually inaugurated the next year, in 1636), and break the line connecting his state to the discredited late Jin dynasty.[16]

If the construction of "Manchuism" was—as with every group identity—a largely artificial process, so was the revival of anti-Manchuism: in order to legitimize their anti-dynastic stance, twentieth-century Han nationalists proclaimed their opposition to the Qing to be a legacy of Ming "patriots" and "loyalists," such as Gu Yanwu 顧炎武 (1613–1682) and Wang Fuzhi 王夫之 (1619–1692), whose works had not surprisingly been republished in the final decades of the nineteenth century—thus embodying a natural response of the "true Chinese" to foreign intrusion. Modern Chinese nationalism used the memories of the seventeenth century's brutalities against the last Han imperial house to arouse a public reaction in the face of contemporary traumas, proving an extremely effective engine for the surge of a new "organic nationalism."[17] It was in the frame of a discourse, dating back to the Song and Ming dynasties, of China as a Han State then, that Western nationalism became a familiar issue within Chinese public opinion.[18] The Hegelian model of a Nation-State as the only possible actor of history began to shape China's future, as well as its past.[19]

As demonstrated by Zou Rong's call-to-arms, then, at the very beginning of the twentieth century the clash between Manchus and Han seemed to be a natural ending to the Chinese crisis, giving a nationalist and ethnic dimension to a conflict that was, substantially, a clash between a central authority and growing local centres of power.[20]

In this context, *The Revolutionary Army* was edited and prefaced by the philologist Zhang Binglin 章炳麟 (1869–1936), who was in those years a preeminent nationalist ideologue. Born in Zhejiang to a literati family, Zhang often liked to recall how his desire to overthrow the Manchus had been aroused by his uncle's tales of heroic resistance against the early Qing. Actually, in his early writings Zhang did not show any particular interest in ethnic or racial questions, maintaining a classical "culturalist" approach to the question of Chinese identity, and even calling for unity between Han and Manchus to save the

---

16 Endymion Wilkinson, *Chinese History. A New Manual* (Cambridge MA: Harvard University Press, 2012), 807.
17 Benjamin I. Schwartz, "Themes in Intellectual History: May Fourth and After," in Ou-Fan Lee and Merle Goldman (eds), *An Intellectual History of Modern China* (Cambridge: Cambridge University Press, 2002, 97–141), 106–108.
18 Wang Ke-wen (ed.), *Modern China. An Encyclopedia of History, Culture and Nationalism* (New York NY: Garland Publishing, 1998), viii.
19 Duara, *Rescuing History*, 17–50.
20 Wang Ke-wen (ed), *Modern China*: ix; on the balance of power between the centre and periphery and its pivotal role in Chinese modern history, also see Crossley, *The Wobbling Pivot*.

country from Western aggression.[21] It was only after 1898 that he became ethnically engaged, although with a "pan-Asian" perspective: in his *Kedilun* 客帝論 ("Treatise on Visiting Emperors," 1900), he still considered the "visiting emperors" of the Qing dynasty as part of the greater Chinese cultural sphere, even if a sort of racial classification began to emerge in his discourse. At this time, his position was therefore not so distant from Liang Qichao's 梁啟超 (1873–1929) recommendation to "tear down the boundaries between Manchus and Han" as set out in the inaugural issue of the journal *Qingyibao* 清議報 ("The China Discussion") in December 1898, a few months after the failure of the Hundred Days' Reform.[22]

It was the tragedy of the Boxer Uprising in 1900 and the calamitous response of the Court to Western intervention that definitively transformed Zhang Binglin into the leader of anti-Manchuist propaganda. In 1902, while Zou Rong was still completing his pamphlet, Zhang organized in Tokyo a "Meeting to Commemorate the 242nd Anniversary of the National Destruction of China" (支那亡國二百四十二年紀念會) to be held on April 26th, the day when the last Ming emperor committed suicide in Beijing.

"That day the nation of Zhou and Han perished," he wrote in a declaration distributed among Chinese students in Tokyo and signed by Sun Yat-sen and Liang Qichao (although the latter—displaying his unwillingness to shift from "cultural nationalism" to "ethnic nationalism"—later asked that his name not be publicized).[23] In those days Zhang significantly revised his previous *Kedilun*. In the new version, the ancient culturalist approach was completely dismantled in favour of a fully racist argument against the alien rulers of Qing: "The Manchus are despicable folk, the people's disdain for them is rooted in their marrow, and they are considered as alien as Europeans and Americans," he wrote, calling for the immediate overthrow of the dynasty.[24] Despite the fact that Zhang later tried to soften his anti-Manchuism, stressing that Han nationalism was not an imperialistic instance (every people, Manchus included, had the right to pursue their own dignity and independence, he argued) and focusing instead on the definition of *guocui* 國粹 (national essence) in terms

---

21 As in *A Treatise on the Urgent Necessity of Learned Societies for the Protection of the Yellow Race*, published on the *Shiwubao* in 1897, quoted in Laitinen, *Chinese Nationalism*, 80.
22 Edward J.M. Rhoads, *Manchus and Han. Ethnic Relations and Political Power in Late Qing and Early Republican China, 1861–1928* (Seattle WA: University of Washington Press, 2000), 3–5.
23 Laitinen, *Chinese Nationalism*, 82.
24 Ibid.: 85.

of cultural heritage, his polemics had already contributed significantly to the spreading of racial hatred among revolutionaries.[25]

From the *Subao* case on, a clear division of the political opposition to the conservative faction of the Court was thus marked out: anti-Manchuist revolutionaries, led by Zhang Binglin, Wang Jingwei 汪精衛,[26] and Sun Yat-sen 孫逸仙 on one side, and reformers still defending the ideal of a Qing constitutional monarchy, like Kang Youwei, on the other. Zou Rong's text is then significant also for showing how Kang himself became a target of nationalists. Included in the edition of *The Revolutionary Army* there was another essay by Zhang Binglin: *Disputing Kang Youwei: A Letter on Revolution*.[27] It was a response to two public letters written by Kang earlier in 1902 to confute the revolutionaries' arguments and their anti-Manchuism.

Kang's main points were the following: the Manchus could not be blamed for all the mistakes and failures of the autocratic imperial system, inherited by the past ages of Han, Tang, Song, and Ming; the Qing had accepted Chinese culture, sharing their power with the Han; finally, and most interestingly, a Han national identity was to be considered a forgery, since the Han themselves had been a mixture of different peoples since the time of the first Empire.[28] While Zhang Binglin was organizing anti-Manchuist commemorations in Japan, Kang was touring the world and collecting funds from overseas Chinese communities in order to "save the Emperor": transforming Guangxu into a constitutional monarch was still his proclaimed intent. In his counter-letter, Zhang denied the acculturation of the Manchus, called Guangxu a "clown" and ironically noted how Kang himself, persecuted by the Qing, was still unable to acknowledge the Han's slavery to alien rulers.[29]

The distance could not be wider. The fracture that opened in 1901 between anti-Manchuist nationalists and reformers was a stark representation of the crisis of Chinese self-consciousness. Their common acknowledgment of the late Qing crisis had opened two different roads. The process through which a new form of ethnic nationalism would replace the venerable culturalism as

---

25   Wang Ke-wen (ed), *Modern China*, 411–412.
26   Wang Jingwei (1883–1944), for years a close associate to Sun Yat-sen, then a prominent member of the Guomindang, he served as President of the Republic of China from 1940 to 1944. In 1905 he published *Minzudi Guomin* (Citizens of a Nation), a systematic effort to define the nation as a race, coalescing Social Darwinism and Hegelian teleology; see Duara, *Rescuing History*, 36–37.
27   Part of the letter was also published in the newspaper *Subao* in June 1903 with the title *The Relationship Between Kang Youwei and Mr. Gioro*, quoted in Laitinen, *Chinese Nationalism*, 86.
28   Laitinen, *Chinese Nationalism*, 94.
29   Ibid.: 96.

the dominant Chinese view of their identity and their place in the world could only be a traumatic one.[30]

3　The *Jiuwanglun* 救亡論: Debunking Han Nationalism

Five years after the "war of letters" between Kang and Zhang, Emperor Guangxu died. Within a few hours he was followed by Empress Dowager Cixi. With a child on the throne and a Manchu prince leading a weak cabinet, faced with the growing instance on "representation" in the provinces, the Qing Empire was almost doomed to fail. For nationalists, it was just a matter of time until the right opportunity presented itself. When that opportunity arose, in Wuchang in October 1911, Zhang's vision of a Han Republic became much more concrete. On the opposing side, even after the death of Guangxu, Kang Youwei did not give up on his ideals. In 1911, while China was experiencing a full-scale revolution, he developed his points from 1902 in a series of ten essays, published together under the title *Jiuwanglun*, "Saving the Country," or more literally "On Avoiding the Death of the Country," in the magazine *Buren* 不忍 ("Compassion").[31]

Wangguo 亡國, the "death of the country," had for centuries been the nightmare of the intellectual and official Chinese elites. It was repeatedly evoked in the face of internal chaos or external invasion to describe the break-up of the entire Confucian civilization, the demise of Chinese legitimacy as a centre of cultural and political power. At the beginning of the twentieth century, Qing rulers were accused by revolutionaries of "selling" China to foreign powers, thus leading once more to the "death of the country." Kang Youwei overthrew this argument, accusing nationalists themselves of smashing China to pieces, ultimately causing its extinction. A republic is "unfit for China," Kang says. A centre of gravity is needed to keep such a vast and diverse country united, and—as Kang himself had been explaining since 1898—a monarch acting as a symbolic head of state was the best solution to put China back on track.[32] Ethnic nationalism—Kang argues—is "poisonous" and "divisive." And blaming the Manchus for the failure of an autocratic system inherited by previous (and ethnically Han) dynasties is at the same time useless and dangerous.

30　See James Townsend, "Chinese Nationalism" in Jonathan Unger and Geremie Barmé (eds.), *Chinese Nationalism* (London: M.E. Sharpe, 1996).

31　*Bu Ren* 不忍 was published in Shanghai from 1913 to 1917, edited by Kang himself together with his disciples Chen Xunyi 陈逊宜, Mai Dinghua 麦鼎华, and Kang Siguan 康思贯.

32　Zarrow, *After Empire*, 32–41.

This argument against nationalism and anti-Manchuism—indirectly presented in the *Datong Shu* as part of much wider philosophical reflection on the pursuit of Equality, and of a political blueprint built upon the idea of transcending the very idea of Nations—is well displayed in the fifth and the sixth essays of *Jiuwanglun*.[33]

In the former, Kang points out that "importing" nationalism from abroad—or reviving its Song-Ming anti-barbarian local roots—is essentially an anti-historical operation, claiming that the true revolution for China would be the establishment of a constitutional monarchy preserving the multi-ethnic nature of *Zhongguo*. It is, therefore, "like adopting an old remedy to cure a new disease," Kang says, and the medicine might eventually become a lethal poison.

> The idea behind this nationalist revolution which is now spreading in our whole country, is nothing but the old Song and Ming theory of "expelling the barbarians." There is something new, which is nothing but the old European theory of nationalism. And we know that both these theories were the products of an autocratic world, being therefore at odds with the principles of constitutionalism.
>
> It is as wrong as healing a new disease with a medicine prepared according to an old formula, which will make the causes of illness even worse; the medicine will eventually poison the patient, leading to death. So, talking about this revolution without examining the causes and circumstances, and culpably relying on old recipes, we risk poisoning ourselves: wouldn't that be so regretful?
>
> Now, we have already made the mistake of taking this evil medicine, and it has already become poisonous; luckily enough, though, it has not yet gone deep inside our body, and we can still recover. But if we do not investigate the different revolutions which spread across Europe's countries in the past, and if we do not study how wars were fought among the thousand nations of the world and how during the last century history has been moving towards constitutionalism and parliamentarism, we will succumb for sure.
>
> To understand the great French revolution we must start from the fact that after Louis XIV France was the strongest country in Europe. Our country is now the weakest: How can we compare ourselves to France, when we are more similar to India?

---

[33] The extracts of the *Jiuwanglun* reported in this essay are taken from *Kang Youwei Zhenglunji*, edited by Tang Zhidiao, Beijing: Zhonghua Shuju, 1981 (2 vols).

Nationalism, if we analyse the past and the present in China and abroad, and if we carefully study the "new law" in Europe and the USA in the last half-century, is absolutely unrepeatable.[34]

Kang then praises the virtues of constitutional monarchy, better suited to China's historical legacy than to a Republic (more on this in the next chapter):

Constitutionalism is a great revolution, the right revolution for a country that has been a monarchy for millenniums. This year's revolution, on the contrary, is nothing but a small revolution; it is a "one people, one dynasty" revolution, with the purpose of taking power back into the hands of the Han people.[35]

Finally, Kang emphasizes that reformism is imbued with a non-violent approach, asking his fellow citizens to carefully evaluate the gains and losses of a revolution that could weaken China and eventually cause its extinction:

Through constitutional reform a great revolution will be accomplished, without sacrificing a single soldier, nor breaking a single arrow or arousing loud voices, but only by pen and tongue: the ruler will return his country back to the people and China will attain stability. Only by being stable can China be strong; revolutionaries, however, are dividing 400 million comrades, smashing ten thousand *li* of land, eradicating five thousand years of civilization, and eventually causing the death of China: the gain will not compensate the losses. Fellow citizens, what are we going to and what are we leaving? What are we getting and what are we losing?[36]

---

[34] Kang Youwei, *Kang Youwei Zhenglunji*, vol. 2, 667–668. My translation. Original text: 今舉國之力持民族革命者，其懷抱知識，不過中國宋、明來據夷之舊論而已。其新者又不過歐人民族之舊論而已，豈知宋、明攘夷，歐人民族之論皆發生於專制之世，而與立憲之義，至反者也。若誤據舊方而服大劑，以醫新病，病原既大相反，則藥劑可毒且死人，言革命者，若知其不考，而誤服舊方，以至毒斃自身也，其為悔應何也。今藥已誤服，毒已大發，幸毒未深而毒可解，考之全歐各國革命之案，稽之大地萬國民族之爭，百年來事未有不歸於定憲法立國會者也，否則敗亡矣。若法大革命而能保者，以承路易十四之后，法為全歐最強之國故也。我則今為最弱之國，豈可引法而自比乎，只有為印度而已矣。主民族者，若能原本古今，考察中外，驗視五十年歐、美之新法，必不遠復也。

[35] Ibid., 668. My translation. Original text: 故言立憲者，大革命也，革數千年國為君有之命。今號革命者，小革命也，僅革一朝一族之命而已，其為復漢人之權利則一也。

[36] Ibid. My translation. Original text: 然而立憲者，不費一兵，不折一矢，不動聲色，僅以筆舌而收大革命之功，君舉其國歸於民，而中國猴安全焉。中國既

In the Essay no. 6 of *Jiuwanglun*, Kang further develops his confutation of anti-Manchuism, focusing on its racial premises. Beginning with the definition of *wangguo*, he shows how Chinese culture actually had not vanished, and had survived centuries of dynastic shifts, wars, rebellions, and divisions. The only case of a near "extinction" of China, Kang argues, was during the Jin and the Yuan rule—not simply because they were "foreigners," but because they tried to eradicate the idea of a Chinese state, throwing the Chinese cultural traditions and political customs into chaos. But the system was eventually preserved, even after the worst crises, and what in ancient times was feared to be the "death of the country" proved to be only a normal phase of internal disorder:

> What in ancient China was called "death of the country" could be either internal or external. Internal menaces were of five kinds: usurpation by a minister, as when Cao Wei usurped the Han or Sima Yan usurped the Wei; change of dynasty by a woman, like Wu Zhao's usurpation of the Tang; revolt of feudal lords, like the Tang Wu uprising at the time of the Yin, or the revolt of Li Yuan during the Sui; peasant revolutions, like when Liu and Xiang overthrew the Qin; internal wars, like the conflicts among the lords of the Warring States or the Spring and Autumn Period, or the turmoil of the Three Kingdoms and the Five Dynasties. All these circumstances were called in ancient China "death of the country." At base, they were just dynastic shifts from one house to another, private accomplishments of one man and his kin; as modern Europeans see it, they were just "internal disorders," not the "loss of the country." Conflicts among foreign nations can also be viewed as "death of the country"; however, if we take as an example the wars among the German feudal states, we can see how they did not break the continuity of a common German civilization. The disorders of the Sixteen Kingdoms and the invasion of the Jin and Yuan, though, really marked the penetration of foreign rulers, who subverted our customs: these actually were the "death of the country." The survival of a country, then, resides in its history, in its habits, in its education; it is not related to its ruler's kin.[37]

---

[37] Ibid., 669. My translation. Original text: 夫中國之舊號稱亡國者，有內亡，有外亡。自內亡國者，其道有五：有以權臣篡位者，若曹魏篡漢，司馬篡魏是也；有以女謁易朝者，若武周篡唐是也；有以侯邦革命者，若湯武之代隋是也；有以草澤革命者，若劉，項之亡秦是也；有以內國相並者，如春秋戰國諸侯之相吞滅，而三國五代之戰伐混一是也。然丹此五倒，中國舊說之所謂

安全則可以強，革命者糜四萬萬之同胞，碎萬裡之土地，榮五千年之文明，而終於亡中國，得失全相反也。吾之國人，何去何就，何取何舍焉。

Kang then turns to Europe: even the strong British Kingdom, he notices, has been ruled for centuries by foreign dynasties! Kang's defence of the Qing rulers through a comparison with European history is useful not only in demonstrating how his international travels since 1898 had contributed to widening his once wholly Confucian horizon, but also in offering a new perspective on nineteenth- and twentieth-century European nationalism itself, showing that it, like its Asian counterparts, was built on largely artificial ground.[38]

> Great Britain is today a strong country, but while the Tang dynasty ruled China, Danish Saxons invaded England; at the end of the Song, the English people were ruled by William the Conqueror, a Norman; in the 16th year of the Kangxi era [1677], William III, a Dutch nobleman, came as a ruler;[39] in Qianlong's time, the British ruler was George I, King of Hannover. So now the British king is of Saxon descent and yet he defends the English people's habits, culture and institutions, preserving a thousand-year-old tradition: changing dynasties and having foreign rulers has not been considered "death of the country." Our China, even through repeated rebellions, is still the same five-thousand-year-old China, with its rites, its literature, its culture, and its habits.[40]

The Qing—Kang says, expressing his traditional "culturalist" view of Chinese history—have adopted Chinese institutional and cultural patterns, preserving Chinese identity as the Hannover have done in Great Britain:

    亡國者，實則易姓移朝，一人一家之私事，今歐人新說，不過視為內亂，不以為亡國者。外國相滅，誠為亡國矣，然此亦如德國封建時之相吞滅，於德國之文明相續無礙也。即謂十六國之亂華，金元之入統，實為外人入主中國，大亂民俗也，真亡國也。然一國之存立，在其歷史風俗教化，不系於一君之姓系也。

[38] On the use of fictional medieval identities in the construction of nineteenth-century European nationalism (with interesting resemblances to what happened in China through the revival of Song and Ming "Han nationalism"), see Patrick J. Geary, *The Myth of Nations. The Medieval Origins of Europe* (Princeton NJ: Princeton University Press, 2002).

[39] In 1677 William III, Prince of Orange, married Mary II of England, although he was proclaimed King of England, Scotland and Ireland only later, on February 13, 1689.

[40] Kang Youei, *Kang Youwei Zhenglunji*, vol 2, 669. My translation. Original text: 今以英之強，而唐時大尼薩遜入主之，宋末時威廉第一以諾曼種入主之，康熙十六年荷蘭侯威廉第三入主之，乾隆時佐治第一以漢那曼王子入主之，今英王則為薩遜王子之種，然而英人之風俗教化政俗，則固英人千年相傳之文明也，不以易朝移姓，外人入主，而認為亡國也。我中國雖屢更革命，而五千年文明之中國，禮樂文章教化風俗如故也。

> Those who have come from the outside, once entered have been changed. Talking about Manchus, in ancient times they were known as the Sushen, being descendants of the Yellow Emperor, too; in Ming times they were outstanding lords and generals, then they came to rule the Central Plains, as Shun was an Eastern barbarian and King Wen was a Western barbarian when he established the Shang. In the field of education, they have guarded the Rites of Zhou and the teaching of Master Kong; in the field of politics, they have used Han and Ming institutions: is this not a dynasty like those founded by Li, by Liu, by Zhao, or by Zhu [Han, Tang, Song, Ming]? They [i.e., the Qing] have preserved China and its five-thousand-year-old civilization, protecting the rites, the texts, the institutions, and the education: as in England, it was just a shift from a dynasty to another.[41]

At the end of the essay, Kang draws more examples from modern European history: foreign rulers—he notices—have often been more effective than "native" ones, using constitutionalism and parliamentarism to give representation and power to their subjects. It happened in Belgium, Greece, Norway, Romania, and Bulgaria, and the same could happen in China, even through the discredited Qing dynasty, he suggests:

> Like England, also Belgium, Romania, Greece, Bulgaria, and Norway do actually have foreign kings, but they have parliaments and cabinets that carry on internal affairs, and everybody recognizes them as civilized and strong countries, not as "dead countries." The English, Belgians, Romanians, Greeks, Bulgarians, and Norwegians, carrying on their own policies, do not view themselves as ruled by "foreigners" nor as "dead states." In the same way, four hundred million Chinese people can have a parliament and a cabinet through which they can exercise political power, and have a nominal sovereign with a salary but with no responsibilities nor possibilities of harming the people; his ethnic group does not matter, it has nothing to do with the survival or the loss of a country.[42]

---

41 Ibid., 669. My translation. Original text: 自外入者，入焉而化之，滿洲雲者，古為肅慎，亦出於皇帝后，其於明時，封號龍虎將軍，然則其入主中夏也，猶舜為東夷之人而代唐、文王為西夷之人而代商雲耳。教化皆守周、孔，政俗皆用漢、明，其一家帝制，不過如劉，李，趙，朱雲耳，五千年文明之中國，禮樂文章政俗教化一切保存，亦如英國也，則亦不過易姓移朝耳。

42 Ibid., 670. My translation. Original text: 大以英於比利時、羅馬尼亞、希臘、布加利牙、那威也，以外人為王，而國民國會，實主內閣，一執其政，天下咸以為文明強盛之國，無以亡國者。英人、比利時人、羅馬尼亞人、希臘人、布加利牙人、那威人自執其政，未嘗以外人為王，而自認為亡國者。若中國四

NATION 105

Kang's whole-hearted appeal was useless. Two months later, the last Qing Emperor was forced to leave the throne, giving way to a new republic. While Zhang Binglin was shifting his attention from anti-Manchuism to anti-imperialism, denouncing the external threats to the new-born Republic of China, Kang persisted in his anti-nationalist and anti-republican cultural fight.

In conclusion, the cross-analysis of these extracts drawn from two texts whose causes and aims are completely different—one, the *Jiuwanglun*, a public intervention against revolutionaries; the other, the *Datong Shu*, an apparently out-of-time Utopia intentionally kept unpublished by the author—display, although from different perspectives, the same philosophical sensibility, shedding light on the profound reasons for Kang Youwei's opposition to the 1911 revolution and especially to its "racist" nuances. First of all, the "nationalist" accusations of Kang being a "conservative" and a "traditionalist" *stricto sensu* seem ungenerous and unmotivated. In the *Book of Great Concord* Kang describes the abolition of family, the public recognition of homosexuality, the establishment of full equality between men and women. Such a Utopia could hardly be the product of a "conservative" mind, especially in a Confucian sense. He was not an anti-Republican either, as will be demonstrated in the next chapter. On the contrary, in his political considerations, he often argues that the "government of the people" is, among the various possible forms of institutional organization, the one closest to the Age of Supreme Peace, pointing to the United States of America or the Swiss Confederation as virtuous examples of this kind, as was pointed out in the *Datong Shu*'s extract on the various forms of unions among countries. No doubt, China in his opinion is not ready yet for *minzhu* 民主 (government by the people)—and this will be the main focus of the next chapter. Despite his loyalism, though, Kang's main concern was not the survival of the Qing dynasty *tout court*, as demonstrated by his proposal to pass the crown to the last descendant of Confucius's lineage, making him an "empty-monarch" serving as the symbolic authority of a constitutional monarchy inspired by the British or Japanese model.[43]

So why did Kang urgently appeal for an immediate stop to the Xinhai Revolution? Was he really betraying his visionary utopianism? Not at all; rather, in his view, the Empire was not ready to become a Republic. Lacking the social, economic, and cultural structures from which republics had stemmed in the West, given the dramatic situation in China, revolution would create nothing but a dangerous vacuum of power—a vacuum that external powers (the West

---

萬萬人，能有國會內閣，以自執其政。但奉一虛銜帝位　給以歲俸，既無責任，不能為惡，無論何種人為之，要與國之存亡得失不相關也。

[43] On Kang's notion of "empty-monarchy" (虛銜帝位) see Zarrow, *After Empire*, 45–55.

and Japan) were all too ready to fill, which would lead to the "extinction of the country," Kang feared. This is the reason behind his attack on nationalists, and the solution to his apparent schizophrenia.

But from a more general point of view, if "nationalism" is to be defined as the construction of an exclusive identity based on blood-race ties, then yes, Kang definitely is an anti-nationalist. As he clearly states in *Datong Shu*, the boundary of race is an "evil" one, possibly the worst, a major source of separation, a detour from the Way towards Great Unity (the fact that he considers the United States and Switzerland as "good examples" of government is significant because these were not typical nineteenth-century "national-states" but multicultural and multilingual confederations).

The revolutionaries' anti-Manchuism, then, was simply unacceptable to a "culturalist-universalist" like Kang, convinced as he was that the survival of China was related to the transmission of its cultural system and the defence of its integrity from external threats, not to the preservation of a "race." If Kang's solution for the future of his country was the reconstruction of a *gong* 公 institutional system, the republic taking form in 1911–1912 appeared to his eyes as the triumph of *si* 私.

Kang's approach to nationalist sentiments is interestingly not too far from recent research on the process of identity creation and on the nature of "nationalism," and his worries on the future of the Chinese Republic seem almost prophetical. In 1911, however, with China fired by the global rhetoric of "competition among races," his voice unsurprisingly was dismissed as a "conservative" echo from the past. His anti-nationalist stance perhaps deserved more attention, though. As was recently pointed out by the outstanding contemporary Chinese thinker Wang Hui—who will be among the protagonists of part three—"if one says that European socialism is a secular religious movement that developed from Christianity to criticize the nation-state, then Kang Youwei's ideal of the Great Community is a theoretical attack that developed from the Confucian tradition and is pitted against autonomous nation-states."[44]

---

44   Viren Murthy, "Modernity against Modernity: Wang Hui's Critical History of Chinese Thought." (*Modern Intellectual History*, 3, 1, 2006, 137–165), 157.

CHAPTER 5

Democracy
"You Don't Wear a Fur in Summer". Between Utopianism and Pragmatism

1 Defining Democracy

"When the Great Way is pursued, a public and common spirit rules all-under-Heaven," reads the *Book of Rites*.[1] As Liang Qichao later wrote in his survey *Intellectual Trends in the Qing Period*—published in 1927 and translated into English by Immanuel Hsü in 1959—if this passage "is translated into modern terms, it contains the idea of democracy, a League of Nations, public upbringing of children, sickness and old-age insurance, communism and the sanctity of labor."[2] And this, as was pointed out in the previous chapters, is exactly the interpretation used by Kang as the philosophical foundation of the *Datong Shu*, and more specifically the justification behind his vision of a democratic world order. In this chapter, the nature of Kang's democratic ideal will be addressed.

The following table from Part Five of the *Datong Shu* describes the process of state-unification (*heguo* 合國) which will occur during the progression to the Age of Concord.

> *Laying the Foundations of the Great Concord in the Age of Chaos:*
> Old countries form leagues.
> Each country's government attains full sovereignty; foreign trade guilds are constituted; in any country, interest groups hold public discussions.
> There are public meetings but no public administrations.
> Every piece of land on the mainland is incorporated into a sovereign country, while the seas have no government.
> As the occasion demands, any country may establish public assemblies.
> Countries are endowed with unrestricted power and autonomy, whereas public assemblies have only consultative power.
> People serve their own country.

---

1 James Legge, *Li Chi: Book of Rites. An encyclopedia of ancient ceremonial usages, religious creeds, and social institutions* (New Hyde Park NY: University Books, 1967 [originally published in 1885]), 366.
2 Liang Qichao 梁启超, *Intellectual trends in the Ch'ing period, translated with introduction and notes by Immanuel C.Y. Hsu.* (Cambridge MA: Harvard University Press, 1970), 96.

Gradually approaching to the Great Concord in the Age of Rising Equality:
New common states are constituted.
The constitution of public administrations is undertaken, there are people serving as representatives and each country has its governing officials.
Isolated lands or islands are incorporated under a government.
The seas are subject to a government administration as well as islands and islets.
As the occasion demands, any country may establish a State: however, two countries cannot be merged into a new State, while a single country can be divided in more than one State.
Countries are endowed with restricted power and autonomy, whereas important issues are tackled by a public government.
People gradually start to neglect the authority of old countries and aspire to a unified government.

Perfecting the Great Concord in the Age of Supreme Equality:
There are no countries, the world is unified.
Every place on earth is subject to a public government, people from everywhere can serve as representatives or discuss government affairs, because there are no boundaries.
The whole world is considered as a common country.
Every place, be it on the land or on the sea, will be part of a common polity.
All previous countries merge into a common government, even the word "country" is relinquished.
With the overcoming of "countries," everything will be autonomously governed by publicly elected officials under a common administration.
With the extinction of old countries, people are citizens of the world while the highest authority dwells in public assemblies.[3]

Kang's praise of what he calls "democracy" is disseminated throughout the book, as demonstrated by these quotations selected by Li Zehou in 1955.[4]

In the world of Great Concord there will be no feudal countries, no rule by military force, no monarchs nor destructive rebellions … No aristocracy

---

3   Kang Youwei, *Datong Shu*, 247.
4   For an analysis of Li Zehou's considerations on the *Datong Shu*, see the next chapter.

nor oppressors and tyrants, looters and corrupted; no private interests, therefore no disputes on properties, businesses or benefits ... No taxes, therefore no need to escape punishment; no social status therefore no humiliations, oppressions, offenders, and retaliations; with no disputes, what punishment is needed?[5]

With no monarchs, nor aristocracy or military leaders (since the dissolution of nations has caused the consequent demise of armies), the task of administrating the planet—which, as Kang shows in detail throughout Part Six of *Datong Shu*, is mainly a question of global planning and statistics—is in the hand of a common government. Its "great decisions are taken by many" (大事從多數決之) as an antidote to individual leaderships and dictatorships; its members are common citizens, except for their administrative duties: the participation in a governmental activity does not imply any advancement of status, nor any hereditary acquisition of prestige or power (職事之外皆世界人，皆平等，無爵位之殊). At any level, they are "selected by representatives" (公政府行政官既由上下議員公舉) who, in turn, are "selected by the people every three years or every year." Banning individual interests in the political, social, and economic sphere is the foundation of Kang's ideal of democracy. The new global government, acting *for* the people and *by* the people, will embody the triumph of *gong* against the centrifugal forces of *si*. If we consider liberal democracy as the solution to the growing competition between divergent private interests rather than their annihilation, then clear philosophical distance appears between Kang's *minzhu* and elaborations of the same theme leading to formulations of liberal democracy.

This philosophical difference is also reflected in Kang's view of racial issues: again, in the aforementioned table, Kang foresees the absorption of the four races (white, yellow, brown, and black) into a single one, which will retain the main features of yellow and white people, whereas the other two will disappear. At a first glance, this may appear as a racist stance, praising the "extinction" of "inferior" human groups; and there are good reasons to consider such a prophecy to be a dark anticipation of twentieth-century history. In Kang's view, though, this racial unification is just another aspect of the global progression towards *Datong*. Differences are not removed through brutal slaughter, but are gradually directed toward a common path. In this sense, Kang's sincere and severe criticism of any "racial" political argument in his many interventions against anti-Manchuism (a key element in the emergence of Chinese

---

5   Li Zehou, "Lun Kang Youwei de Datong Shu", 143.

nationalism as an ethnic, rather than cultural, identity) which was underlined in the previous chapter, belongs to the same approach to the issue of "diversity."

In a nutshell, we may define Kang's political theory as the invention of a "global imperial democracy": the ancient ideal of the *tianxia*[6] is projected in utopian terms to a setting in which sovereignty is shifted from the physical figure of the emperor to the ideal of "public-mindedness" or *gong*. Nationalists and republicans, according to Kang, support a view of democracy which is infused with selfishness, or *si*, and it would break up China, causing a reversion to the Age of Chaos.

This may help us understand the stunning contradiction between his utopian one-world republican democracy on the one side, and his actual political struggle in China for the defence of the monarchy on the other, which was particularly visible after the Xinhai Revolution. In 1917, almost two decades after the Hundred Days reforms, Kang tried to return to the political stage in person, again as a defender of the Empire. In the intervening nineteen years, though, China had changed profoundly and the veteran reformer appeared now as a staunch nostalgic.

2   Kang's Realist Approach: Democracy Can Wait

On July 1, 1917, general Zhang Xun 張勛, a former protegee of Yuan Shikai 袁世凱, marched on Beijing and reinstalled Xuantong 宣統, the last emperor of the Qing, on the throne. Kang, who had been opposing nationalist republicans (and Yuan Shikai's ambitions) for more than a decade, arrived in Beijing four days before the announcement of the restoration, having since June urged Zhang Xun several times to take the capital by force.[7] Promptly drafting an edict celebrating the restoration, Kang at the same time resumed his main proposals for a comprehensive reform of the Empire, which by the way was to be called the "Chinese Empire" (中華帝國) rather than Great Qing.[8] His edicts—ignored by Zhang Xun himself—suffered an even worse fate than those of nineteen years earlier: if in 1898 Kang's attempt to change China had lasted barely three months, this time it did not outlive two weeks. By July 12, the Republic was back in Beijing.

As farcical as it may seem, however, the abortive restoration of 1917 is a significant symptom of China's chaotic situation after the death of Yuan Shikai,

---

6   On this, see below Chapter 8.
7   Hsiao, *A Modern China and a New World*, 253.
8   Zarrow, *After Empire*, 262–263. On Zhang Xun also see Wang Ke-wen (ed), *Modern China*, 272.

DEMOCRACY   111

who had acted as the only remaining centre of gravity of a young Republic: the country was again on the verge of conflagration, poised to be divided among the new warlords. Yuan's failed imperial restoration, moreover, had demonstrated how fragile Republicanism still was from an ideological point of view: the taboo of the "return of the emperor" had been readily infringed, and monarchical ideas, thanks to the Republican failures, had proven to be still alive and usable for political purposes. The *coup d'état* cost Kang dearly: already in dire straits with the new *intelligentsia*, he was now definitively labelled an anti-Republican nostalgic conservative.

In an attempt to rebut these critiques, in *Buren* that same year Kang published a long essay in three parts expressing his view on Republicanism and democracy: *Gonghe Pingyi* 共和評議, *Impartial Words on Republicanism*.[9] Written while he was a political refugee in the American Legation, and issued in Shanghai as a book in 1918, it adds new considerations to earlier arguments on Chinese and international politics.[10]

The third section of this work, in particular ("On how the *Book of Great Concord*, that I wrote thirty years ago, firstly addressed the issues of democracy and Republic, and how it was too advanced for Chinese people") is both a passionate defence of Kang's commitment to democracy and a lucid analysis of China's structural weaknesses. In the second paragraph of this section, Kang directly addresses his fellow citizens, using the *Datong Shu*—widely quoted throughout the essay—as proof of his sincere commitment to the development of a Chinese democracy in the future.

> My fellow citizens, you say that I am defending monarchy against democracy? What about the fact that thirty years ago I wrote about the Great Concord, exposing the theory of a world in which people share suzerainty? I was the first, in our country. My *Book of Great Concord*, which describes the three ages of the world, was published in the eighth issue of this journal, in the eighth month of 1913, and I ask you, my compatriots, to read it carefully. If you will read it, how will you be able to say that I have opposed democracy?[11]

---

9   This is the translation proposed by Hsiao, *A Modern China and a New World*.
10 Hsiao, *A Modern China and a New World*, 257.
11 Kang Youwei, *Kang Youwei zhenglunji*, vol. 2, 1047. My translation. Original text: 吾國民乎？得無以我偏主民主，而攻民主乎？然吾三十年前，發大同之說，明天下為公民有之義，舉國莫我先也。吾《大同書》言合國三世表，已於癸丑八月印在第八卷中，請吾國民疑我者細讀之。吾國民覺此乎，吾豈偏攻共和民主者乎？

So why did he actively pursue the restoration of monarchism in China while considering the abolition of kings and emperors as a necessary step toward a global Concord? The answer is summarized in the following section, where Kang introduces his main point: establishing democracy is a matter of time and circumstances, and China is not yet ready.

> I did not dare to speak publicly of democracy, believing that its time had not yet come. As the Invariable Mean says, "vast and profound is the quell out of which time flows." And in the Analects, it is said that: "The phoenix sits on the mountain's peak, oh times, oh times!" The Book of Changes reads: "Great thing indeed is to follow the times." Fur in winter, hemp in summer: this is people's normal clothing. If I wore a fur in June, would not I die from heat? And if I wore hemp in January, would not I suffer cold? So I believe that this hour, in which we confront ourselves with the Great Powers, is not the hour of democracy for us. It is not that I don't have hemp or fur: I store them in the cupboard, waiting for their time to come; similarly, I have in great esteem the discourses on democracy and on Republic, but I have stored them, waiting to use them when the time of Great Concord comes.
>
> Today, my fellow citizens wrongly believe that democracy is fit for this time; but wearing a fur in summer you die from the heat, wearing hemp in December you die from cold. I see it, and dread. I cannot help weeping at their bitter fate, urging them to change their clothes.[12]

Republicanism and democracy must be a product of their own circumstances. They cannot be imported nor transplanted, Kang points out:

> I think that for thousands of reasons it [establishing democracy and Republic in China] is not possible; because among one hundred Republics you will not find two equals, due to historical, geographical, and cultural factors [a Republic] cannot be imitated nor is there a universal technique to preserve it.[13]

---

12 Ibid. My translation. Original text: 然我且不敢言民主共和者，誠以未至其時也。《中庸》曰："浦博淵泉，而時出之。"上《論》末章曰："山梁雌雉，時哉時哉。"《易》曰："時之為義大矣哉。"夫冬裘夏葛，人之常服也，若五月披裘則喝死，十二月衣葛寒侵，吾以今列國競爭之時，非行用民主之時也。吾非無裘葛也，藏之篋笥，待其時而用之，吾於至珍民主共和之說，亦藏之篋笥，待大同時而用之。今吾國民，誤民主於今，則五月披裘，當喝死也，十二月衣葛，當冷死也。吾見而懼之，不能不苦口流涕，而勸其易服也。

13 Ibid. My translation. Original text: 吾即以為萬不可行，百國共和，又無一同者，吾即自有歷史地理風俗，不可效人，則無一術維持共和矣。

According to Kang's self-defence, then, the effort in 1917 to reinstall the Manchu dynasty on the throne, albeit on new premises, should not be seen as contradicting his utopian dream of a global democracy. Rather, it is based on a pragmatic evaluation of the actual Chinese circumstances. The utopia of a Great Concord is not betrayed but rather "maintained," waiting for the right time to come. While the unquestioned goal of history is unity, the idea that it could be achieved through China simply dismissing the Empire is far from evident, Kang argues; and even less so if the new Chinese State is to be based on "racial" and "divisive" premises, as he frequently underlines in his anti-Republican essays.

Kang's proposal for the institutional resurgence and reform of the Empire is clearly defined in the following passage, where he displays his passion for world and comparative history, certainly nurtured by his international peregrinations since the exile of 1898, and documented in his biography and his travel diaries.[14] Again, the starting point is a classical quotation: a hexagram from the *Book of Changes* (the "headless dragons") serves as an introduction to the author's own theory of constitutional monarchism.[15]

> I imagined it for China, thinking carefully, and studying deeply, considering the features of uncountable countries, collecting good examples, ancient and modern, and finally building my own theory. For long time I have retained it, but now I intend to hand it over to you, my fellow citizens. Confucius thus comments on the *qian* hexagram from the *Book of Changes*: "To see dragons with no head. Auspicious." The Commentary of the Images says: "*Qian* originally uses nine and rules the world." Where do its political implications lead us to? In Greece, where there was an assembly of people chosen for their merits; in Rome, where there were a Senate and a triumvirate, with senators all chosen for their political prominence or for their personal reputation. In Germany, where seven Prince-electors used to nominate the king; in Switzerland, where there are seven ministers who in turn act as president for a year-long mandate; in the United States of America, where each State chooses two delegates for the Senate,

---

14 For an account of Kang's journeys, see Lo Jung-pang (ed), *K'ang Yu-wei*. In the *Datong Shu*, large sections dealing with the historical evolution of the world up to the twentieth century might be considered as "comparative history" rather than "utopian fiction," as already pointed out above in the Introduction.

15 The image of "headless dragons" has been interpreted diversely throughout the centuries, as a group of dragons physically with no head or as a group without a head, or a leader. Kang seems to follow the latter reading, so as to justify his ideal of an "empty monarchy." Legge has a completely different translation: "If the host of dragons (thus) appearing were to divest themselves of their heads, there would be good fortune."

which is charged with supervising the President and controlling him on foreign policy and great issues; in France, where the President has ceremonial functions but no actual power and administrative functions belong to the cabinet; at the time of Tang Yao,[16] who consulted with the four Yues for important issues; and at the time of the Zhou, when the Republic of Zhou-Shao was established.[17]

Now, inspired by the sentence of Master Kong, and taking into account the foreign systems of Greece, Rome, Switzerland, America, and France, as well as the domestic ones of Tang Yao and the Republic of Zhou-Shao, melting them together and harmonizing their different flavours, can [the result] be something fit for us? Aside from a National Assembly, I therefore propose to establish a Senate as the highest institutional body of the country, with the 22 provinces plus Internal Mongolia, Tibet, and Qinghai sending a representative each; and if there is someone of great virtue and of great learning whose provincial seat has already been filled, he can nonetheless be nominated by the Senate as a member of the assembly; of the 28 members, seven are chosen in turn as standing members; the administration of the State is divided into five offices: one is called Foreign Affairs, dealing with the great issues of foreign relations; one is called War, declaring wars and making peace, with the Marshall of the Army being subject to the cabinet; one is called Law, deciding on great judicial matters; one is called Political Stability, deciding on political litigations; one is called Education, being responsible for national education and not subject to the policies of the cabinet; in addition, a president and a vice-president of the assembly are chosen, following the Swiss system, where in case of illness or absence of the president, the vice-president acts as his substitute.[18]

---

16 Tang Yao, one of the Five Legendary Emperors, who according to the myth lived around 2200 BC.

17 In the ninth century BC, following a rebellion against the tyranny of King Li of Zhou, the new king—Xuan of Zhou—decided to share his power with Duke Mu of Shao and Duke Ding of Zhou; this institutional experiment was later dubbed "Zhou-Shao Republic" (周召共和). This episode is mentioned by Sima Qian in the *Shiji*.

18 Kang Youwei, *Kang Youwei zhenglunji*, vol. 2, 1047–1048. My translation. Original text: 吾為中國計之，昧昧我思之，沈沈吾畫之，斟酌萬國之宜，薈萃古今之美，無亦有一創說焉。懷抱之久，今願以敬獻吾國民。孔子系《易》之乾曰："見群龍無首。吉。" 象曰："乾元用九，天下治也。" 此其政治之極軌那？其在希臘，則有賢人會議；其在羅馬，則有元老院及三頭政治，其元老皆選專於政治而有重望者焉。德國則有七選侯以選立王者，其在瑞士則以七部長，歲選議長；其在美國則以每週選二人為上議院議員，以監督總統，握其外交及大政；其在法國則有代表王之虛總統與責任內閣；其在唐堯則大政咨於四岳；

The 1917 project, when seen from this perspective, was not a simple dynastic restoration, as it may have seemed to those who were nostalgic for the Qing (such as Zhang Xun himself, by the way). Rather, it implied an almost revolutionary change of perspective: the power of the monarch had to be scooped out, leaving only his sacral charisma and ceremonial duties. Such an institutional asset serves as the main feature of Kang's theory of the empty-monarch in which, following a fully Statist approach, Kang moves sacrality "from the king to the State."[19] Quoting the *Book of Changes*, the "head" is cut off and the Empire is transformed into a public-minded (*gong* 公) polity ruled through a diffused and multi-layered institutional system: such an asset may be even closer to the Age of Supreme Peace than a fragile Republic built on wrong premises and incapable of reforming the country, and functioning rather as a screen for old-fashioned authoritarianism (as the years of Yuan Shikai's rule over China had suggested): "Introduced without an intervening age of constitutional monarchy, and amid great confusion, to a largely unprepared population, the Republic, not surprisingly, malfunctioned."[20] Consequently—in Kang's opinion—restoring and adjusting the Empire might be a way to gain time and prepare China for the Age of Rising Peace without causing the country to collapse backward to chaos. The solution is constitutional monarchy, as Kang had already claimed in the *Jiuwanglun*.

The historical linearity pointing to the Great Concord does not imply a sort of "institutional linearity," then: the republic may be more chaotic and even less democratic than a "commonwealth" monarchy. This point, in particular, is developed in the first paragraph of *Gonghe Pingyi*'s third essay, "Rome and England both passed from democracy to monarchy, attaining a new strength"— another example of Kang's fascination with comparative and global history *ante litteram*.

其在周室則周召共和。吾今上桌孔子"群龍無首"之言，外採希臘、羅馬、德、瑞、美、法之制，內採唐虞四岳，周召共和之法，合一爐而冶之，調眾味而和之，其貨可行乎。請於國會而外，立元老院為最高機關，凡廿而行省，及內外蒙古、西藏、青海、各公舉一人，入充元老，其有大功德、大文學，雖其省額滿，亦可由元老公請入院，額數以廿八人為度，輪選七人為常，駐辦事員分五司焉：一曰外交，凡有外交結約之大事者斷焉；一曰兵，凡開戰議和，及參謀部元帥府隸焉；一曰法律，凡大審判決焉；一曰平政，凡政之訟決焉；一曰教，凡國教任，凡不隸於內閣之大政隸之，更公舉一議長，一副議長，其議長之制如瑞士，其議長以病或事缺席，則副議長代之。

19 Chang Hao, *Chinese Intellectuals in Crisis: Search for Order and Meaning, 1890–1911* (Oakland CA: University of California Press, 1981), 5–6.
20 Pines, *The Everlasting Empire*, 168.

Those who say that establishing a monarchical system after democracy is not possible, shall change their mind. Was not Rome, in ancient times, a democracy? Since Augustus, though, it became an autocratic monarchy, and it prospered, expanding its rule over thousands of *li*, governing Europe until the age of Constantine: for two thousand years it was a great Empire. Until recent times, England and Wales were small and uncultured democratic countries. Then monarchy was established and in 300 years the kingdom conquered the Netherlands, later conquering India and colonizing Canada and Oceania: it is today a great country, whose flag waves everywhere in the world.[21] Now, can we deny that Rome and England are both countries ruled by law? From small and weak barbaric countries to great and powerful empires: is not this what we call progressing? But maybe it is not enough to convince those who believe that after democracy it is impossible to establish monarchy. Germany, for example, today exerts a huge influence: it has just taken the city of Riga away from the Czar, and is now heading to the Russian capital with its army. A democracy which cannot exert its full control over the country can hardly be strong. The United States of America are the best example of a democratic system; however, they have declared war on Germany, sending their citizens to the battlefield for many months,[22] because when war is unavoidable, that is not the moment for people's rule [democracy]. As for today, what time is it for us? Isn't this the time of war, for our country? Please, my fellow citizens, follow and value these considerations.[23]

Finally, in the third section of the third essay of *Gonghe Pingyi*—explicitly entitled "Chinese people, citizens of a country which has never been a democracy, ignore what a Republic is and that's why they are foolishly losing their

---

21   This point of England being a republic which successfully turned to monarchism is widely used by Kang; see for example his telegram to Feng Guozhang, mentioned in Hsiao, *A Modern China and a New World*, 255.
22   Kang refers here to World War I.
23   Kang Youwei, *Kang Youwei zhenglunji*, vol. 2, 1046. My translation. Original text: 或謂民主之后不可改君主，改則退化，其謬至易知矣。羅馬之先，豈非民主乎？而自奧古士多之后，改為專制君主，羅馬乃盛，拓地萬裡，為歐正統，至君士但丁，二千年為大帝國矣。至今英克林威爾民主也，在小國未文明時，其后英改為郡主，垂今三百年矣，始收荷蘭，滅印度，定加拿大及澳洲，英乃曰大，英旗於日月出入。羅馬與英，豈不足稱法乎？由弱小蠻，進為文明霸國，非進化乎？此之不足，而謬云民主之后，不可改為君主。今德國已勝勢，取俄裡加，已為全軍扑俄京。蓋民主之國勢難統御，無能強其國者。美為民主政體至今美矣，然日號其民，欲與德戰，而招兵數月，故國爭未免之時，非行民主制之時也。今何時乎？豈非國爭時乎？請懸記其得失以覘之。

DEMOCRACY   117

struggle"—Kang returns to many of the points previously examined (i.e., the need for a full comprehension of Republicanism as a product of specific historical and social circumstances, the peculiarities of twentieth-century China and the dangers of an extemporary or "copied" democracy), adding specific accusations against contemporary Republican and nationalist intellectuals. They may claim to be sincere democrats, but they still act as imperial censors, condemning and ostracizing counter-current thinkers like himself, Kang declares:

> My fellow intellectuals, aiming for high discourses and pressing the times, are forcing it [i.e., the establishment of a Republic] without having actually reflected critically upon it, even for one single day. [...] You can establish a school following a teacher only after receiving the teaching [from him]; you can set up a strategy only if you are trained in it. That's because in order to pass on their knowledge, their experiences and their activities, people need to master them through many years of study and many years of exercise: only then they can actually be able to put them into practice.
>
> Every art is subtle and studying it seems hard for a long time, thus a republican system is a similarly manifold, subtle, and abstruse matter. Recently, among our country's scholars of America and Europe, many have used Japanese translations as short-cuts, but Japan does not have a Republican system and [those translations] do not give details on Republicanism! So, if before Xinhai Revolution in China there was not a single book on the concept of Republic, since then, in the whole country there has not been a single true scholar of Republicanism yet. [...] Following my return to China I have met not a few scholars: old students know much about China and ignore the outer world; new ones have a superficial knowledge of the outer world and do not understand China. Talking about "foreign studies," Europe, America, Asia, and Africa are different and distant, it is difficult to visit them all, their systems are manifold and ever-changing, it is difficult to study them all. Talking about the Republic, under its name only a general idea is included and by examining its actual content you may see its inevitable variations, the whole course of its institutional forms, its pros and cons, as well as the reciprocal followings and imitations: among the many Republican countries throughout history, not a single one is similar to another, and even Rome did not follow the example of Greece. The seventy-two cities of the Hanseatic League did not follow Rome, the Commune of Florence did not follow Germany, the Swiss Confederation did not follow the Italian Communes, the United States did not follow Switzerland, France did not

follow America, Portugal did not follow France, and the twenty American Republics may look similar from the outside but from the inside are actually different; coming to the European revolutions, they followed the American and French examples, they took the essence of Republic, distilling it and catching its spirit without necessarily copying its formal appearance, and this ultimately shows how extensive the transformative capacities of Republicanism are. Name and reality differ, but those who only have a superficial knowledge ignore it and are mislead. So, the Republican system considers the nation as a public affair and the country as a people, it is a peaceful common vision, being for this different from autocracy. France is a purely republican country, but among the parties today [represented] in Parliament there is still a party marked as "monarchical"; moreover, the German Empire is considered by many to be an autocracy. The German socialist party is now represented in Parliament and publicly discusses democracy ... French Monarchists express their own views although republicans have extensive prejudices against them, condemning and debating their ideas. Because a Republic is to be considered as the representation of the ideas and visions of the entire people, putting together their multiplicity, it cannot force everyone to promote democracy. If there are taboos, that is a suppression of citizens, it is an autocracy, not a Republic. Our country since 1912 has reformed its institutional system, becoming a Republic, and nobody dared to discuss it. If someone does not advocate democracy and Republic, and he says so openly, he is immediately viewed as a traitor, as in the former Empire those who talked about democracy were considered rebels. The intellectuals of our country have preserved the bad habits of the Empire, and albeit enchanted by Republic they are actually practicing autocracy. Then, somebody should dare to ponder on the pros and cons of the Republic, to ask whether it is fit for China's geography, habits, history, and sensibility, to examine it critically, inviting intellectuals and scholars from all over the country to reflect on it again and again, balancing gains and losses and only then implementing it. But even though they have not analysed it thoroughly yet, and even though they ignore whether it is possible to implement and enforce it, they wish to attain the benefits and security of Republic—which they consider as a sine qua non for the interests of the country and the wealth of the people—therefore causing trouble and losses. [...] Now, we will not here reply to the ancient scholars' attacks on democracy; and yet, how can I deny that among the numerous Chinese modern intellectuals there is not a single one who has a clear understanding of what a Republic is? Because if they had a deep knowledge of its perils, they would first of all admit that it is completely unfit for China. They would be denounced publicly as if they were rebels: thus, seeking to protect themselves, they are not brave enough to speak openly; aspiring for rank and wealth and hoping to jump aboard this Republic to gain some power, they do not dare to express themselves.[24]

The conclusion, for Kang, is unquestionable: at that moment, "Republicanism and China cannot stand together":

> For six years democracy has brought disasters to our country, and its advocates have trapped 400 million Chinese within this tragedy; those who are aware of it and yet don't talk—some for fear, some out of interest—do not love their country anymore. To say it simply, Republic

---

24 Kang Youwei, *Kang Youwei zhenglunji*, vol. 2, 1049–1051. My translation. Original text: 然猶必立學從師以受之，設局整陳以操之，入傳習所、試驗場、作工廠以習之，需以數年之學力，尚須實地練習者數年，然后乃施之實用焉，然后可佔其能否。夫以工藝之微，學之猶若是至難且久也，況夫共和政治之深繁奧賾也。近者吾國求歐、美之學，多假途於日本之譯本，而日本既非共和政體，其於共和政皆語焉而不詳，故辛亥以前，吾國竟無共和政體之一書，即辛亥以后，全國亦未有共和政體之一學。[...] 吾歸國以來，所接人士，不為少矣，其舊學者，多知中而寡知外；其新學者，略知外而不知中。就言外學，則歐、美、亞、非，地勢遼遠，游者難於遍至，國體整變，學者難於盡悉。就言共和，舉其廣名，則大略若同，考其內實，則無不變異，其立法之本末，成效之得失，相師互鑒，而古今萬國之共和，無一同者，故羅馬不師希臘也。德之漢堡七十二市府，不師羅也，意之佛羅練士五市府，不師德國也，瑞士聯邦，不師意大利之五市府也，美不師瑞，法不師美，葡不師法，而美洲之二十共和國，外全相似，內實不同，全歐洲諸國之革命，則盡以美洲、法國為戒，取共和之精華，而去其糟粕，得其神意，而不必泥其形似，此尤共和變化之至者矣。名實少異，宜淺識者不知而反惑之。且夫共和之制，以國為公有，全國之民，和平公義也，此所以異於專制也。故法國為純粹共和之國，而今議院之政黨，尚有特標明為王黨者，甚至德之帝國，幾為專制矣。而德之社會黨，乃於議員公言民主之制，而奧無論也。法之王黨，各發其心思議論，雖共和黨之偏至極端者有駁難而無非議之。蓋以共和者，為代表全國人之心思議論，從其多數而行之，非強人人之必言民主也。若有所禁，則是遏抑國民也，是專制也，非共和也。吾國自壬子以后，改國體為民主共和，無人敢議之者。其有不言民主共和，而他及者，即視若悖逆，有若昔日帝國之言民主，視為叛亂焉。蓋吾國之學者，皆染中國帝國之余風，雖心醉共和，而實行專制若也。然則誰敢以共和之得失利害，宜於中國地理風俗歷史人情與否，考而辯之，更安能集一國學士大夫、通人才士講求反復，窮極得失，而后行之。夫既未嘗考辯講求，不知其可否而強行之，而欲其得共和之宜，受共和之安，以為國利民福，必不可得也，故召亂敗也。[...] 夫舊學之攻民主者不論，雖然，吾國新學者至多，吾豈敢謂其無一通共和者.蓋新學者深知其苦，而謂萬不可行於中國者固有矣。然以得罪於眾，等於叛逆，以保身家，故不敢昌言，或心既利祿，欲乘民國而圖權利，至不敢微言。

and China cannot stand together. When the Republic was established, China was lost; if the Republic endures, China will disappear. My fellow citizens, please, think about it with a fair mind, if you still love China.[25]

3 Kang and Beyond: Confucianism and Democracy

In the 1950s, having fled to Hong Kong from the mainland after the proclamation of the People's Republic of China—before definitively moving to Taiwan—historian Qian Mu 錢穆 (1895–1990) completed one of his most significant essays: *Chinese Political System Through the Ages: A Critical Evaluation* (中國歷代政治得失). Qian's stance was clear: using Western categories, such as "democracy," to describe and evaluate the trajectory of Chinese political culture throughout the centuries was an essentially wrong approach. Anticipating the debate on the "exportability of democracy," Qian pointed to the differences in the social, cultural, and ideological settings from which Western and Chinese institutional experiments stemmed. Whereas, theoretically and generally speaking, the West established "contractual" institutions, with a dialectic interaction between the people and the rulers (with the former attempting to control the latter through various means), the Chinese subjects—according to Qian—have rather chosen to "trust" their ruler(s), thus producing a hierarchical and familial sociopolitical system based more on "responsibility" and "moral expectations" than on reciprocal suspicion or the search for a balance of powers.[26]

Defying the mainstream bias towards Chinese autocracy, Qian moved his argument even further: China had experienced its own kind of "representative democracy," embodied in the examination system as implemented from the Song dynasty to the last years of the Qing; this peculiar form of interaction between literati and the State, in Qian's view, supplied the Empire with a sort of "meritocratic government," providing a link between the gentry and the

---

25 Ibid., 1051. My translation. Original text: 夫是以民主之害國殃民者六年，而議共和者無之，是以陷中國四萬萬人至於此慘也，有所畏，有所利，知而不言，皆不愛國而已。要之一言，民國於中國不並立，民國成則中國敗矣，民國存則中國亡矣，吾國民愛中國乎，其平心思之。

26 For a summary of Qian's position in the debate on "Confucian Democracy," see Deng Lilan 邓丽兰, *Rujiao minzhu yihuo xianzheng minzhu—shixi Zhang Junmai yu Qian Mu gyanyu Zhongguo chuantong zhengzhi zhi lunzheng* 儒教民主，抑或宪政民主—试析张君劢于钱穆关于中国传统政治之论争 (Tianjin 天津: Nankai Daxue Zhongguo shehuishi yanjiu zhongxin, 2009).

central administration.[27] Qian's interpretation of Chinese history, later valued as a significant contribution to the emergence of a New Confucianist approach to the discourse on East Asian institutional models and their possible evolution, as original as it may be, is certainly indebted to previous reflections generated by the first philosophical encounter between traditional Confucianism (for all that this might mean) and modern Western political thought.

Without considering the widely discussed re-readings of Classicism, such as the Mencian theory of *minben* 民本 or "people-at-the-basis,"[28] or the debate on the "democratic" function of grassroot rebellions throughout Imperial history,[29] the first noteworthy contact between Western theories of democracy and Chinese political tradition took place during the final decades of the Great Qing's rule over China. Democracy, and its by-product Republicanism, in those years entered the debate on China's future as a symbol of Western supremacy in the eyes of the country's new intellectual forces, who were passionately trying to repair the crumbling imperial system. The impact of John Fryer's translation of *Political Economy*, with its three-stage evolutionary theory of institutional systems (monarchy, oligarchy, and democracy) can from this point of view be considered a watershed.[30] In a few years, while the Court was impotently witnessing the break-up of China, the apparent defeat of Zhang Zhidong's *ti-yong* theory ("Chinese essence, Western tools"), on the basis of which the *yangwu* movement's efforts to modernize China had thrived for three decades without opening up a discussion about the imperial system, opened the doors to the ultimate discussion on the responsibilities of the traditional political culture *as a whole* in the decline of the country.

As already remarked, for Kang and his followers the most urgent matter—before and after 1898—was to help build "public-minded rulership" (*gong* 公), in contrast to the "selfish" (*si* 私) vision of power which, in his opinion, had progressively weakened the Empire. Clearly, direct participation in the State by the *whole body* of the Chinese people was not on the table: seen in this light,

---

27 Qian Mu 钱穆, *Zhongguo lidai zhengzhi deshi* 中国历代政治得失 (Beijing: Jiuzhou chubanshe, 2012), 98–99.

28 As Andrew Nathan correctly pointed out, it must be stressed that *minben* "has never meant people's rights (*minquan*) or people's rule (*minzhu*)." Andrew Nathan, *Chinese Democracy* (New York NY: Alfred Knopf, 1985), 127.

29 Yuri Pines notes that "rebellions can be interpreted as a peculiar (and very costly) readjustment system, a kind of bloody popular 'election'"; at the same time "any new rebel-turning-emperor served as a proof that there was no real alternative to the political system established in the aftermath of the Warring States." Pines, *The Everlasting Empire*, 161.

30 On this, and more generally on late-Imperial and early-Republican political and philosophical debate, see Zarrow, *After Empire*.

then, democracy "has a lot more to do with the empowerment of the people in the state than it does with a concept of top-down state power."[31] Kang's reform of monarchy in this sense is much closer to Statism than to a generic plea for democracy.

Yet, in the *Datong Shu*, as summarized by the "table on mankind's progression to equality" examined at the beginning of this chapter, Kang prophesied that the "end of history" will manifest itself as a global democracy, a one-world Republic tearing down barriers and boundaries. Even while revising and completing his utopia, though, on the political stage Kang acted as a critic of Republicanism, publicly confronting Sun Yat-sen and Yuan Shikai, and even attempting in person to reinstall the last Qing emperor, as in the failed coup of 1917.

In this framework, the interest of *Gonghe Pingyi* does not lie exclusively in its being an anti-Republican manifesto. Kang himself used this work to present his comprehensive view on the future of China, justifying his imperial sentiments within a country which had just got rid of the Empire in the name of modernity. And his argumentation presents many interesting points.

Most importantly, as Kang underlines in the last passage of *Gonghe Pingyi*, Republicanism and democracy are "practices" which need training (*cao* 操) in order to be successfully mastered. In his synthesis, Kang "rested his arguments sometimes on theoretical grounds, that is, political change must be compatible with the historical circumstances prevailing at a given period of time," consequently viewing Republicanism as something that "was intrinsically desirable but lay beyond China's immediate reach."[32]

Furthermore, Kang's attack on fellow intellectuals who act with no respect for the Chinese situation perhaps recalls more recent confrontations over the "exportation" of democracy in alien contexts. "Few, if any, Western liberal democratic theorists in the post-World War II era have sought to learn from the traditions and experiences of East Asian societies […] and defenders of 'Asian values' are viewed as archaic or politically dangerous."[33] This contemporary indictment of Western intellectuals' "provincialism" may have sounded familiar to Kang, who—as we have seen—directed similar accusations against Chinese

---

31 Anthony Kane, "The Creation of Modern China: the Nationalist vs Communist Roads." In *Conference on the evolution of democracy in China—sponsored by Carnegie Council on Ethics and International Affairs and Pacific Cultural Foundation* (Taipei: Pacific Cultural Foundation, 1990), 8.
32 Hsiao, *A Modern China and a New World*, 220.
33 Daniel Bell, *Beyond Liberal Democracy: Political Thinking for an East Asian Context* (Princeton NJ: Princeton University Press, 2006), 4.

political theorists: copying the West in order to compete is not the solution. China must recover through its own remedies.

We should also bear in mind that *minzhu* and *gonghe* can indicate a plurality of theories and actual institutional formulations across different contexts, as Kang himself observes throughout his work. Once more anticipating more recent approaches to the same issues, Kang acknowledges that if democracy is to be considered as a peculiarly European or American manifestation, then it has nothing to do with China, due to the extreme dissimilarities in historical evolution between the East and the West. Nevertheless, where democracy is freed of its "Western-superiority" veneer and conjugated in accordance with the differences and complexities of different geographical and historical situations (as Kang and Qian Mu both argue), then it may also be considered as having its own form, being an already extant piece of the Chinese historical experience. If Qian finds some seeds of democracy in the Song dynasty public exam system, Kang considers the virtuous Zhou kings to be examples of democracy no less worthy of attention than those from France or the United States. The lingering question, though, is whether a meritocratic oligarchy can be considered a form of "democracy."[34] To Kang, a constitutional monarchy with a nominal emperor at the apex who legitimates a constitutional mechanism of checks and balances, could be more public-minded (and therefore "democratic") than an autocratic Republic, nominally democratic but in reality providing a battlefield for divisive and exploitative forces.

So, this evident divergence between the project of a constitutional monarchy and the dream of a global democracy is explained by Kang as a difference in terms of *time* rather than *ideals* or *values*. Showing a pragmatic approach to historical evolution (which is why Hsiao defines him a "gradualist"), Kang states that democracy and Republic will eventually thrive on a global scale, but he is also convinced that each community will reach that point according to its own rhythm and pace. Democracy and Republicanism are not *wrong* or *right* on their own terms: they can only be valued in relation to the circumstances generating and sustaining them. Understanding the "vast and deep source of time," as the *Invariable Mean* prescribes, is the only way to spot the right solution to save a country on the brink of collapse. Kang thus stresses the importance of *timeliness* as one of the most important virtues in politics,

---

34   For a recent view on the issue of meritocracy vs democracy in a "Confucian" context, see Daniel Bell and Li, Chenyang (eds), *The East Asian Challenge for Democracy: Political Meritocracy in Comparative Perspective* (Cambridge: Cambridge University Press, 2013).

making his connection to classical Chinese philosophy (and strategy) once more explicit.[35]

In the debate on whether Confucianism can generate democracy—which, far from being a historical curiosity, has been a key point in recent decades, both in Taiwan and in the PRC—Kang again assumed a purely Confucian and "universalistic" approach: his main concern was not the definition of a Chinese cultural model (a "national essence") as opposed to the Western one, but the understanding of how China can generate her own democratic system over the long run. His aim was the construction of a strong Chinese state according to a more general framework of global historical evolution.

"Superficially, democracy may appear as a universal value, in an 'every street leads to Rome' fashion; and in today's world, the political systems realized by numerous countries may seem to have similar features, all to be known as 'democracies'. However, the historical roots of each country's realization of democracy are actually different, and the effects of democracy in each country's modern and contemporary historical development are equally dissimilar."[36] Almost a century after the publication of *Gonghe Pingyi*, and more than fifty years after Qian Mu's reflections, such was the premise of the sociologist Fang Ning 房宁 in the introduction to his essay *Chinese Experience with Democracy*. Underlining China's historical, geographical, social, and cultural peculiarities in comparison to the West, and stressing how democracy can be inflected differently in different places and times, Fang shares Kang's inclination towards the contextualization of political systems (although his conclusion negates the possibility for China to have a multiparty system, the converse of that envisioned by Kang in his constitutional monarchy project).

Kang's focus on the creation of a *gong* polity and his vision of *Datong*, on the other hand, have been used by Wang Hui, a "new-left" intellectual (who will be discussed in more detail in Chapter 8) who supports grassroot democracy experiments in the PRC and calls for the emergence of "social groups" rather than "political parties," as a counterbalance to the capital-driven CCP.[37] The fact that

---

35   On the importance of *shi* 势 (momentum, disposition) in Chinese traditional strategy, and its implications for the construction of a concept of "efficacity" rather different from the Western one, see François Jullien, *Traité de l'efficacité* (Paris: Grasset & Fasquelle, 1997).

36   《从表面上看，民主似乎是一种"普世价值"，似乎"条条大路通罗马"，当今世界上多数国家采取的政治制度在形式上是类似的，都被称为民主政治。但是，实际上各国实行民主政治的历史原因有差别的，民主政治在各国近现代历史发展所起的作用也不尽相同。》 Fang Ning 房宁, *Minzhu de Zhongguo jingyan* 民主的中国经验 (Beijing: Zhongguo shehui kexue chubanshe, 2013), 1–2. My translation.

37   On both Fang and Wang, see Mark Leonard, *What does China think?* (London: Fourth Estate, 2007).

two intellectuals providing substantially different solutions for contemporary China can both claim a part of Kang's legacy certainly shows the latter's pivotal role—his political failures and shortsightedness notwithstanding—in the shaping of modern and contemporary Chinese thought.

Being more focused on the comprehension of the ever-changing circumstances in *time*, than on the definition of fixed identities in *space*, Kang was unsurprisingly isolated in a world set on fire by the quest for national values seen as the reasons behind each country's failures or successes. However, such an approach—together with his comparative interests, the "deconstruction" of democracy, and the theory of *gong*—makes Kang a forerunner of later reflections on the controversial topic of "democracy in China." This rich and complex ideological legacy certainly underscores the troubled and still unresolved passage of China from Empire to "after Empire" (to quote Peter Zarrow's book). And it would be ungenerous not to recognize Kang's importance as a witness to and interpreter of his troubled time, or to underestimate the significance of his intellectual wanderings between utopianism and realism as embodying a fundamental feature of Chinese intellectual and political history, both before and after 1911.

CHAPTER 6

Socialism
Confucian Equality, from the Well-fields to the Communes

1 Kang, a Confucian Communist?

The history of the introduction of socialism into China, of its assimilation and its final victory under the cloak of "Maoism," is not the theme of the present book. However, the presence of socialist instances and ideals in Kang's utopianism can be counted as one of the most interesting aspects of the *Datong Shu*, and certainly one of the most debated ones.

For a background analysis, it is useful to underline that the first Chinese reference to Western socialism can be found in an essay by the well-known scholar and translator Yan Fu 嚴復 (1854–1921), entitled *Yuan qiang* 原強, "The Origin of Strength," written in 1895 and published in the Tianjin-based newspaper *Zhibao* 直報. In this essay—as explained by Li Yu-ning in *The Introduction of Socialism into China*—Yan noted how scientific progress in the West had led to extreme economic inequality, which in turn had given rise to what he called the "parties for the equalization of the rich and the poor" (*jun pinfu zhi dang* 均貧富之黨). Like Yan Fu, Kang Youwei also viewed the emergence of socialist schools of thoughts throughout the West as a response to a growing economic disparity between rich and poor, mainly caused by the "use of machines to make things, thus completely replacing the work of artisans."[1]

Kang, who in his first political works translated "socialism" as *renqun zhi shuo* 人群之說 and communism as *qunchan zhi shuo* 群產之說,[2] clearly foresaw the emergence of "modern" social conflicts as one of the key historical dynamics which would craft the future of mankind on a global scale:

> In recent years there has been a sudden rise of struggles by labour unions to coerce the capitalists in Europe and America. This is only the beginning. The formation of labour unions will certainly increase in the future. One may fear that this will lead to the calamity of bloody conflicts … A hundred years hence it will certainly draw the attention of the entire world. Therefore nowadays socialist and communist doctrines are

---

[1] Quoted in Hsiao, *A Modern China and a New World*, 109.
[2] Li Yu-ning, *The Introduction of Socialism into China* (New York NY: Columbia University Press, 1971), 3.

gaining increasing popularity, which will constitute a most important subject of discussion.[3]

Kang acknowledged the existence of economic inequalities in Asia as well (thus confirming once more his "global" approach to history as compared to other thinkers, both Western and Chinese, who focused instead on an ostensible Chinese "uniqueness" in terms of social development). From the fact that people in the old Empire could "buy and sell land," inequality stemmed. The well-field system was conceived to tackle this issue, but it had been successfully implemented only in the most remote past (and again, but with less success, at the time of the Wang Mang reforms in the first century CE), Kang observed.[4] Land ownership, then, appeared in Kang's eyes to be one of the main aspects in the construction of a "new world" as imagined in the *Datong Shu*, giving this work a powerful socialist nuance.

Among Kang's major works, the *Book of Great Concord*, to use Hsiao Kung-chuan's words, indeed displays "a clear note of socialism"; and Kang himself, albeit showing a "quite hazy and fragmentary knowledge" of the doctrine, became "an outstanding forerunner of the socialist movement in modern China" thanks to this book.[5] It is not surprising, then, that—even if Kang was commonly labelled as a "Confucian reformer" following his failed attempt of 1898—his prophecy of the Age of Supreme Equality was to gain him special attention in the PRC years, when—as will be described in more detail in the next chapter—his "Confucian-communist" utopia became a challenging subject of study for several recent intellectuals.

Although the roots of Kang's philosophy of history and of his concern for social and political development should be interpreted as purely (although to some extent heretically) Confucian rather than Marxist,[6] the final result is the prophecy of a definitely "socialist" world order, which includes the abolition of private property and family, and the global planning of any economic activity, unquestionably echoing Communist aspirations and utopias. In Kang's vision of the future, only an extreme form of socialism, enforced by a capillary global State, can save the world from the threat of starvation and potential extinction caused by an unprecedented growth in the human population.

---

3 Hsiao, *A Modern China and a New World*, 109.
4 Ibid. The full passage summarized here by Hsiao will be translated later in this chapter.
5 Hsiao, *A Modern China and a New World*, 126.
6 See above, Chapter 1.

2 "Everything Public under Heaven"

In Part Six of the *Datong Shu*[7] the economic issues, and their "socialist" solutions, are presented by the author in full detail. Here, after in the previous chapters having analysed the causes of human suffering and the progression of mankind toward larger and more "democratic" forms of political unity, the author describes the functioning of the one-world state in economic and productive terms. Retrieving the venerable Confucian ideal of *gong* and using it as an antidote to the emergence of social inequalities caused by the "modern economy," Kang denounces the roots of the Chinese crisis, starting from the issue of land property, and envisions its solution: the creation of an efficient generator of "public-oriented" policies, capable of planning every aspect of the productive process, from the choice of crops to the daily life of citizen-workers.

> People rely on farming, crafting, trading, but the ingenuity in earning money has been progressively refined, and now the reliance on industry has almost doubled. Until recently, each activity has been increasing its productivity and refining its techniques: common farmers, craftsmen, and traders have been able to attend schools and farmers have been able to use new tools and fertilizers. Construction techniques, for example, have become remarkable: dirigibles sail the skies, railways shrink the distances, wireless communications cross the seas; in comparison with the "old" world, this is a "new" one indeed. The flow of trade is bigger, steamboats are spreading, goods are transported everywhere across the five continents and new enterprises which have never been achieved for millenniums are flourishing everywhere. Culture evolves day by day, and the past is left behind. As remarkable as these new techniques can be, they are just a superficial aspect of this new world, and they cannot help the deprivations suffered by common people, nor the lack of public mindedness.[8]

---

7   In the Zhonghua edition it figures as Part Seven.
8   Kang Youwei, *Datong Shu*, 262. My translation. Original text: 人生之所賴，農出之，工作之，商運之，資生之學日精，則實業之依倍切。至於近世，農工商業獎勸日加，講求日精，凡農工商皆有學校，農耕皆用機器化料。若公事之精，製造之奇，汽球登天，鐵軌縮地，無線之電渡海，比於中古有若新世界矣。商運之大，輪舶紛馳，物品交通，遍於五洲，皆創數千年未有之異境。文明日進，誠過疇昔。然新業雖瑰偉，不過世界之外觀，於民生獨人之因苦，公德之缺乏，未能略有補救也。

The stress on the Confucian value of "public-mindedness" is evident here. This aspect of Kang's thought has become part of an interesting debate on the Confucian roots of contemporary Chinese utopianism. Reflecting on the Confucian ideological sources of egalitarian views, Gao Ruiquan 高瑞泉 has pointed out that Chinese Classicism—albeit active within a social context that "cannot be defined as egalitarian"[9]—still provided some interesting examples of egalitarian concerns. Whereas the existence of a public examination system presented a striking difference with European feudalism (this point was also underlined by Qian Mu, as discussed in Chapter 5), the traditional Confucian system of values, unquestionably based on agrarianism and on the reduction of differences between rich and poor, and with a consequent bias against the excesses of private wealth, is not so distant from modern socialist blueprints. Gao himself quotes the *Datong Shu* as a significant example of this link between two such apparently distant cultural constructs as Confucianism and Communism (and he is just one among many scholars who have devoted their studies to these aspects). There is no doubt, of course, that Chinese Classicism appears more hierarchically structured than fully egalitarian Christianity—as argued among others by Jacques Gernet—and the "ritualist veneration" prescribed by the Classics is a clear manifestation of such a hierarchical vision of society as fully elaborated by Xunzi 荀子, Gao explains.[10] We know that many of the most prominent figures in the history of Chinese Classicism, starting from Master Kong himself, albeit holding to the traditional "ritualist" view of society, have underlined the importance of "balance" (and therefore equality) in order to stabilize social orders. Mencius in particular produced the well-known *minben* 民本 theory, by which the people have to be considered by the ruler as the foundation of his power and the centre of his concerns. This care for the people's needs (often sponsored for reasons of political stability, more than for a humanitarian afflatus), spurred the famous Classicist criticism that "rich people own pieces of land one after another, while the poor have land just enough to stick an awl into it" (富者地連阡陌，貧者無立錐之地).[11] So the paradox underlined by Gao (and by many scholars investigating the Confucian echoes in Chinese socialism) lies in how Western liberalism, focusing on individual freedom and on the "equality of opportunities," has generated an economic system in which the difference between rich and poor is acceptable, while Confucianists (both ancient and modern), although preaching "ritual

---

9 Gao Ruiquan 高瑞泉, "Lun pingdeng guannian de rujia sixiang ziyuan 论平等观念的儒家思想资源". (Shehui kexue, 4, 2009, 120–129).
10 Ibid., 122.
11 Ibid.

hierarchies," have come to criticize the emergence of economic disparities. Even an adversary of Kang like Zhang Binglin (see chapter 4) used to state that the Chinese imperial system's social structure was closer to a concept of "equality" than even the Western or Japanese constitutional states.[12] In other words, in the Confucian worldview, the "status inequality" prescribed through the ideal of *li* 礼 is balanced by the importance of *ren* 仁 and by the praise of a compassionate ruler: the famous—and often overestimated—Confucian aversion to merchants' profits is rooted in such a philosophical construction, then. And Kang's utopia, preaching the abolition of private interests in any field, drawing on Confucian ideals, perfectly fits in this framework.

It is relatively easy to draw a causal relationship between a major concern with the issue of equality (*pingdeng*) and the following elaboration of *datong*-oriented political elaborations. As Kang himself wrote, "as for concord and equality, first you have concord and then you can have equality."[13]

If China's most severe problem is lack of equality, then a society based on the ideal of concord, or of an extensive Commonweal in which all differences—from the biological to the artificial—are annihilated, is the only possible solution. This simple conceptual mechanism may help us position Kang in relation to some of the other late Qing and early republican intellectuals. His disciple Tan Sitong clearly shares Kang's concerns, whereas Liang Qichao appears to be more sensitive to the issue of "freedom" (*ziyou*) than to equality—which would explain the scarcity of references to the concept of *datong* in his works and his pre-eminent focus on the problem of democracy and citizenship.[14]

Sun Yat-sen would appear, in this sense, to be closer to Kang than might be suggested by the confrontation between the two over the question of what a "nation" is. Sun uses the concept of *datong* extensively in his writings. We can detect a pattern in his use of the term which is not dissimilar from Kang's: a concept is taken from the lexicon of the Classics and remodelled according to new contingencies and with the use of new ideological tools. Yet, in Sun's case, the contribution of Western philosophy is definitely more substantial and more intentional, and it is then used as a piece of a wider concept of political order, translated into a general political blueprint. Like Kang, Sun uses the concept of *datong* as a vehicle for a comprehensive, and "utopian," paradigm in the description of his supreme political goal: the abolition of Chinese inequalities.

---

12 See Zhang Taiyan's *Daiyi ranfou lun* 代議然否論, quoted in Gao Ruiqian, "Lun pingdeng guanian", 122.
13 同字、'平字'，先同而后能平。Kang Youwei, *Kang Youwei zhenglunji*, vol. 2, 594.
14 Wei Yixia 魏义霞 and Gao Zhiwen 高志文, "Sun Zhonghsan de datonglixiang ji qi yiyi: jianyu Kang Youwei dengren bijiao 孙中山的大同理想及其意义—兼与康有为等人比较." (*Heilongjiang shehui kexue* 128, 5, 2011, 5–9), 5.

It should be noted that in Sun's approach, it is "external" inequality that plays the more significant role. In other words, while Kang is still inspired by a universal framework in which the fight against inequality naturally expands from one level to another, from the family to the *tianxia*, resulting in global governance, Sun's reflections are more visibly nation-oriented. Inequality is expressed and addressed from the point of view of the Nation (and more specifically of the Han-nation): this includes inequality internal to the state (social tensions, resulting in his *minsheng* principle, or political unbalances, resulting in his *minquan* principle) as well as that external to it (in terms of international relations, thus producing Sun's principle of *minzu*, tightly connected to the fight for "independence"). Once this conceptual difference is highlighted, the divergence between Kang and Sun when discussing the "nation" might appear more understandable.

The comparison between the connection between equality and *datong* in Kang and Sun is an essential preliminary for understanding their triangular relationship with a third character who theorized (and implemented) a *datong*-oriented political program, and who did it in a more concrete way than the formers: Mao Zedong.

The debate on the main source used by Mao to craft his own concept of *datong* is still open. Kang himself might have been a source of inspiration, as well as Tan Sitong, as Mao explicitly expressed his admiration for their reforms in his youth. Already in 1917, in a letter to Li Jinxi, he wrote: "*Datong* is our purpose. Kang described *datong* but could not find the way to it". However, if Mao's *datong* represents the same ideal goal as Kang's (summarized by the *Liyun* slogan of *tianxia wei gong*), the path is the problem. Mao's blueprint for reaching and implementing a state of *datong* clearly entails a conflictive and dialectical view of history inspired by Marx, rather than a natural view of progress as the Sage's ability to perceive and accompany change that Kang had inherited from the *Yijing*. The same question applies to the relationship between Mao and Sun, and between Sun and Kang. The latter was mentioned when discussing nationalism; the former is still under scrutiny by scholars. Like Mao, Sun used *datong* as a portmanteau word for his political project, which in turn provided Mao with a more specific set of conceptual tools linking the Confucian vocabulary to a "modern" lexicon representing issues such as nationalism, mass participation, and welfare.

In the next passage from Part Six, Kang focuses on agriculture, investigating the causes of inequality and displaying again his unprecedented attention to global dynamics and international comparison: lamenting the absence of any efficient form of "public control" over land, he nods to the Mencian legacy represented by the well-field system of the Zhou; in parallel, he makes an interesting reference to the particular nature of America's historical evolution when compared to the Chinese (or continental European) experience: the possibility of opening up new lands was a key factor in the United States' successful evolution, he says.

> Now, we shall talk about agriculture. In China people can buy and sell land. Since everyone can obtain a small piece of land, it is difficult to use machinery to farm. Not to mention the fact that there are no farming schools yet, there is no knowledge of how to improve production, the landlords usually do not farm themselves because many of them are tenants, the leasing rates are expensive, floods and droughts may occur; even working the entire year with callused hands and feet while the whole family doubles its efforts, farmers can't raise their livestock; even eating yams and cooking gruels, they won't appease their hunger; forced to sell their children to pay taxes and levies, pale and in tattered clothing, their suffering is hard to describe. If schools for farmers were established, if the species of crops were better known, if fertilizers were perfected and machineries were used more diffusely, as in Europe or in America, yet the fields would still be too small, making it difficult to attain ultimate uniformity: large fields would go uncultivated while small ones would still cause fruitless efforts, and those who own no piece of land would still be used as farmers, suffering cold, wandering and ravening like beggars. This is not specific to China: except for America, where a newly opened land provides large fields, almost every country cannot avoid such a situation. Confucius was worried about this, therefore elaborating the well-field system, but those who came after him did not care about people suffering cold and hunger. So that pattern could not be applied to the new territories. As Confucius said, "Through equality there is no poverty": this is the highest principle. Later Confucians constantly developed the theory of equalizing the fields and developed the methods to divide each field; Wang Mang did not follow this way, presumptuously abandoning these prescriptions, and chaos was aroused. The theories on livelihood by the foreigner Mr. Fourier,[15] prescribe that a big field of ten *li*—devised as a

---

15   In the original text, Kang mentions "Mr. Fu, the Englishman"; however this is a clear reference to Charles Fourier (1772–1837), the French philosopher who inspired the creation of utopian socialist communities in the United States throughout the nineteenth century. Fourier's thought presents many common points with Kang's: the evolutionary view of history, moving from Chaos to Harmony; the struggle for the abolition of private property; an egalitarian view of women's status, with a consequent denunciation of the traditional family and praise of sexual freedom. Among the modern European thinkers, Fourier

well-field—may sustain one thousand people: his ideas are moved by universal empathy (*ren*), but they cannot be implemented. Then, when people start to sell and buy properties, having their own *private* properties, the distance between rich and poor is far from levelled, ultimately resulting in the lack of equality.[16]

Proceeding from these observations, in the same part of the book Kang develops his own "Confucian-communist" formula of a fully *public-oriented* and *planned* economic system, enumerating the benefits of a successful fight against inequality in every productive sector, from agriculture to industry. The philosophical premise of this praise of commonality is presented in the following passage, entitled "Comparing private production to public production in agriculture, industry, and commerce," where the author denounces the limits of the economic models produced by what he calls the old world, starting from the traditionally prominent sector of agriculture:[17]

> We shall now compare private production to public production.
>
> **Agriculture.** In a private mode of production there are those who cultivate a lot and those who cultivate less, so their productivity is uneven, as is their labour. In addition to that, market fluctuations are variable, it is difficult to predict sales and farmers cannot decide in advance what

---

seems to be the closest to Kang's vision of social and historical development. For a survey of Fourier's utopianism, see Charles Fourier *Design for Utopia: Selected Writings*. (Studies in the Libertarian and Utopian Tradition, New York: Schocken, 1971).

16 Kang Youwei, *Datong Shu*, 262–263. My translation. Original text: 今以農夫言之。中國許人買賣田產，故人各得小區之地，難於用機器以為耕。無論農學未開，不知改良，而田主率非自耕，多為佃戶，出租既貴，水旱非時，終歲勞動，胼手胝足，舉家兼勤，不足事畜，食薯煮粥，猶不充飢，甚者鬻子以償租稅，菜色褸衣，其因苦有不忍言者。即使農學遍設，物種大明，化料備具，機器大用，與歐美齊，而田區既小，終難均一，大田者或多荒蕪，而小區者徒勞心力，或且無田以為耕，飢寒乞丐，流離溝壑。此不惟中國為然，自美洲新辟得有大田外，各國殆皆不能免焉。而亞洲各舊國，地少人多，殆尤甚者也。孔子昔已憂之，故創井田之法，而后人人不憂飢寒。而此方格之事，非新辟之國實不能行。若孔子所謂"蓋均無貧"，則義之至也。后儒曰發均田之說，又為限民田之法，王莽不得其道而妄行之，則造以致亂。英人傅氏之論生計，欲以十裡養千人為大井田，其意仁甚，然亦不可行也。蓋許人民買賣私產，既各有私產，則貧富不齊，終無由均。

17 In the Shanghai version this passage is divided between different chapters, while in the Jiangsu edition of 1985—reprinted by the Renmin University Press in 2010 and used as the main reference here—it is presented as one single chapter. It was not fully translated by Thompson, but only summarized, perhaps for its excessive Maoist echoes? Indeed, this excerpt is the best point of departure to discuss Kang's particular "Confucian communism."

crop is more convenient to cultivate, consequently wasting their surplus. Wood and fruit, fish and poultry: if they are not sold, they lose their quality; but if farmers cannot predict it in advance, they cannot plan their production. Therefore, for the minority of them it is a matter of lack of planning and missed opportunities; for the majority, though, it means a reckless waste of products and labour. If we sum up all the farmers of the world, their numbers will grow a thousand times. If we sum up the missed opportunities of each single farmer, the waste of production and of labour of each single farmer, the result will be millions of wasted products, of missed opportunities and useless hours of labour, and hundreds of thousands of unused products and devalued tools. With global statistical planning these problems would be definitively solved: would not it be like building uncountable embankments along the Yellow River? If we don't follow the way of Commonality and continue to allow the troubles caused by the existence of a private mode of production, though, the situation for farmers will be unbearable.

Commerce follows the same pattern. The absence of a big plan "based on statistics"—on a national scale in the Age of Comfort, but ultimately global as the world moves to the stage of its final perfection—appears as the reason for inequalities and poverty. The market, he says, has to be "ruled according to the people's needs." An interest in the diminution of wasted goods also witnesses an (unexpected) environmental consciousness on Kang's part, and adds to the prophetic tone of the book.

Commerce. Since individuals run their own businesses, free to open their activity and to choose their employees, they cannot merge their activities, because it would be impossible to plan and foresee the needs of an entire population. If planning were possible, though, each shop would strengthen its profits, overcoming the incapacity to store a wide arrange of goods in advance to anticipate people's requests, which now causes stored goods not to be requested, or requested goods not to be stored, with the result of over-capacity in some shops and under-capacity in others as it now happens to many people.

With over-supply on one side and under-capacity on the other, the same good's price fluctuates: under-supply makes its price higher, while over-supply makes it cheaper: there may be sharp individuals who get rich because of this, but more and more families lose their business. So, people lose their money, productivity is uneven, and human dignity is unequal. When people lose their business they bring poverty and suffering to their family, to the extent that they may even die for this and cause unhappiness to the world. But when there is over-supply of any kind of goods, their prolonged accumulation produces corruption: merchants have interest in keeping them and do not give them away lightheartedly, instead producing falsifications and selling them to people; there are laws prohibiting this practice, yet they manage to escape any control. When this kind of corruption involves food and medicines, it harms people's health and well-being; when it involves machineries, the dimension of its destructive consequences is indescribable. Also those selling any other good, besides food, medicines, and machinery, may be corrupted, cheating and harming people: aren't they like worms corroding the world and the attainment of the Supreme Equality? Even if governments could exert their control, avoiding the accumulation of surpluses, corrupt traders could simply discard their goods, causing, again, a reckless waste.

In the world of the Supreme Peace, all continents will be linked, the population will grow enormously, and the need of goods and tools will be vast. Uncountable human beings on one side, limited natural resources on the other; what we calculate today as the daily needs of an individual (for example: flour, meat, and sugar daily consumption, or the quantity of iron, cotton, silk, leather, wood, bamboo, metal, stone, feathers, herbs, bones, drugs, colours, and tools needed, and all the thousand life necessities) will exceed the capacity of the world to generate them and the capacity of men to produce them. So everything will have to be fixed in advance, corrupted people will have to be cast aside, the land will not be distributed to private individuals, and the global rulership, based on statistics, will consider making profit from other individuals as a mistaken policy, a stupid error! Describing the *Datong*, Confucius said: "It is hateful to waste accumulated goods, they must not be stored for oneself."[18] So, if traders all over the world started distributing the goods they have long been accumulating, and if each one of them decided to give them back and make them available, according to the necessities of people, would not this increase the health of citizens a thousand times? What could be more efficient than this, in fighting poverty? But it is impossible, unless we rule the market according to the way of the Great Concord.

Industry. Each worker has his own organization, their number is different from one region to another, and the majority is underpaid while only few of them are well remunerated; capitalists exploit them: workers carry on the production all together, but their low wages are unsustainable.

---

18   This is a quotation from the *Liji*.

If they refused to work, though, they would not make a living, starving and wandering like bandits. And each factory has its own plans of production, so that large-scale planning is impossible. Without planning, each factory makes its own products autonomously: as a result, some goods are too common and others are too rare, some goods are brand new and others are too old, some goods are despised and others are highly praised. If they are abundant or despised, their value is low; if they are rare or praised, their value is high. This creates a gap between those who have money to buy them and those who don't, thus engendering inequalities and differences of status between rich and poor, which is far from the model of Supreme Equality. Then the more common or the more despised goods are often falsified or counterfeited, as it also happens with machinery or medicines: when there is corruption, its bad consequences are uncountable. For any kind of product there is corruption and counterfeiting! If they are not counterfeited nor stored, they are thrown away. So, if we summed the goods that are produced by all the workers in the world and then thrown away, they would pile up, countless like the sands of the Ganges! What an uncountable waste of labour, of spirit, of natural resources, not to mention the waste of clothes and food consumed by workers! Goods must be necessary and there should be no useless production: would not such a way of production benefit immensely our fellow citizens of the world? And yet uncountable goods are produced by workers and then discarded; it is like rejecting people, labour, spirit, resources, and food. Again, what a reckless waste it is! If statistics were applied globally, if people worked for the public good, but a day-by-day planning policy was not implemented, that would be a mistake, a useless attempt, because it would not abolish the existence of private industry.[19]

---

19 Kang Youwei, *Datong Shu*, 265–268. My translation. Original text: 今以獨人之營業與公司之營業比較之。以農業言。獨人之營業，則有耕多者，有耕少者，其耕率不均，其勞作不均。外之售貨好惡無常，人之銷率多少難定，則耕者亦無從定其自耕之地及種之宜，於是有余粟滯留者矣。木材果實，畜牧漁魚，銷售與否，多寡孰宜，無從周知，無從預算。於是少則見乏而失時，多則暴殄天物而勞於無用。合大地之農人數萬萬，將來則有十百倍於此數者。一人之乏而失時，一人之殄物而枉勞，積之十百萬萬人，則有十百萬萬之殄物、失時、枉勞者矣。有十百萬萬人之殄物、失時、枉勞，則百事失其用，萬品失其珍。以大地統計學算之，其所失敗，豈止恆河沙無量數而已哉！然則不本於大同而循有家私產之害，但中於農者為不可言也。以商業言之。商人各自經營，各自開店用夥，無能統一，於一地之人口所需什器，不能得其統算之實。既能統算，而各店競利，不能不豫儲廣蓄以待人之取求，所儲蓄者人未必求，人求者未必儲蓄，不獨甲店有余而乙店不足，抑且人人皆在有余不足之中。夫有余於此，則必不足於彼，於是同一物也，不足則昂涌，有余則

Having dealt with the substantial flaws characterizing—in the author's eyes—what we would now call the "private sector," in the following section Kang describes in more detail how the "public-minded" world of Great Concord he envisioned will actually be organized from an economic point of view. At that time, "any activity will have returned to the public sphere" (農工商之業，必歸之公), he announces. The old Confucian ideal of equality turns modern: the challenge of modernity transforms the well-field system of the Zhou into the sort of Communist prophecy that thinkers like Li Zehou would find to be not so distant from a Maoist programme.

賤退，雖有狡智億中致富之人，而因此敗家失業者多矣。夫既有贏虧，則人產難均，而一切人格治法即不能平；敗家事業，則全家之憂患疾病中之，甚且死亡繼之而人不能樂。即在百物有余雍積久必腐敗，商人好利，必不輕棄飾欺作偽，仍售於人，雖有律限，不能盡察。以腐敗之食物藥物與人，則可致疾病而衛生有礙；以腐敗之機器與人，則其誤害之大尤不可言矣。即自藥物、食物、機物外一切器之腐敗者，誤人誤事，作偽生欺，豈可令其存於天壤間而為太平之蠹哉？且政府即能查察，余貨不售，則必棄之，是為暴殄天物。夫以一店之余物已不可言，若合大地之商店於貨而統算之，其為恆河沙無量數，殆不知加幾零位而不能盡也。當太平之世，大地全通，生人繁殖，需用物品益為浩繁。夫以生人之數無量而大地之產有涯，今以一人之用品計之，如一日需食粉質幾何，肉質幾何，糖質幾何，銷料幾何；需衣布帛幾何，絨料幾何，皮料幾何；需用木料、竹料幾何，金料、石料幾何，羽毛料、草料、骨料幾何，丹青料幾何，藥料幾何，機器料幾何；萬品千匯為人所需者，出之於地，作之於人，皆有定數，而徒供無量之腐敗棄擲，非徒大地不給，亦治大地統計學為同人謀利益者所大失策也，愚謬甚矣！孔子為大同之策曰：貨惡其棄於地也，不必藏於己。夫以全地商店久積有余之貨皆當棄地者，而一一移用而為有用，以供生人之需，其所以為同胞厚生者增幾倍哉？以此為恤貧，復何恤貧之有？故不本於大同而豫治商業者，不可得也。以工業言之。又工人各自為謀，各地工人多少不同，多則價賤，少則價昂，資本家既苦之，而工人同一操業，而價賤者無以足用。若其求工不得者不能謀生，飢寒交迫馴為盜賊，其害益甚矣。即大作廠機場之各自為謀，亦不能統算者也。不能統算矣，則各自制物，則必至甲物多而有余，乙物少而不足，或應更新而仍守舊，或已見棄而仍力作。其有余而見棄者則價必賤，不足而更新者價必昂。既有貴賤，則貧富必不均而人格必不平，無由致太平之治。且其有余見棄者，必化偽欺人，而壞其心術，若機器、藥物之有詐偽，若有腐敗，貽害無算。夫凡百什器，皆豈可腐敗而欺人哉！若不欺人而不售，則必棄之。夫以全地之工人統算，其作器之見棄，其為恆河沙無量數，不知加幾零位矣！夫工人之作器，費日力無算，弊精神無算，費備用之百器無算，無量數之工人之需衣食器用者無算。若以之作器，器必有用，必不虛作，其益於全地同胞豈有涯量？而今以無量之工人之作器而棄之，是棄無量數之人，其無量數之日力，其無量數之精神及其他一切無量數之衣食宮室器用也，又豈止暴殄天物而已哉！為大地統計學者，為人民謀公益者，雖日謀之計之而無以為策也，惟有失謬無算而已，無術救之矣，不去人之私工故也。

Now, if we want to attain the Great Concord, first we have to overcome any private production. That's why agriculture, commerce, and industry must return to the public sphere. If all the fields of the world are managed as public property it will be impossible for anybody to own or purchase them. The central government will establish a Ministry of Agriculture in charge of all the cultivable pieces of land around the world, and each administrative level will establish its Department for Agriculture and supervise their division; its offices and branches will be established for every fixed amount of *li*. Each of these levels will install its officials. Students of agriculture will be examined by those offices and if they pass the exam they will be given a piece of land to be cultivated. The amount of cultivated land will vary according to the machinery developed at the time. They will be used for any kind of grains and plants and livestock and fishery. They will work and study in the same place; those who can't stand both activities will be substituted by someone else, because as the number of employees increases, a new grade of perfection will be needed. So, as the population increases, the farming activity will flourish, more new territories will be opened up and techniques will be perfected. Every small administrative unit will routinely call a meeting of its agriculture officials to examine gains and losses; every year, it will communicate its revenues to the central Ministry of Agricultural Affairs which in turn will pass them to the Ministry of Industry and Commerce. The Ministry will calculate the amount of daily supplies needed by the world population, in addition to those needed to repair the damages of natural calamities; it will also consider the most suitable sites of production (among hills and swamps, coastal areas and deserts, fertile plains and dry zones) for any kind of crops, fruits, livestock, and fishery; then the Ministry will compare the yearly data on land production provided by every administrative subdivision's rural bureau, providing a general estimate and communicating it back to the Ministry of Agriculture. The latter will check and ratify the decision; then it will inform every subdivision of its quotas of production, passing down to the smallest unit's agricultural bureau the information on which plants, crops, and animals must be grown or bred according to the geographical features of the place. Jiangnan is suitable for paddy rice, Hebei for wheat, Jiangsu and Zhejiang for mulberry, Sichuan for herbs, Guangdong for flowers and fruits, Siam and Annam and Myanmar for husked rice, northern Kouwai is good for animal farming, the coast for fishing, Shanxi for salt and coal, India for the five cereals, the islands of Nanyang for sugarcane, gems, and pepper. Similarly, we can describe the most suitable products for any country of the world.[20]

3   Central Planning and Local Autonomy

In the following section Kang shows once more—as he did in the previously cited comparisons of political systems in the world—his deep (and somehow naive, albeit anticipatory of more recent trends) interest in a global and comparative approach to history. Besides Kang's taste for encyclopaedic displays of foreign knowledge, following the steps of Lin Zexu and Wei Yuan, we can detect in the following passage a curious echo of the Chinese tradition of local gazetteers, which described in detail the geographical and economic peculiarities of Chinese provinces or localities. That same tone is here adopted and expanded by Kang on a worldwide scale: his survey covers the various regions of the five continents, in a scholarly description of the crops best suited to any region in the world.

> Generally speaking, in the tropics rainfall is abundant and vegetation is florid; its typical products include cotton, indigo, sugar, sappan wood, palms, coconuts, bananas, sandalwood, and any kind of spices. In temperate zones, vegetation is slightly less luxuriant but there is still plenty of

---

20   Kang Youwei, *Datong Shu*, 268–269. My translation. Original text: 夫欲至大同，必去人之私產而后可。凡農工商之業，必歸之公。舉天下之田地皆為公有，人無得私有而私買賣之。政府立農部而總天下之農田各度界小政府皆立農曹而分掌之，數十裡皆立農局，數裡立農分局，皆置吏以司之。其學校之學農學者，皆學於農局之中，學之考驗有成，則農局吏授之田而與之耕。其耕田之多寡，與時新之機器相推遷。其百谷、草木、牧畜、漁魚皆然。其職業與學堂之堂生相等，其不足則兼職，取之兼業之人；其有余酌職業而增之，以求致精。人愈多則農業愈增，辟地愈多，講求愈精。各小政府以時聚農官議而損益之，歲時以其界內所出之材產告之公政府農部，移告之工商部。商部以全國人民所需之食品用品統計若干，與其意外水旱天災彌補若干，凡百谷、果木、牧畜、漁產之用物，何地宜於何品，何地不宜於何品，若山陵、原隰、川海、沙漠、腴瘠、燥濕出產幾何，皆據各分政府之農曹所報之地質出產，以累年之比較而定期農額，統計而預算之，定應用若干，移之農部。農部核定，因各度界之地質宜應種植、牧畜、漁產若干，令各度界如其定額而行之，下之各度界小政府之農曹，令各小度界如額種植、牧畜、漁產，如中國江南之宜稻，河北之宜麥，江浙之宜桑，四川之宜蘗，廣東之宜花果，暹羅、安南、緬甸之宜米，北口外之宜畜牧，沿海之宜漁鹽，山西之宜鹽煤，印度之宜五谷，南洋各島之宜蔗、珈非、胡椒。宜多添各洲各國產物以發明之。

food and useful products, such as maples, elms, willows, pines, cypresses, laurels, camphor trees, firs and birches, mulberry, hemp, potatoes and sugarcane, nuts, peaches, rice and wheat. In the frigid zone vegetation is scarce: Siberia is suitable for pines and wheat, Northern Korea produces ginseng. In Persia, the climate is wet and it favours the production of rice, sugar, tobacco and opium, peaches, pears and plums, apricots and prunes and dates. In Afghanistan, warm regions produce cotton and rice while the cold ones are abundant in wheat, sugarcane, melons, and grapes. Arabia is rich in dates and coffee. Turkey produces wheat, grapes, oranges and olives, pines and cypresses. As we can see, Asia is abundant in flowers, plants, and spices. The French territory is good for agriculture: it produces wheat, corn, mulberry, tobacco, grapes, olives, and apples. England is first in the world for oats production. In Spain, sugarcane, chestnuts, and olives grow as well as oranges, mulberry, indigo plants, grapes, cotton, and rice. Wine is Portugal's most noticeable product. Italy's oranges, lemons, wheat, corn, and potatoes are unmatched, and its production of cotton, tea, and mulberry is also abundant. In Greece they grow rice, cotton, and tobacco, in Switzerland barley and potatoes along with a rich production of timber. In Germany there are many kinds of grapes, while Austria and Hungary produce wheat, barley, cereals, hemp, and tobacco. Sweden's radish is the best in the world. Russia, the Netherlands, and Denmark have any kind of wheat, but Holland also produces tobacco and hemp while Russia is rich in wood and timber. Belgium produces hops. In the northern regions of continental Europe you can find pines, cypresses, hazels, elms, and a kind of small willow. In Tropical Africa there are ten-year-old high plants of cotton, big coconut trees and dates; in the interior of the continent you can find coffee and walnuts, while in northern Africa's coastal areas olives and peaches are widespread. Egypt produces cereals, indigo, cotton, and sugar. In America people cultivate corn, wheat, cotton, sugar, rice, tobacco, potatoes, and any kind of fruit. In Peru the situation is similar but the majority of people breed chickens. Mexico produces sappan wood, maize, tobacco, sugarcane, and coffee, but rice is also abundant. The islands of Western India are particularly rich in typical tropical products: the sugar produced in Cuba is the first in the world, but the island is also famous for its abundant sandalwood and coffee, and for its production of tobacco, oranges, and pineapples. Columbia is outstanding for its coconuts, which are possibly used as hats, but the country is also unmatched in South America for its indigo, cotton, coffee, tobacco, sugarcane, and for its gum trees and sandalwood. Chile and Argentina produce a huge amount of wheat, grapes, and sugarcane. On the island of

Java the breadfruit grows. Australia produces rubber trees, grapes, wheat and corn, cotton, sugar, tobacco, rice, and any kind of fruit.

This is just an outline, but it is clear that any of the five continents has its own characteristics and each of their regions is more suitable for a specific type of plant or animal. So, any administrative unit's rural bureau will summon its offices of agriculture and will publicly discuss how to program cultivation and animal breeding, planning and fixing quotas of production for every single farm. How many workers are needed, how much fertilizer, how many tools and machineries, how much wasteland must be brought under cultivation, how many plants, crops, and animals for each species are sufficient, how many mills and factories have to be built: all will be decided and fixed down to the last detail.[21]

After this immodest display of knowledge, Kang turns back to more concrete and salient political issues, as he outlines a blueprint for the decentralization of State activities: in the following passage he deals with agriculture, but the same pattern is applied later in the text to any other human activity, from schooling

---

21 Kang Youwei, *Datong Shu*, 269–270. My translation. Original text: 大凡熱帶雨多，卑木最繁盛，則生棉花、藍靛、糖、蘇木、棕櫚、椰、蕉、黑白檀及諸香料。溫帶繁植稍次之，而食物、用物乃最多，若楓、榆、柳、櫸、鬆、柏、桂、樟、杉、樺、桑、麻、薯、蔗、桃、米、麥之類是也。寒帶植物少，西伯利亞宜鬆及麥，長白、高麗宜參。若波斯氣侯溫濕，產米、蔗、煙、罌粟、桃、李、梨、杏、梅、棗。阿拉伯盛棗及加非。土耳其產小麥、葡萄、橙、欖、鬆、柏。蓋花卉香料，亞洲為盛矣。法國地宜農，產麥、玉蜀黍、桑、煙、葡萄、欖、林檎。英宜燕麥甲各國。西班牙產蔗、栗、欖、橙、桑、藍、葡萄、棉、米。葡萄牙之葡萄酒為絕美之專產。若橙、檸檬、小麥、玉蜀黍、馬鈴薯，意大利略同，而棉、茶、桑為大。希臘產米、棉、煙。瑞士產裸麥、洋芋，而又富於堅材。日耳曼多種葡萄，又與澳大利、匈牙利產小麥、裸麥、谷、麻、煙。瑞典蘿卜最美。俄羅斯、荷蘭、丹墨多各種麥，而荷有煙、麻，俄富於材木焉。比利時產忽布。大率歐洲北部有鬆、柏、榆及矮小之楊柳也。非洲熱帶，有數十年之大棉、大椰樹、棗樹，內地則加非、胡桃，北岸則欖、桃。埃及產五谷、藍、棉、蔗。美洲產玉蜀黍、小麥、棉、蔗、米、煙、馬鈴薯及諸果，秘魯同之而雞那最多。墨西哥產蘇木、玉蜀黍、煙、蔗、加非，而米尤盛。西印度諸島尤饒，兼熱帶諸物產，扣勃島產糖冠天下，黑檀、加非尤盛，而煙、橙、鳳梨各有矣。科侖比亞以椰為著，可制帽；其藍、棉、加非、煙、蔗，又若樹膠、蘇木，則南美洲所獨矣。智力、阿根廷產大小麥、葡萄、蔗。夏娃尼島產面包果。澳大利亞洲產竹橡、葡萄、小麥、玉蜀黍、棉、蔗、煙、米及諸果。此其大略也。凡五洲土產，各有所宜，分其地質之宜而種植、牧畜、漁取之。各小政府農曹召各農局公商界內種植、牧畜、漁取稱額之法，統計而決算之，分之各地農場。應用農人若干，應備化料若干，應備農具機器若干，應開墾若干，應分別種百谷、果菜、樹木、畜雞、鴨、鵝、魚、牛、馬、羊、豕若干，廠場若干，各分其職而專為之，及其瑣細。

to industrial production. The scheme is simple: the one-world government will collect data from the individual regions and will fix quotas of production and general political outlines. However, in the limits of its assigned duties, every unit will then be "self-sufficient," in terms of the division of work and the redistribution of resources among its citizens, also providing housing, education, and health care (following a global standard that leaves no space for inequality between one region and the others). The ability to unify global planning and self-government indeed constitutes a fundamental piece of Kang's vision, and it also provides an interesting starting point for reflecting on modern utopianism and its political realization in China.

> Any administrative unit will have an autonomous government and will establish a rural unit, under which rural bureaus will be established every ten kilometres and, below them, farms will be established within every kilometre. They will distribute rice, wheat, cereal crops, fruits and vegetables, fisheries and cattle, and the work will be organized through directors, elders, vice-directors, members of the brigade, administrators, secretaries, officials, and apprentices. Directors will supervise general activities, elders will manage the division of work, vice-directors will be their assistants, brigades will carry out their group activities, administrators will collect and store up goods, and secretaries will collect data and record them. Single farms will be charged with tilling and planting. Their extension will not be fixed in advance: as their techniques become more and more refined, as they open new roads and as the strength of their members increases, the communes will become larger. Rural units at each level will have an office supervising the quality of the soil, arranging human settlements according to a careful analysis of the distribution of mountains, plains, marshes, rivers, in order to avoid disparities in soil fertility or in meteorological conditions.[22]

The tension between the need for a central administration and the necessity of including the "local" dimension in the political process, emerging in Kang's

---

22 Kang Youwei, *Datong Shu*, 270–271. My translation. Original text: 每度界為一自治政府，立一農曹，其下數十裡為一農局，其下數裡為一農場。其為稻、麥、黍、百谷、花果、草木、漁產、牧畜，各置分司，皆有主、伯、亞、旅、府、史、胥、徒以司之。主者總辦也，伯者分司之提調也，亞者副之助之也，旅者群執事也，府者收藏者也，史者統計及記事者也。其農場者，農田種植之所也。裡數不定者，機器愈精，道路愈辟，人之智力愈強，則農場愈廣也。每度農曹皆有地質調查局，將其本度內之山陵、原隰、墳衍、川海、人居為小模形，別其肥瘠及泥沙、水石之差，風雨、霜露之度，以色別而詳識之。

text in utopian and extreme terms, can be seen as one of the main concerns of Chinese intellectuals and statesmen of the modern era. Pamela Crossley has constructed her recent interpretive history of modern China around this bipolar pattern (the core vs. the peripheries) and her analysis of Maoism as one of the most energetic attempts to "recentralize China and permanently prevent a reversion to the narrow loyalties of place and region that had poisoned the country for so long—and which the developmentalist would have perpetuated with their centers of resource concentration, their enclaves of specialists and professionals,"[23] further proves the common concerns, and sometimes the common solutions, shared by Kang and the Chairman. The stress on the ideal of *Datong* posed by Mao in the 1950s, while "the hand of the state began to lie more heavily on the countryside"[24] until by 1956 there were no private enterprises at all, echoes Kang's "Confucian" socialist recipes and his praise for "the return of every activity to the public sphere," even while claiming allegiance to completely different ideological and cultural categories. The pattern of a one-world central government distributing administrative duties to a number of progressively more "local" units—the latter functioning in a way resembling Maoist communes—moves the old imperial ideal of *minben* 民本, then, to a global level, while an impersonal and "democratic" government of equals is charged with the old sacred duty of the Emperor to ensure social balance. The ideological route leading from the "rule of the Emperor" to the "rule of the Party" is thus paved by the Confucianist Kang, albeit unwittingly.

As was pointed out with regard to the discourse on democracy—where the aspiration to a *gong* polity is doomed to clash with our "modern" understanding—it is not easy to insert Kang's view on the emergence of a socialist and public-minded policy into any Western category. Certainly we can say that Kang's social ideal gravitates around "the elimination of political, racial, sexual and national barriers, not so much because these hierarchies were evil as because all differentiation of phenomena obscures the truth that on the level of philosophic truth 'reality' is 'one'," as Charlotte Furth has convincingly put it.[25] Whatever his philosophical premise, though, the result is astoundingly similar to the Maoist dream of publicly controlled State-production, which was implemented up to its tragic endings in the 1950s and 1960s. Following this thread, the possible interpretation of such an unexpected affinity, in other words the much-debated "Communist" legacy of Kang's *Datong*, will be discussed in more detail in the next chapter.

---

23   Crossley, *The Wobbling Pivot*, 237.
24   Ibid., 215.
25   Furth, "Intellectual Change", 22.

PART 3

Legacies

CHAPTER 7

The Red Concord
Kang Youwei and Mao Zedong, Meeting in the Land of Utopia?

1   Kang vs Mao: the Benevolent Gaze of Li Zehou

The "prophecy" of a socialist world order, presented in the previous chapter, unsurprisingly became a matter of discussion for Chinese intellectuals and China scholars after the establishment of the People's Republic of China in 1949, as already mentioned. The key question here is this: Can we really consider Kang's utopia—extending Confucian care for "equality" to an almost communist extent—as an anticipation of Mao's struggle for the eradication of social differences? In other words, can Kang be labelled as an "unconscious" or unwitting communist, a thinker who produced his utopianism with the sincere aim to overcome the inequalities of his era? Or was this just a childish (and hypocritical) bourgeois fantasy, a cowardly flight from reality into a faraway world of tomorrow? These questions spurred a philosophical and political debate in the 1950s, when the "Great Leap Forward" put that same ideal of *Datong* at the forefront of a vast ideological campaign launched by Mao himself, and Kang Youwei's thought suddenly became the object of vibrant disputation.

In "On Kang Youwei's Book of Great Concord" (论康有为的大同书), published in 1955 in the ninth issue of the journal *Wenshizhe* 文史哲, a young Li Zehou 李泽厚, later to become one of the most prominent and widely discussed thinkers in the People's Republic of China, provided an in-depth analysis of Kang's utopianism. Although informed by Marxism, Li distinguishes himself from the orthodox Marxist view which had labelled Kang a "conservative" whose utopianism was nothing more than a capitalist *divertissement*, and instead gave a more benevolent and objective appraisal of Kang's thought. In this text the 25-year-old Li openly criticizes many of his contemporaries' interpretations of the *Datong Shu* as well as their critiques of the late Qing reformers' in general, thus proving himself to be a young and independent thinker, and somehow anticipating his later collision with the Party.[1]

---

1   An interesting, although very short, summary of Li's thought can be found in John Zijiang Ding, "Li Zehou: Chinese Aesthetics from a Post-Marxist and Confucian Perspective," in Chung-ying Cheng and Nicholas Bunnin (eds), *Contemporary Chinese Philosophy* (Oxford: Blackwell, 2002).

> Before the diffusion of Marxism, modern China had witnessed three main currents of anti-imperialist and anti-feudal thought. Accordingly, modern China had also witnessed and experienced three forms of socialist utopianism: the agrarian-socialist utopia of the Taiping Kingdom, Kang Youwei's bourgeois and liberal progressive utopia of *Datong Shu*, and the Universal Welfare utopia of Sun Yat-sen's petty-bourgeois revolutionary party. These three socialist idealisms appeared in succession and represent a historical phenomenon of particular significance in social terms. They appeared under different circumstances, in different situations and at different stages, each of them strongly expressing, through its unique aspects, the hatred of the Chinese people against an exploitative system and their aspiration for a better life, as well as depicting the objective challenges faced by Chinese society at the time and the actual trends in its economic development. Thorough research into modern Chinese socialist utopianism is therefore highly significant for an understanding of modern Chinese political and intellectual history, being also a magnificent page in the history of the contribution of the modern Chinese nation to the global advance of socialism.[2]

After this introductory remark, Li gets to one of the key points of his analysis, expounding the reasons why Kang's significant utopia is so often "misread." In fact, the existence of contradictory aspects in Kang's philosophy is undeniable, and his biography, fractured by the post-1898 exile, has proved to accommodate easily the tale of a two-faced life: the reformer and the utopian, the conservative and the socialist. But it is sufficient to recall the complexity of the *Datong Shu*'s ideative process mentioned in the Introduction (begun in the late 1880s, almost completed in 1902, partially published in the 1910s, then revised and published posthumously in 1935) to understand how fragile such a distinction may appear. As I tried to demonstrate with regard to his political positions, Kang's production does not fit into a "before" and "after" 1898 pattern; rather, it appears as a complex fabric constantly redefining Chinese identity faced with "modernity."

Instead of dividing it chronologically, some scholars have elaborated a thematic separation in Kang's production. Such is the case for the contemporary scholar Bai Rui 白瑞, for example: in order to bypass Kang's apparent contradictions, Bai interpreted his philosophy as a sort of "two-level building." A "compromising" reformism—the actual effort to strengthen China—on the

---

2 Li Zehou, "Lun Kang Youwei de Datong Shu", 127.

one side, and an "utopistic" view of mankind's future on the other.[3] Hsiao's approach is similar, and Kang himself hints at the distinction to be made between his public thought and his most private beliefs. Yet these two spheres cannot be considered as "two worlds apart," since they form a unique structure, unified by the global vision of historical evolution which was underlined in the previous chapters. Each stage sheds light on the other, with Kang somehow shifting from one level to the other throughout the decades without ever abandoning the comprehensive structure of his thought. Li Zehou's analysis of Kang's philosophy belongs to this interpretive direction:

> Kang Youwei's socialist utopia is well displayed and summarized in his *Datong Shu*, which is therefore one of his most significant works. At the same time, though, the *Datong Shu* is one of his most misread and misinterpreted works, and such a misunderstanding is clear throughout some of the essays which have recently dealt with this book. For example, someone has argued that the *Book of Great Concord* is a "utopian ideal of agrarian socialism";[4] others have described Kang's theory as "drifting away from the fundamentals of socialism";[5] someone has credited Kang Youwei for trying to "give the Chinese bourgeoisie a way of escape";[6] someone else has even described the purpose of Kang's book as the attempt to "deceive and anesthetize the masses, in order to mitigate the revolutionary tide."[7] All these different views have generated a confused perception. Actually, the Datong Shu, through the format of a utopia, expresses Kang's early anti-feudal progressive and bourgeois ideal in its naked aspect: this is the book's content and its specificity. So, if we say that Kang's Hundred-Days manifesto was the last effort to summarize the whole political programme of the eighteenth-century reformers, we can affirm that his *Datong Shu* was the first attempt to provide reformism with a utopia aspiration. These two "faces" present a great distance and many contradictions (and this fact has puzzled many observers); however, at the same time they form a single unity.[8]

---

3 Bai Rui, *Xunqiu chuantong zhengzhi de xiandai zhuanxing*.
4 Reference to Li Rui 李锐, "Comrade Mao Zedong's early revolutionary movement" 毛泽东同志的初期革命活动 in 中国青年, 3, 1953, 9.
5 Reference to Ji Wenfu 嵇文甫, "Youlile de xueshuo 游离了的学说" (*Xinshixue tongxun* 新史学通讯 1953), 6.
6 Reference to Fan Wenlan 范文澜 (*Zhongguo jindaishi* 中国近代史), 322.
7 Reference to Mao Jianxun 毛健予, "Wenti jie'an 问题解答" (*Xinshixue tongxun*, 1953), 19.
8 Li Zehou, "Lun Kang Youwei de Datong Shu", 128.

Given the fact that this reinterpretation of the old Confucian vision of *datong* undoubtedly figures as one of the highest products of late Qing reformers in terms of its ideological breadth and political projection, how then can the emergence of this utopianism in an anti-revolutionary class be explained from a Marxist point of view, without accusing Kang's thought of being the philosophical product of an emerging capitalist class? First of all, Li argues that Kang and his contemporaries "were facing a period of unprecedented change and creative chaos, when everything was quickly collapsing, reshaping, or transforming; this new stage, never experienced before, caused people to be dazzled and deluded as they started to doubt their once-solid beliefs: this is not a minor issue but a complex and major question."[9] Then, Li defines Kang's escape to Utopia as a proof of the limits of an "unripe class": this strenuous jump into a "dreamed world," consciously kept apart from any "public" political agenda, somehow served as an indirect self-denunciation of the limits of a "national bourgeoisie" striving to reform its country, Li writes.

> On the one side, in the imaginary world of *Datong Shu* we can certainly detect the weak and compromising essence of reformism; on the other, though, the ideal of *datong* greatly exceeded the actual expectations of the reformers, setting forth ideas and positions which they did not dare to address in their political platforms. Through the idea of *datong* and the old theory of the "three epochs," Kang indeed "found an ideal, an artistic form, and a dream to prevent a narrow-minded bourgeoisie being self-contradicted by those views of his own, and also to preserve his enthusiasm on the stage of a great historical tragedy," as Karl Marx had said about Louis Bonaparte. The optimistic aspiration to a world of "great concord" thus became the main ideological principle and the practical driving force guiding the core group of reformist intellectuals (i.e., Tan Sitong's "left wing" and Kang's own direct disciples): they considered themselves to be acting as glorious martyrs for the sake of mankind. The liberal utopianism of the reformers, then, was produced by the weak body of a class in which "the spirit was willing but the flesh was weak,"[10] so to speak, displaying its specific immaturity. As Lenin wrote in his *Two Kinds of Utopianism*, "utopias proceed from the ongoing struggle against old systems, against the slavery of peasants, against political oppression ... At the same time they are produced by low classes who do not take an independent position in this struggle. Utopias and fantasies

---

9   Ibid.
10 "心有余而力不足"。

are produced by such lack of independence, by such a *weakness*." This is exactly the objective class basis of Kang Youwei's utopianism.[11]

In fact, reading the *Datong Shu*'s chapters dealing with economy, production, and society one can hardly deny their "affinity" with Marxist concerns, apart from their Confucian pedigree. And that is exactly what Li does in another section of his youthful essay, where he focuses on those economic aspects of the Great Concord (mentioned and translated in the previous chapter), highlighting the assonance with Maoist blueprints: Kang expresses a materialistic view of human history, albeit drawing it from Classicism—or so the author argues, trying to intertwine the Mencian threads of the *Datong Shu* with Marxism. That is made evident by the fact that Kang's ideal of *Datong* implies the full realization of *material* necessities, which are in his view inseparable from the *spiritual* importance of global equality. And this is not so distant from Marx, Li underlines:

> In his vehement attack on the sufferings caused by the old society, Kang unfolds his optimistic social project of Great Concord. The philosophical foundation of his blueprint is the bourgeois theory of human nature ("people desire to eliminate evil"): "The meaning of life is to avoid suffering and to attain happiness, there is no other way than this." The *Datong Shu* gets rid of the hypocritical exteriority of feudalistic values, waving the banner of a simple and natural humanism, pointing out the righteousness and rationality of mankind's "pursuit of happiness" and opposing the reactionary theory of asceticism and frugality, sponsored by the feudalistic landlords throughout the centuries. The basis of Kang's imagined world of Great Concord, then, is the highest grade of perfection of a *material* culture, where scientific progress is described as extremely developed and human life is described as extremely satisfactory and people have fulfilled their material (clothes, food, houses, transportation) and spiritual (culture, education, entertainment) necessities. [...] One cannot easily dismiss all this as a "capitalistic degeneration"; this beautiful image produced by an utopian illusion is—from an objective point of view— the beautiful and powerful ode of a new bourgeoise class to a capitalistic society which was at that time attaining a high grade of industrialization. [...] Kang's dream of a "leisure park world" and his belief in the inevitability of social progress resonate with the actual social aspirations of his time and reflect the pursuit of happiness of wide popular masses,

---

11   Li Zehou, "Lun Kang Youwei de Datong Shu": 135–136.

demonstrating how the structure of the world of *Datong* rests on a material development: this is undoubtedly something that we can define as "correct" and "advanced." And it also marks a fundamental difference between Kang's *Datong Shu* and the "System of Imperial Fields." Kang provides further evidence of his utopia's fundaments when he recognizes that the public ownership of work and capital is at the basis of the Great Concord. And in the *Datong Shu*, workers enjoy a high social position.[12]

Li goes on to analyse the socialist elements in *Datong Shu* in more detail, extensively quoting the original text:

> In the world of Great Concord, as Kang points out, there is no exploiting nor oppression, there are no "private interests" and "damaging the public good through personal interests is prohibited" (to cite the commentary on the *Liyun*). In his utopia, the power deriving from property (財產的所有權) is entirely owned by a public government (*gong zhengfu*, 公政府). As Kang writes: "Every activity, agriculture, industry and commerce, will return to the public sphere"; "every piece of land in the world will be *public*"; "the infrastructure built by hundreds of workers will return to them: they cannot be private property of any individual"; "there cannot be private enterprises: every economic activity in the world will be controlled by the ministry of industry of the public government." Production and distribution will be planned: "There will be no surplus of products, no corruption nor waste." In Kang's words: "In the Age of Concord, the world will be public, there will be no classes, everybody will be equal." Clearly, this is a *grand* socialist utopia, which exceeds by far the structural constraints of the "feudalistic" oppressing class and clearly demonstrates the courage of the emerging bourgeoise in its search for the truth and in its challenge to transcend its own interests. It is a mighty philosophical expression of the Chinese people's aversion to exploitation and its desire to break free from any form of oppression. Therefore the *Datong Shu* is endowed with a rich *popular* content.[13]

Undeniably presenting itself as a socialist and people-oriented prophecy, the *Book of Great Concord* deserves more than the snubs it has received from Marxist intellectuals, Li argues in his concluding remarks:

---

12   Ibid., 132–134.
13   Ibid., 135.

> In conclusion, the economic assumptions and basic principles of Kang's utopia can be described through the words used by Engels speaking of Saint-Simon: "here we can see the far-reaching look of a man of talent." Addressing the economic issues of *datong*, Kang acknowledged that the fulfilment of Great Concord can only be realized on the basis of a highly developed material culture, in which the forces of production have been greatly empowered: only then will people be able to get rid of poverty and enjoy happiness. He predicted that politics would have soon started to gravitate around a matter of economics: the regulation of production; and he expressed in a simple way the great principle that everyone ought to work. Of course, Kang is not as farsighted as Saint-Simon, who detected precisely the class struggle between work and capital in a capitalistic society, as well as the conflict of interests lying behind the existence of a private mode of production. Kang's reformist utopia is, in this sense, more limited.[14]

But Li's analysis is not limited to economic socialism. Equally interesting is his survey of the *political* implications of Kang's utopia. Here, the author conveys his own optimism concerning the possibility of constructing a system in China which is simultaneously socialist and democratic, a utopia which he will fully express starting from the 1980s. "The question of the political principles underlying the world of Great Concord undoubtedly represent an issue of major importance," Li points out in his earlier work on Kang.

> In the world of Great Concord, there are no families: each individual is brought up and educated in a Common House which will also be his place of work. But what kind of thing is this "community" at the end? How is it concretely embodied? Is it somehow related to the constitutional monarchy promoted by Kang in his early political activism? It is clear that in the "community" (*gong*) of Great Concord, the content and nature of a "common government" is of great importance. In his utopia, Kang unexpectedly unfolds before our eyes a thorough road map to a *democratic* world. I say *unexpectedly*, because such a democratic thought, referred to someone who we usually consider as a mature conservative who defended monarchy and advocated a reformism with severe limitations to the "rule by the people," is something that really defies our expectations. Here, Kang fully exposes the huge contradictions between his philosophy and his political action. Kang defined himself as "the first actual

---

14   Ibid., 136.

proposer, in China, of 'civil rights' (*minquan*) as a general principle."[15] During his youth, through his disciples and friends, and through books like *Confucius as a Reformer*, he tried to propagate a bourgeois reflection on democracy. For example, in *Confucius as a Reformer* he states: "Yao and Shun considered as the highest human attainment the establishment of Supreme Equality through democracy. [...] Confucius brought order to the Age of Emerging Equality following the example of King Wen to establish a compassionate (*ren* 仁) monarchy, but at the same time he was looking forward to the Age of Supreme Equality, following the example of Yao and Shun to promote democracy."

In his Commentary to the *Liji*, Kang writes: "So, the world will be a single country and people of this global nation will enjoy public and common utilities; not a single individual nor a single family will own private properties whatsoever. The masses will publicly select the worthy and promote the capable to fill positions of responsibility, which will not become an hereditary possession to their sons or brothers: this will be the general rule of government." However, if we say that in Kang's public writings the democratic approach is veiled under the cult of the Sages—a timid way to present them—then, in his "secret and concealed" utopian vision, that kind of philosophy appears bare and bold.[16]

The complex issue of the possible "totalitarian" outcomes of Kang's one-world vision, is rapidly (too rapidly, perhaps) discarded by Li:

> Above all, Kang clearly states that the one-world government is in first place a mechanism (*jiguan*, 機關) for the cultural and economical administration of society, and not a strong and oppressive state apparatus (*guojia jiqi*, 國家機器).[17]

Kang's view on democracy—Li argues, quoting extensively from Part Six of the *Datong Shu*—is based on the assumption that "a free and happy life can be attained only on the basis of principles like 'human equality' and 'unrestricted individual rights.'" As for Kang's socialist concerns, his democratic thought reveals "the political aspiration of the emerging bourgeoisie" and "embodies

---

15 This is a quotation from Kang's *Letter to the Conference of Chinese Communities in the Americas on the Necessity for China to Pursue Constitutional Monarchy Instead of Revolution*.
16 Li Zehou, "Lun Kang Youwei de Datong Shu", 142–143.
17 Ibid.

their opposition to a reactionary, feudalistic, and authoritarian system." Such a philosophical construction, combining socialist and liberal elements, displays a "noteworthy progressive nature," Li says speaking (provocatively?) to his Marxist comrades:

> From another point of view, we must consider that the author of *Datong Shu*, when describing the most perfect "democracy," immediately points out that such a democracy cannot be a sudden attainment but must be preceded by another stage, a constitutional monarchy limiting the power of the ruler. A similar stance was expressed by a young Liang Qichao, who made a clear-cut differentiation between democracy (*minzhu*) and civil rights (*minquan*), acknowledging that they must "proceed in good order" and "cannot be achieved overnight."[18]

"The world of Concord is built on the economic basis of collectivism; but on the other side, it is founded on a social pattern that we could call 'absolute freedom,'" Li then writes. And indeed this synthetical definition catches all the fascinating (and still unresolved) ambivalence of Kang's utopia, and it also anticipates the tough and dramatic political confrontation on the possible coexistence of a communist society with some form of "democracy" that would flare up in the following decades.[19]

As benevolent as Li's look at Kang's utopianism could be, it is still the look of a Marxist thinker. In his conclusions, then, Li moderates his enthusiasm for the world of Supreme Equality by admitting that, at the end of the day, Kang Youwei was speaking on behalf of the bourgeoisie: his socialism was in some measure "spurious," but nonetheless represented a *progressive* and *advanced* intellectual product of modern China, much more consistent than the "naive utopianism" expressed by the Taiping rebels, Li argues:

> Kang Youwei's ideal of a Great Concord, in its position on the possible "peaceful coexistence" with the feudal class or its "extreme disdain for mass movements" might seem to resemble the political idealism and the so-called utopianism of Tsarist Russia's liberals, criticized by Lenin in *Two Kinds of Utopias*. However, Kang's utopianism certainly does not "corrupt the democratic consciousness of the masses, concealing a new form of oppression under the glittering veil of the pursuit of selfish

---

18 Li Zehou, "Lun Kang Youwei de Datong Shu", 143. The quotation by Liang Qichao is from "Principles of change from autocracy to democracy": 论君政民政相嬗之理。

19 On this, see Chapter 5.

desires," to use Lenin's words. The *Datong Shu* does not contain such political implications, as demonstrated by the fact that Kang decided not to make it public. This book marks an important step in the history of modern Chinese socialist idealism and it is far more advanced than the naive agrarian socialist utopianism of the Taiping rebellion. The *Book of Great Concord* elaborates a theory of historical development based on the understanding of social necessities, thus pointing to a world based on the economic foundation of a highly developed material civilization, inspired by the general principles of universal employment and public ownership, and politically structured as a democracy in which every individual is considered free and equal. To a certain extent, the *Datong Shu* aptly expressed the common aspiration to a better life of both advanced intellectuals and Chinese common people, as well as their shared trust in scientific progress, their aversion to feudal autocracy and their pursuit of rights and democracy. The *subjective* form of socialist utopianism is filled with the *objective* content of a theory of democracy. The same is valid for Sun Yat-sen's thought, as Lenin pointed out in his essay *Democracy and Populism in China*: Chinese modern socialists can be defined as socialists only from a *subjective* point of view, since they react against oppression and exploitation; however, from an *objective* point of view, their agenda is the fight against a "specific historical form of exploitation, i.e., the feudal system." Utopian socialism was a strong philosophical reaction to oppression and exploitation: the ideal of Great Concord was a cry against feudalism. In conclusion, it is clear that the *Datong Shu* could not be a critique of capitalistic society, and it is not actually inspired by socialism but by capitalism; having said that, it is the sincere and coherent ode of an enlightened mind longing for the joyful destiny of a country walking toward a brighter future.[20]

Li Zehou's interest in Kang's utopianism was not exhausted by this essay, though. Two years later, the young philosopher chose to return to the *Datong Shu*, this time with another intention. His aim was to mount a polemic aimed directly against another prominent Communist thinker, Tang Zhidiao 汤志钧, who had criticized Li's "benevolent" interpretation of the *Datong Shu*, brusquely dismissing the *Book of Great Concord* as a "reactionary" piece of literature. Li in response criticizes Tang's entire scholarship on the *Datong Shu* as "inconsistent and baseless." The following extracts represent an interesting example of that exchange of ideas: it is both a scholarly debate on Kang and,

---

20   Li Zehou, "Lun Kang Youwei de Datong Shu", 148–149.

most importantly, a testimony to the energetic philosophical confrontation among the Communist intelligentsia of the 1950s.

> Mr. Tang Zhidiao's paper *On Kang Youwei's Book of Great Concord* (published this year in the first issue of *Philosophy of Cultural History*) advances some criticism of my previous essay *Discussion on Kang Youwei's Book of Great Concord*, touching fundamental questions with regard to the evaluation of the *Datong Shu*. In other words: is the *Datong Shu* a fundamentally progressive or reactionary book? The point of divergence is that for Tang Zhidiao the philosophical foundation of Kang's book is reactionary, serving as the theoretical basis for his late years' activity of "lulling the masses," "contrasting the revolution," and "defending monarchy to restore the Empire" (these are quotations from Tang's article). I cannot agree with this view, since I am convinced that in its main content the *Datong Shu* basically expresses the progressive thought of young Kang, advocating for bourgeoise democracy and liberalism. Now, I will briefly address some of Mr. Tang's remarks.
>
> First of all, I consider Mr. Tang's methodology of research as absolutely inappropriate. He does not rely on any analysis of the *Datong Shu*'s actual content, rather using a purely chronological examination of its dating as the point of departure for his discussion. The *Datong Shu*—Tang argues—was "completed" in 1901–1902, during Kang's exile following the failure of the Hundred Days reform, a time when the emergence of revolutionaries spurred Kang's "reactionary" attitude: "He supported Guangxu, feared a popular uprising and wished to draw an ideal boundary: that's why he wrote the *Datong Shu*," Tang writes, and *consequently* the *Datong Shu* is defined as reactionary. In the article, there is no reference to the *Datong Shu*'s contents, there are no observations nor concrete responses to my own analysis of those contents. There is no substantial research on the philosophical content of Kang's text nor of its specific connections to his contemporary social and historical situation: the author simply uses the philological examination of the *Datong Shu*'s writing process as the only element in shaping his own judgment on the book's value. Honestly, any theory built on these premises is quite dangerous. Have we forgotten the erroneous methodology of Mr. Yu Pingbo's researches on the *Dream of the Red Chamber*?[21]

---

21 Li Zehou, "Datong Shu de pingjia wenti yu xiezuo niandai 大同书的评价问题与'写作年代." (*Wenshizhe*, 1957). Included in *Zhongguo jindai sixiangshi lun* 中国近代思想史论 (Beijing: Renmin chubanshe, 1979), 149–150.

The debate on the *Datong Shu*'s composition, which was addressed in the Introduction to the present book, is understood by Li as involving something more complex than a simple dating: it indirectly demands a judgment on the whole of Kang's production, and on the intentions behind his political action after the failure of the Hundred Days. Tang's version of the facts (the *Datong Shu* was completed while Kang was already a "reactionary," fighting against the Republic) vehemently discredits the entire purpose that ostensibly lay behind the author's utopianism.

In his studies of Kang's *Datong Shu*, presented above, Li Zehou not only provides some interesting hints about the internal debate among Communist intellectuals on the relationship between tradition and modernity; he also anticipates the revival of interest in late Qing reformers that he and some of his fellow intellectuals will encourage in the decade stretching from the end of Maoism to the Tian'anmen protests in 1989, while bidding "farewell to revolution" (*gaobie geming*, 告别革命).[22] This will be a cultural effort tightly intertwined with more general reflection on the possibility of reforming China, harmonizing the revolution with a care for individual freedom.

As far as Li's own system of thought is concerned, the 1955 and 1957 essays also supply a significant example of the author's youthful development. Defined as a "post-Marxist anthropological ontology," Li's view tries to "combine the most important aspects of traditional Chinese philosophy with those of Western philosophy and to establish a methodology for the study of philosophy that embraces both Chinese and Western thought," as recently summarized by a scholar of contemporary Chinese philosophy.[23] Li's early interest in Kang's elaborations on the concept of *Datong* would certainly resonate in his more mature elaboration on the "philosophy of the future" which, again to use John Ding's words, aims at "overcoming tragic conflicts and dissensions between human beings and nature, society and individuals, emotion and reason, history and psychology, and ideal and reality" through an "analysis of the objective history of social development."[24] We could say that Kang's philosophical "road map"—examining the global history of mankind, from chaos to concord—is not far from Li's own purpose.

Additionally, in Li's attempts at demolishing some of the fences erected between Maoism (or Marxism in general) and Chinese Classicism by their

22 See Tze-ki Hon, *Revolution as Restoration. Guocui xuebao and China's Path to Modernity, 1905–1911* (Leiden: Brill, 2013), 1. On Li's intervention in the debate on *gaobie geming*, see Li Zehou and Liu Zaifu, *Gaobie geming: ershi shiji duitan lu* 告别革命：二十世纪对谈录 (Taipei: Maitian Press, 1999).
23 Ding, "Li Zehou".
24 Ding, "Li Zehou", 252.

respective supporters, we can detect a sort of "accommodative" attitude. It is this attitude that, according to Jing Wang's account of Li Zehou's general approach to tradition, is the pivot of the philosopher's intellectual production:

> Li Zehou's double call for "constructing two civilizations" (the material and spiritual civilization) is symptomatic of his accommodative streak that always seeks to merge materialism and idealism in a continuum reminiscent of middle-of-the-road Confucian eclecticism. Therefore, instead of valorizing Li Zehou's philosophy as a site of contestation, I suggest that we examine it as a site of conciliation where an ongoing process of ideological negotiation among historical materialism, idealism, and Confucian rationalism takes shape. Bearing in mind his penchant for the philosophy of the unity of Heaven and (hu)man, we should anticipate that Li Zehou's theoretical practice faithfully enacts the Confucianist instinct for reconciliation. The meeting of classical Marxist with reformist Confucian ideology thus sets the moral tenor of his philosophy of modernity.[25]

Such an attitude received harsh criticisms from both the left and the right; the former criticized "what they consider to be his pseudo-Marxism," while the latter condemned him "for degenerating into the dogmatism of outworn Marxism," with other less politicized critics considering "his theoretical frameworks to be a 'mixed stew of Marx, Kant and other philosophers' or, at most, a 'creative imitation' of those figures."[26] This was a destiny similar to that of Kang, by the way. Meanwhile, if Li Zehou tried to "save" the author of the *Datong Shu* and late Qing reformism from the excessively stern political judgment of the Marxists, cleaving to an objective (and "accommodative") approach, in those very same years some scholars outside the PRC were fighting a battle to "protect" Kang from any possible communist embrace.

2 Kang vs Mao: Saving the *Datong Shu* from Communism

In 1967, while Mao was launching his Great Cultural Revolution and Li Zehou was further elaborating his own approach to Marxism, Lawrence Thompson—who had translated a significant portion of the *Datong Shu* nine years

---

25 Jing Wang, *High Culture Fever: Politics, Aesthetics, and Ideology in Deng's China* (Berkeley, CA: University of California Press, 1996), 94.
26 Ding "Li Zehou", 257.

before—wrote a short but incisive essay to *deny* the existence of any Marxist nuance in Kang's utopia. In no way can Communists claim, even indirectly, his utopian legacy, he claimed; Kang's and Marx's visions "differ completely."

> Marx advocates a revolutionary seizure of power by the proletariat which will result in centralization of the means of production and eventually in a "vast association of the whole nation"; K'ang believes that the basis for the establishment of One World is replacement of the family system by the system of public institutions, and feels confident that the ideal polity will come about in the natural course of evolution.[27]

This view was not isolated. On the contrary, it has been often shared—and again for clear political reasons—among scholars of Chinese thought outside mainland China since 1949. An outstanding example of this kind of judgment can be found in Hsiao Kung-chuan's study of Kang's philosophy, published less than ten years after Thompson's paper and sharing much of those ideas:

> in the first two decades of the present century diverse currents of socialist thought, ranging from utopian socialism to Marxism, from capitalism tempered with socialization to unmitigated communism, found expression in the writings of Chinese intellectuals. Kang's Great Community stood perhaps as the most systematic and imaginative socialist construct of all. More radical than Hu Shi's "liberal socialism," it might be characterized as "democratic communism" and as such was much more akin in spirit to utopian socialism than to revolutionary Marxism. This observation should suffice to warn against giving more credit to Kang than he deserved, as some recent writers seem to be doing. One of them has suggested that Kang's ideal of the Great Community is indistinguishable from "Western Communism"; another claims that Mao Zedong "has borrowed heavily for his ideas for commune" from Kang Youwei.[28]

In the first two quotations, Hsiao refers to Kyoson Tsuchida, who in his *Contemporary Thought of Japan and China* (1927) asserted that Kang's *Datong* was "the same social ideal as in Western Communism or anarchism." According to Hsiao these are "untrue" considerations. Even though Kang shares some similar points of view with anarchists—such as his attention to the value of "universal love" or his idea of abolishing families and marriage in the name of

---

27   Thompson, *Ta-tung shu*, 351.
28   Hsiao, *A Modern China and a New World*, 494–495.

individual freedom—"there is a crucial difference between the two: the latter called for the abolition of government, whereas the former envisaged a comprehensive world government."[29]

The second claim—that Mao borrowed heavily from Kang—is addressed by Hsiao in the following terms:

> There are of course striking points of contact between the Great Community and Communist society, beyond obvious structural similarities. Both are universalistic ideals based on the assumption that human development is rigidly unilinear. But such similarities do not obscure the fundamental differences between the two.[30]

Explicitly nodding at Thompson here, Hsiao underlines how, in his opinion, Kang's assumptions are "widely different from those of the Marxist," because "the essentially humanistic outlook of K'ang was diametrically opposite to the Communists' brutally cynical view of man and society." Hsiao's conclusion is clear cut: "K'ang therefore was inherently unacceptable to Mao Tse-tung as Mao would certainly been unacceptable to K'ang Yu-wei."[31] In other words, "K'ang's philosophical standpoint was diametrically opposed to that of the Communists and his ideas of abolishing the family and private property were based on the 'idealistic' notion of universal love, instead of the Marxist doctrine of class war."[32]

Such a staunch anti-Maoist attitude—certainly not "accommodative," and on the contrary uncompromisingly cutting any possible thread linking Kang and Mao's utopianisms—evidently bespeaks the necessity (from Thompson's and Hsiao's point of view) to separate Maoism from the roots of Chinese identity, using Classicism as a defensive trench against Communist China in the years when the rhetoric of *datong* was being used by Mao and his followers as an ideological tool in their revolutionary enterprise.

However, the debate on the relationship between Kang and Mao would not end with Hsiao's clear stance. A few years later, while analysing the *Datong Shu* in his essay on democracy and authoritarianism in China, the Berkeley researcher Wen-Shun Chi would argue that "there are reasons to believe that Mao was heavily or almost exclusively influenced by Kang in establishing the

---

29   Ibid., 495, note 314.
30   Ibid., 495.
31   Ibid.
32   Ibid., 132.

communes."³³ And more than two decades later, new connections between the Confucianist and the Communist would be sketched in China.

3   Kang vs Mao: Unconscious Classicism and Unwitting Socialism?

In 2010 the *Journal of the Hunan University of Technology* published a paper by two scholars, Xia Tingting and Du Juhui, who attempted a comparison between Mao Zedong's social idealities and Kang Youwei's utopianism as expressed in the *Datong Shu*. Mao himself had even had some words of approval for Kang's reformism (not Kang's utopianism, ironically, since the *Datong Shu* was not published until 1935), prior to his revolutionary turn in the 1920s. And later the Chairman would remark on the limited significance of *Datong Shu*, observing that Kang "did not and could not find the way to achieve Great Harmony."³⁴ So the question of how much "communism" is contained in the *Datong Shu* has loomed over any study of Kang's "late" thought for a long time, both before and after the establishment of the PRC, as the confrontation between Li Zehou and Tang Zhidiao demonstrates (although Mao and his thought did not explicitly appear on stage in that debate, for obvious political reasons).

In their paper, Xia and Du start from a very traditional (from a Marxist point of view) premise: Kang, far from being a socialist or a communist, was the most prominent figure among those "capitalist reformers" who had unsuccessfully tried to change China at the end of the nineteenth century through their "traditional" and "bourgeois" tools.³⁵ Despite this prologue in which they clarify that Kang's and Mao's political activities were at odds with each other from a "class" viewpoint, the authors then admit that a kind of a relationship between the two can be detected: the Chairman, in the years of his intellectual formation, had "unconsciously" (不自觉地) received some influence from Kang's theory of *datong* and of Confucian progressivism in general.³⁶ The definition of the contribution of Classicism to the development of Maoism as an "unconscious" process may to our eyes appear somewhat naïve. What is interesting in this approach, though, is the fact that, by such rhetorical *escamotage*, Xia and Du seem to provide Maoism with a sort of "excuse" for the unmistakable classical

---

33   Chi Wen-shun, *Ideological conflicts in Modern China. Democracy and Authoritarianism* (New Brunswick: Transaction Publishers, 1992), 30.
34   Mao, *Selected works*, vol. 4, 414, quoted in Hsiao, *A Modern China and a New World*, 132.
35   Xia Tingting 夏婷婷 and Du Juhui 杜菊辉, "Mao Zedong yu Kang Youwei shehui sixiangguan zhi bijiao 毛泽东与康有为社会思想观之比较." (*Hunan Gongxue Daxue xueban*, 15, 6, 2010, 78–81), 78.
36   Ibid.

echoes emerging out of almost every aspect of the Chairman's thought and political theories (a fact on which much has been written in the last decades). So, in this particular case, Mao's assumed "unconsciousness" in his borrowing from Classicism may fill the gap which separates the Communist leader from the "bourgeois" and "Confucianist" Kang. Having shortened the distance between the two, then, the authors proceed in good order to examine the similarities and differences between their utopias, dodging the risk of breaking any political taboo. The key, according to Xia and Du, is the consideration that Mao and Kang "both received the influence of Chinese classicism (儒)":

> Kang Youwei had studied Confucian thought since his childhood, being influenced by traditional culture and being familiar with the Classics: Confucianism and traditional culture, then, were deeply rooted in his thought. Of course, Kang wasn't a mainstream classicist and his constant aim was not a philological exegesis but the search for the spirit of the Classics, and through the reformulation of Western and Buddhist contents he finally built his own peculiar social vision of *Datong*. Kang himself, in his autobiography, had briefly sketched the formation of his own idea of *Datong*. It was meant to be in Kang's words the result of reflection on "the profound meanings of Master Kong's words, the deep foundations of Classicism and Buddhism, the entrance of new Western models into China and the limits of the theory of Heaven and Man."[37] After having "unrolled the analysis to a global context and after having applied it to the present and the past,"[38] the theory of *Datong* had finally been conceived.

References to Li Zehou's approach to Kang's thought might be discerned in this paper, albeit rather timid ones, and with no direct mention of Li's own essays. What is interesting here is the cautious attempt at redefining the relationship between Tradition and Revolution, in a moment when Confucius becomes the protector of a new wave of Chinese nationalism and Kang is no longer a "conservative" deserving of blame, but perhaps even an example whose guidance it is once more possible to seek (more will be said on this in the next chapter). In 2011, Li Zehou's approach to this issue again emerges—explicitly, this time—in the words of, Evans Chan 陳耀成, a contemporary film director based in Hong Kong and producer of a documentary on Kang's "cosmopolitan" and "utopian"

---

37 Kang Youwei, *Kang Nanhai Zibian Nianpu*, 1992.
38 Ibid.

phase entitled *Datong: The Great Society* 大同：康有為在瑞典. In an interview with Peter Zarrow, Chan says:

> Kang's legacy is complex. If his reform efforts failed during the 1911 Revolution, but have survived as an illusory path not taken by "China," his speculative utopian program was realized to a fault in revolutionary China during the Great Leap Forward. Mao's relationship with Kang, fraught with respect and rivalry, was one of the most astonishing things I uncovered during my research. Apparently, Mao found his initial calling after reading Kang's *Datong Shu* in 1917, when he was 24. He wrote to a friend stating Datong to be his political goal, while citing the Confucian evolutionist paradigm developed by Kang. Understandably, that has been suppressed throughout his career, probably because of his insistence on his originality, but apparently also due to an urge to hide his original calling's Confucian underpinning in the Marxist-Leninist revolutionary rat race, in both his theoretical one-up-man-ship within the party, and later in his state-building rivalry with the Soviet Union. But Kang cannot be blamed for the Great Leap Forward's barbarous atrocities by design or ignorance, because of his own leeriness of a forcible utopianism. [...] More recently Li Zehou hailed Kang as the greatest modern Chinese philosopher. And he made a strong case for rehabilitating Kang politically in his book *Goodbye to Revolution* (告別革命, 1995) by maintaining that Kang's might have been a better option for China. A number of viewers seem to feel that that is my film's position.[39]

In conclusion, this discussion on Kang's socialism is just a small piece in the much wider mosaic depicting the relationship between the CPC's mainstream Marxist ideology and the legacy of the Confucian and Classical tradition inherited from the Imperial age.

First of all, it confirms that Mao's thought did not grow as an entirely exogenous product within Chinese intellectual life, since in his earlier intellectual elaboration—as seems to be proved by his apparent connection to Kang—the Chairman inserted (unconsciously or not) a number of traditional elements. Even in the harshest moments of his ideological fights, traditional threads can often be traced, although veiled under the Communist rhetoric. As Stuart Schram has argued in his analysis of Maoism's early formative process, the Communist leader and many of his "revolutionary" colleagues "remained deeply marked both by the faith in the intrinsic capacities of the Chinese

---

[39] See the full text of Peter Zarrow's interview at: www.thechinabeat.org (December 2011).

people, and by the *traditional modes of thought* which they had repudiated"; therefore "they were fated to live in circumstances of permanent political and cultural ambiguity and instability."[40] In the late 1910s, years before becoming the head of Communist China, Mao had praised the only three people who had an idea about how to rule modern China as a whole: Yuan Shikai, Sun Yat-sen, and Kang Youwei. Among them, Mao acknowledged, only the latter had basic principles (*benyuan* 本原) and a broad perspective, although his proposals were restricted to the realm of rhetoric.[41] Again, in 1917, while stressing the importance of "little people" (*xiaoren* 小人) versus the hierarchical values of Confucian "gentlemen" (*junzi* 君子), Mao made an explicit reference to the ideal of *Datong* as the supreme goal of revolution: here, he clearly showed his "persistent attachment to elements of the Chinese tradition,"[42] even while talking about his ultimate plans for the future of the country.[43] Beside their common interest in the language of Confucian utopianism, Mao and Kang also shared a similar interest in Western thought and global historical patterns, albeit from different viewpoints. As was pointed out earlier, Kang's view of "modernity" was largely a "materialistic" one, focused on scientific, social, and political progress more than on purely philosophical or metaphysical considerations: this aspect was readily underlined by Li Zehou in order to make Kang's utopianism appear closer to Marxism. However, that stress on economic and technological development may have been influenced by the kind of Liberalism which had been imported to China through the translations of Yan Fu, more than by Marxism *tout court*. As strange as it might seem, Mao Zedong himself was not immune from that source of inspiration. As pointed out by Stuart Schram in his analysis of an article written by Mao in 1919 on "the great union of the popular masses," if a discernible philosophical bias is to be found in such a work, it lies "neither in Marx nor in Kropotkin, but in the ideas of Western liberals as transmitted and transmuted by some Chinese writers of the late nineteenth and early twentieth century," like Yan Fu and Kang's disciple Liang Qichao.[44] "Mao was never, at any time after 1918 or 1919, a nationalist solely, or primarily, interested in China's 'wealth and power.' But neither was he

---

40 Stuart Schram, "Mao Tse-t'ung's Thought to 1949," in Ou-Fan Lee and Merle Goldman (eds), *An Intellectual History of Modern China* (Cambridge: Cambridge University Press, 2002, 267–348), 268.
41 Mao, *Correspondence*: 19–21, also quoted in Schram "Mao Tse-t'ung's Thought", 272.
42 Maurice Meisner, *Mao Zedong: A Political And Intellectual Portrait* (Cambridge: Polity Press, 2007), 17.
43 Schram, "Mao Tse-t'ung's Thought", 273.
44 Ibid., 275.

a 'proletarian' revolutionary like M.N. Roy, who never thought in terms of the nation," Schram concludes.[45]

Secondly, the debate on Kang and Mao contributes to defining the limits of a purely political interpretation of the history of Chinese modern philosophy based on Western categories. The more recent trends in global history, and in global intellectual history, may help us to understand in a new way the forces that, from the American Revolution to World War I, shocked and reshaped social and political orders all around the world.[46] In the case of Mao and Kang, one cannot overlook the emergence of Statism—a major trend of nineteenth-century global history—as a common feature of their political and philosophical blueprints. From this point of view, Mao and Kang both seem to share—from different social backgrounds and with different political agendas, of course—the same powerful ideological tensions pervading Chinese public opinion at the turn of the twentieth century. Both thinkers, notwithstanding their clear differences in terms of their actual political goals, were revolving around the burning questions of the time: Can the quest for "modernity" free China from the gravitation of such a strong and rooted tradition as Chinese Classicism (Confucianism, or the Central Tradition, or more generally the "imperial system")? Can a de-legitimated social and political system be rebuilt without the risk of "losing the country"? Can the effort of transforming China into a strong nation be reconciled with the aspiration (prevalently Confucian/imperial in Kang's mind, more influenced by Marxist internationalism in Mao's) to universal equality and stability?

Once the ideological schemes placing the Communist revolutionary and the conservative Confucianist on the opposite sides of the aisle are set aside, then, the comparison between Mao and Kang may appear in a new light, as involving two complex figures who strove to provide answers (sometimes similar, sometimes quite different) to the same questions, and who were both influenced by internal and foreign currents of thought, although to different degrees and with different ideological references. Doubtless Mao's view of an economic system sustained by the "blank page" of the masses rather than by the work of experts or specialists would have been unacceptable to a Confucianist like Kang, whose conception of economic planning is based on "knowledge" and not on "revolution," and more explicitly on a global extension of a (democratized) bureaucracy, rather than on cadres or party leaders. But still, keeping in mind that Mao's plan was an *actual* political action, while Kang produced an utopian book whose prescriptions might have been realized far in the future,

---

45   Ibid., 279.
46   See Osterhammel, *The Transformation of the World*.

the points of contact between the two visions cannot be overlooked. In other words, rather than meeting "unconsciously," they can be said to embody the very same pivotal moment in Chinese intellectual history, and to be part of the same global intellectual history: their philosophical threads, which would eventually meet in the realm of utopia, were an effort to articulate differently the same aspiration: finding a place for China in a new world order. In conclusion, in order to assess the actual dimension of Kang's and Mao's familiarity with each other, it could be advisable to turn the perspective on its head: instead of taking the differences for granted and focusing (sometimes embarrassingly) on the "unexpected" connections between the Communist and the Confucian, it might be more useful to grant the existence of a similar background and a similar climate (both in global and local terms), focusing instead on how those shared concerns developed over different paths, sometimes diverging and sometimes proceeding in parallel. "From the 1980s Chinese historians were actively engaged in two projects: to retrieve indigenous elements in Chinese thought that anticipate a Western-style Enlightenment and to explain the causes of Maoism," Viren Murthy notes. And may be clarified by this brief survey on the *liaison dangereuse* between Mao and Kang may help to better understand the synchronous emergence of these two tendencies in Chinese contemporary scholarship.[47]

47   Murthy, "Modernity against Modernity", 141.

CHAPTER 8

A *Datong* for the Third Millennium
Globalism versus Nationalism

1 Kang and Wang Hui: in Search of Another Modernity

The last quotation of the previous paragraph comes from Viren Murthy's review of one of the most widely discussed and complex examples of recent Chinese scholarship on Chinese thought: *The Rise of Modern Chinese Thought* 中国现代思想的兴起, by Wang Hui 汪辉 (1959–). A prominent member of the so-called "new left," former editor of the journal *Dushu* 读书, in his magisterial survey of Chinese modern thought Wang "highlights the role of intellectual history as critique and attempts to recover repressed elements of the past in order to question the structures that govern the present."[1] The significance of such an approach, not just in terms of Chinese history but from a global perspective as well, are again underlined by Murthy in his review: "Although Wang's work takes China as its focus his genealogical method of critique addresses, because he constantly underscores the global nature of modernity, a more generally relevant problematic. In particular, Wang's work suggests that, in other parts of the world, including the West, overcoming capitalist modernity and imagining alternatives will be inextricably linked to retrieving resources that modernity rejects or forgets and rethinking these forgotten resources in light of the present."[2]

Whereas Li Zehou in the 1980s had said "farewell to Revolution," abandoning the idea of revolution itself as a solution to the problems of China, in his essays Wang chooses a different approach. Wang's philosophical quest does not aim at putting "an end to history" or at putting "an end to the relevance of revolutionary politics altogether"; rather, it is an attempt at denouncing "the end of the possibility for twentieth-century solutions to contemporary problems," Rebecca Karl argues.[3] In his critique of what he calls the "depoliticization of politics"—in other words, the blind faith in economic development as the magic spell to solve the long-standing Chinese problem with so-called "modernity"—Wang insists throughout his works that "history matters" and

---
1 Murthy, "Modernity against Modernity", 136.
2 Ibid.: 137.
3 Rebecca Karl, Foreword to Wang Hui, *The End of Revolution: China and the Limits of Modernity* (London: Verso, 2009), 1–2.

that "the problem of modernity *is* the problem of mass democracy (in its many potential forms) and not merely of economic development."[4] Additionally, on the previously addressed issue of the relationship between Confucianism and Maoism (or revolution in general), Wang understands the Chinese revolutionary legacy as Janus-faced: "On the one hand it inherits and continues the critical legacy of late Qing intellectuals who drew on a number of resources, Chinese, Western, and hybrid, to resist aspects of modernity. However, on the other, the Chinese revolution also inherits and institutionalizes the uncritical rejection of tradition, which goes hand in hand with a progressivist vision of history based on the nation state, a vision that is inextricably linked to the capitalist modernity that the revolution was supposedly resisting."[5]

This kind of approach to the much-debated categories of "tradition" and "modernity" is the consequence of historical changes in the PRC. After the end of the Maoist utopian struggle, the emergence of a renewed interested in traditional values and in how they could be moulded to address the issue of "modernization," which had been timidly appearing since the first years of Deng Xiaoping's reformism, eventually spurred a rediscovery of imperial thinkers in general and in late Qing "Confucian modernism" in particular. In fact, Confucius was no longer an enemy (he could indeed be considered an ally, as he is today), and so were the Confucians. Their philosophical endeavours could even prove useful in the redefinition of Chinese values and as an anticipation of the historical trajectory of China. After the year 2000, the grand return of Confucianism to the stage of Chinese political and ideological life was no longer a hint nor an academic suggestion, but a widespread certainty. And among those thinkers who most convincingly started to use Classical categories to reshape the political debate, Wang Hui is certainly one of the most prominent. And he has often showed an explicit interest in Kang Youwei, a figure who brings together many disparate strands in Wang's book. The most salient of these strands is the definition by Kang of a "universal principle" (公里) as the theoretical possibility to define a common path for China and the rest of the "modern" world. As has repeatedly been pointed out throughout this book, Kang's reinvention of imperial Confucianism in a "universal" way—from his interest in global and comparative history to the Utopia conveyed by the *Datong Shu*—can definitely be considered to be the core of his philosophical and political agenda: "The general principle combines the Western discourse of science and Confucian visions of the cosmos. Because of the polysemic

---

4 Ibid.
5 Murthy, "Modernity against Modernity", 143.

nature of this concept, late Qing intellectuals could use it to point to a post-national utopia even as they made it integral to the nation-building project."

From this viewpoint, Wang's interest in the *Datong Shu* and in Kang's use of the ideal of "commonality" as an antidote to divisive trends such as nationalism or today's neo-liberalism is fully understandable. In that Utopia, Wang "clearly sees the unavoidable authoritarian characteristics of the modern state and the deep-seated authoritarianism of the theory of the modern state. This is an attempt to transcend the capitalist modernity that China is now in the midst of eagerly pursuing. It is a plan for an anti-modern modernity. It is a religious reaction to the process of China's becoming organized as a secularized capitalism."

Wang Hui's connection to Kang is also detectable in their common "Statist" attitude in opposition to a more radical view conveyed by neo-liberal Chinese stances: "This is the sense in which a Japanese supporter of Chinese neo-liberalism, Ogata Kou, contends that in China, unlike in America, it is the neo-liberal proponents of small government who are radical, since they go against the tradition of state socialism, while the so-called New Leftists, such as Wang Hui, are conservative, since they reinforce the ideology of the state."[6] Equally, the two thinkers share an optimist view by which "democratic institutions"—and Wang's ideal of democracy is clearly related to Kang's one, both being indebted to the ideal of *gong*, as was said in Chapter 5—will eventually bridge the gap between the need for a "strong State" and the aspiration for equality. Whereas Kang's target was the reformulation of imperial institutions, Wang aims at influencing the reforms implemented by the Communist Party. Both of them, though, seem to invoke a "different modernity" if the "normal" one is to be considered the "global capitalist" asset. In conclusion, Viren Murthy's words serve again as a good synthesis of Wang's interpretation of the role played by the *Datong Shu* in Chinese intellectual history, both then and now: "Kang then combined a Confucian idea of re-imagining the past as an ideal with a future-oriented concept of time, namely evolutionary time, to project a utopian future, which would show the *limitations of the global capitalist present*."[7] Kang Youwei's attack on the inequalities and the "predatory energies" of the long nineteenth century serve Wang as a means to craft his critique of twenty-first-century globalization and its neo-liberal repercussions in the Chinese political discourse. Another prominent Chinese thinker will use Kang's denunciation for a global critique of our contemporary world dis-order, as we will see in the next section.

---

6   Ibid., 140. Emphasis in original.
7   Ibid., 158.

2   Kang and Zhao Tingyang: *Tianxia* Revisited

In 2013 the *Journal of East China Normal University* published a paper by Liu Liangjian, a scholar of modern Chinese philosophy, on the "world order" (世界政治秩序) envisioned in the *Datong Shu*. In this "new philosophical dream" (哲学新梦)—the author argues—Kang Youwei defied the international order of the long nineteenth century by praising the dismantlement of borders in a process of global unification. Having acknowledged Kang's Buddhist influences in the description of human suffering and of its overcoming,[8] and after underlining his position *against* nationalism as a divisive force, Liu then moves to an interesting comparison between Kang and a more recent, and equally well-known, Confucian thinker: Zhao Tingyang 赵汀阳 (1961–).

Zhao, a researcher at the Chinese Academy of Social Sciences, is among those thinkers who are attempting to transform Classical Chinese philosophy into a viable ideology for the contemporary world, and came to the forefront of the debate on China's place in the world thanks to his 2005 book *The System of Tianxia* (*Tianxia tixi* 天下体系). Four years later, in *Researches on a Broken World* (*Huai Shijie Yanjiu* 坏世界研究), he would further develop those theories, outlining his political philosophy in a more comprehensive way. Zhao's philosophical theory of international relations had a huge impact on China's community of international relations scholars, due, in part, "to the fact that Chinese scholars in this field have not been able to produce a theory as sophisticated as his, even though this has been on their agenda for some time."[9] In Zhao Tingyang's own words, "the historical significance of 'rethinking China' lies in recovering China's own ability to think, reconstructing its world views, values, and methodologies, and thinking about China's future, Chinese concepts about the future, and China's role and responsibilities in the world.'"[10] The philosopher, echoing Kang Youwei's dream of a *datong* world, "argues that *tianxia* theory offers an alternative, far better model of a future world order that takes into account the interests of the entire world, whatever its constituent elements."[11] More specifically, the *tianxia* system—rooted in a sort of revived Confucian universalism—develops along the following lines:

---

8   Liu Liangjian 刘梁剑, "Kang Youwei 'Datongshu' yu shijie zhengzhi zhixu yuanli: zhexue xinmeng" 康有为《大同书》与世界政治秩序原理：哲学新梦. (*Journal of East China Normal University*, 2, 2013, 52–58), 53. On this, see also above, Chapter 2.

9   Zhang Feng, "The Tianxia System: World Order in a Chinese Utopia." *Global Asia*, 2009.

10   Zhao Tingyang 赵汀阳, *Tianxia Tixi: Shijie zhidu zhexue daolun* 天下体系：世界制度哲学导论 (Nanjing: Jiangsu Jiaoyu Chubanshe, 2005), 7.

11   Zhang, "The Tianxia System".

1) make the common interests of the whole a priority over individual interests, so that the benefits of joining the system will always be greater than the benefits of leaving it;
2) create a structure of harmony where individual interests are so interlocking and mutually constituted that anyone's gain will always result in a gain for others, and anyone's loss will always lead to a loss for others;
3) create common values by being inclusive of all cultures while denying the dominance of any one of them, so as to transform enemies into friends and realize world peace.[12]

So, turning back to Liu's article, any proposed connection between Kang's utopianism and Zhao's attempt at building a world-view based on Confucianism is more than justified. This is indeed Liu's point. Kang Youwei's scheme is echoed by Zhao Tingyang, whose theory of the *tianxia* system, although still an introductory sketch, spurred vivid interest both in China and in the English-speaking world; it resembles Kang's denunciation of an "inter-national" (国际) order in which there is "no law nor heaven" and conflict is the moving force. However, the early-twentieth-century crisis, which the author of the *Datong Shu* interpreted as the burst of divisive forces, is addressed by Zhao in slightly different terms. In his view, the problem is not the existence of "nations" themselves, but the unbalanced emergence of a global sensibility.[13] The following is a significant extract from Zhao Tingyang's major work:

> Today, from a political sense, a "one-world" has not been realized yet in terms of institutional organization, governing structures, political order; at the same time, in a merely geographical or material sense, the world has already become a sort of wasteland with none in charge, a common resource which can be arbitrarily plundered or contended by anyone, a battlefield on which conquerors are marching through. This is indeed the greatest problem of our contemporary world: a world which is "disordered" from an institutional point of view and which lacks any political principle, can only be a world driven by violence.[14]

According to Zhao's lexicon, *tianxia* refers to an "ordered" world; a world which has passed from "chaos" to "cosmos"; a world which is fully structured as a global polity, including from an institutional point of view: and this, again, is very

---

12 Ibid.
13 Liu Liangjian, "Kang Youwei yu Datongshu", 54.
14 Zhao Tingyang, *Tianxia tiyi*, 12.

familiar from Kang's vision of a strictly organized one-world government which does not leave any space for private interests or selfish forces (see Chapter 5). However, it must be said that Zhao Tingyang's commitment to the ideal of a universal polity is much less detailed than Kang's Utopia: the specific form in which the *tianxia* will be realized is blurred in Zhao's texts.[15] Zhao's image of political units (*danwei* 单位) beneath the *tianxia*, which in the author's words will not resemble "nation-States" (民族国家) but will merely be "territorial governments" (地方性统治), unquestionably echoes Kang's prophecy of a purely geographical distribution of power in the Age of Concord, deprived of any identity-building materials. What is most significant about Zhao's familiarity with Kang's imagined future, though, is its connection to a new mood in the Chinese self-image.[16] In 2008 Beijing hosted the Olympics, signalling the will of China to make a great comeback to the world stage. The presidency of Hu Jintao was marked by a robust stress on concepts like "harmonious society," "multipolar world," and "peaceful development." China was eager to return to the light of world politics—after decades of "nurturing the shade" as prescribed by Deng Xiaoping—but in a tranquil and open manner. Not coincidentally, Wang Hui and Zhao Tingyang both use some of Kang's keywords to convey a democratic, humane, and universal interpretation of Confucianism and, more generally, of what we could call Chinese identity. And both of them are indebted to Kang's attempt at deconstructing Western modernity in favour of a Universal modernity. As Wang Ban 王班 of Stanford University has recently argued while commenting upon the political implications of the *Datong Shu*, Kang's "revised Confucian universalism could provide a non-Western path to save the world from the vicissitudes of Western modernization."[17] This quest for a new pattern of modernity and for a new kind of global order, inspired by a reinterpretation of Classicism in universal terms, albeit still alive among a number of Chinese intellectuals and policy-makers, was forced to the rear by the rise of a much stronger nationalist agenda in the recent years of Xi Jinping's ascension to power. Even at this time, though, echoes of Kang's legacy can be heard, although serving different causes.

---

15   Liangjian, "Kang Youwei yu Datongshu", 55.
16   See Marc Andre Matten, *Imagining a Postnational World. Hegemony and Space in Modern China* (Leiden: Brill, 2016).
17   Xie Fang 解芳, "Rethinking Tianxia," Report of the Workshop on 'Culture, International Relations, And World History: Rethinking Chinese Perceptions Of World Order' (Stanford University CA, 6–11 May 2011).

174   CHAPTER 8

3   Kang and Gan Chunsong: a Confucianist Nostalgia

The "return of Confucius" to the political and ideological stage can be rightly considered as the most striking intellectual innovation in Chinese intellectual life at the beginning of the new century.[18] Although individual pieces of the Classical tradition had never been fully rooted out, even during the revolutionary twentieth century—as the previous paragraphs have tried to demonstrate—the public recognition of Confucius as a relevant and valuable figure is a much larger phenomenon than a high-profile scholarly debate. In today's China, Confucianism is accepted as a mass product, as a significant element in the construction of a new/traditional Chinese identity, both internally and externally on the global stage. However, as might be expected, this kind of Confucian nationalism by which the Master has become the pivot of a *specific and well-defined* identity contrasts strongly with the aforementioned use of Confucian ideals in pursuit of a *universal* concept of *tianxia*. In this light, Confucianism assumes an almost religious nuance, appearing as a form of State-cult rather than a philosophical aspiration. In this sense, Xi Jinping's sponsorship of tradition is close to Kang's 1898 project for a State-Confucianism—as part of China's march towards the Age of Rising Equality—rather than to the prophecy of the *Datong Shu*. This link is made explicit by Gan Chunsong 干春松 (1965–), a contemporary Chinese scholar who has devoted his studies to the emergence of *kongjiao* 孔教 in late imperial China and on its political implications in term of a successful State-building process. In his essay *Defending the Cult, Establishing the Country* (保教立国) published in 2015, Gan addressed the present-day significance of Kang's "anticipatory" (超前的) interest in matters such as how to put China together, how to make central and local powers function, how to harmonize different nationalities, and so forth. The following is an extract from Gan's foreword: here, Wang Hui's interpretation of the connection between late Qing struggles and the challenge for contemporary China's is echoed, although from a different perspective and with different purposes.

> Certainly, approaching the end of the twentieth century, and even more after the beginning of the twenty-first, following the continuous development of Chinese society and economy people started to experience the difficulty of using present models to understand the Chinese political and economic model, and therefore understood that in order to analyse

---

18   See Maurizio Scarpari, *Ritorno a Confucio. La Cina di oggi fra tradizione e mercato* (Bologna: Il Mulino, 2015).

those political and economic peculiarities a careful look at our traditional culture was necessary. At the same time, multiple theories on "modernity" (现代性) caused the emergence of multiple ideological trends dealing with the issue of "legitimacy" (合法性) which generated the bankruptcy of the mainstream system of values and spurred the flourishing of diverse social discourses. It is exactly against this background that in mainland China the revival of Confucianism has constantly developed through the last years. Differently from the New Confucianists in Hong Kong and Taiwan who inclined toward the propagation of "virtue and morality" (道德心性), New Confucianists in mainland China have a stronger inclination toward politics and pragmatism; this tendency is not found only in the theories of New Confucianist academics, but is also visible in religious, educational, and political implementations. And its values are not orientated exclusively towards the discussion on the reception of "modernity," but they also harbour a strongly revisionary approach to "modernity" itself. From this tendency, Kang Youwei eventually received attention from political parties considered both as similar and different from his orientations, and by historians who carefully excavated his life and works and finally removed from them the label of "obsolescence"; Kang's political activism and theories, then, impart a guiding significance to the present. We could even say that a sort of "New Kanghism" (新康有为主义) has emerged. If by New Kanghism we intend a discourse that does not merely add new labels but also shakes off the previous ones, then we have to reject a *new* reading based on ideological models as well; we need to assess carefully the problems faced by Kang Youwei himself, and that's why the essays presented in this book all focus on the issue of State-building (建国). The issue of State-building can be divided into two sub-questions: 1) how can China be transformed from an Empire into a modern nation-State; 2) how can this newly built nation be organized in terms of internal order and administrative structure. Kang Youwei clearly recognized that the world faced by China at that time was structured upon the international competition among States; and that world based on confrontation was called by Kang the "new world." Facing that "new world," Kang acknowledged that he should have kept his cherished dream of a Global Concord undeclared: the world of *datong*, albeit best suited to the Confucian theory of *tianxia*, could not fit in with the actual needs of the Age of Comfort.[19]

---

19 Gan Chunsong 干春松, *Baojiao liguo: Kang Youwei de xiandai fanglüe* 保教立国：康有为的现代方略 (Beijing: Sanlian shudian, 2015), 3-4.

According to Gan, then, Kang's significance for the political debate in contemporary China (which in his opinion is huge, to the extent that he even identifies a New Kanghist current) does not lie in his "universalist" aspiration, as argued by Zhao Tingyang. Nor does he consider Kang's critique of modernity to be the foundation of an anti-neoliberal discourse on grassroots democracy and "common good policies," as theorized by Wang Hui. Rather, here it is Kang Youwei's approach to the issue of State-building that is seen as a most valuable precursor to today's challenges. As argued by Fang Ning in relation to democracy,[20] in Gan's eyes China is not ready yet for the anti-nationalist and "globalist" Age of Concord, as indeed it was not at Kang's time. Competition among nations is still alive, Gan points out. So, the discourses of Zhao and Wang are too anticipatory: State-building processes still require to be accomplished before China can move to the next stage.

This is of course consistent with Gan's interest in Kang's project of a Confucian Church, which is at the centre of his book: among the many extracts from Kang's writing presented and commented upon by Gan, the following two (one from the *Introduction to Confucian Church* 孔教會序 of 1912, the second from an article published on the *Zhongguo xuehui bao* 中國學會報 in 1913) are good examples of how the *Kongjiao* project of late Qing and early Republican times—which does not *disclaim* but *logically precedes* Kang's utopianism, as it was repeatedly pointed out—might serve the leaders of contemporary China much better than the prophecy of a world with no borders nor identities.

> So, to establish a State and to sustain the lives of its citizens, the backbone of a great religion is needed. A religion which can change common habits, enter people's hearts, serve as a model of behaviour, for death and for life; a religion by which the people can be ruled. This is something that cannot be achieved through politics.[21]
>
> Then, what is the national spirit of China? It is in the doctrines of Confucius. They are a coherent system made up of social theories, physics, politics, and heavenly principles. They are a Rite.[22]

The idea of building a Chinese State religion may have prevented China from falling apart during the crisis of the Empire, as Kang Youwei advocated; and it may well help the PRC, should its ideological glue or its materialistic frenzy be

---

20 See above, Chapter 6.
21 Kang Youwei, *Kongjiaohui xu*, quoted in Gan Chunsong, *Baojiao liguo*, 59.
22 Kang Youwei, *Zhongguo xuehui bao tici*, quoted in Gan Chunsong, *Baojiao liguo*, 61.

one day exhausted, Gan seems to hint.[23] This might confirm Wang Hui's intuition that, at the end of the day, the challenges faced by Kang are not so different from those confronting today's China, and they raise the same unresolved questions about what China is and what it should be. Finally, the concurrent interest in Kang's ideas shown by both "nationalist" and "cosmopolitanist" thinkers in contemporary China further demonstrates that nationalism and internationalism in late-nineteenth-century China were indeed, as Rebecca Karl has pointed out in her studies, the two sides of the same coin.[24] And in Kang's case, these two seemingly contradicting forces are harmonized in a unique philosophical structure, theorizing the strengthening of China as coherent with (and not in tension with) its growing participation in world politics.

---

23   For a recent and extensive survey of Kang's *kongjiao* project, see Tang Wenming 唐文明, *Fujiao zaikuan: Kang Youwei kongjiao sixiang shenlun* 敷教在宽：康有为孔教思想申论 (Beijing: Zhongguo renmin daxue chubanshe, 2012). It is worth noting that Tang makes Gan's point even more explicit in his conclusions, hinting that Confucianism as a State-cult may well serve as a safe and traditional alternative should Communism exhaust its cohesive force in China.

24   See Karl, *Staging the World*.

Conclusions

The long journey of the *Datong Shu* and of its ideas—flowing from the *Annals of Lu* to Wang Hui's reflections on the future of Communist China—is far from finished, then. In this book I tried to follow part of that flow, focusing on Kang Youwei's ideal of a Great Concord, both from an "internal" point of view—placing the *Datong Shu* in the context of Kang's entire production—and from an "external" perspective—focusing on the correlation between this work and the intellectual debate in early-twentieth-century China or even in today's PRC.

In the first two chapters, I tried to identify the philosophical seeds of the *Datong Shu* with the aid of Kang's lectures on Classicism; I also examined his much-debated relationship with Buddhism, seen as part of his attempt at reorganizing Tradition. My conclusion is that the ideal goal of *Datong*, as the ultimate expression of Empathy and human progression, must be considered as a salient piece of Kang's own reinterpretation of Classicism, not as an "extreme" nor an "escapist" appendix. His prophecy flows logically from the philosophical and political premises of his Esoteric Classicism, following the way paved by Dong Zhongshu and his New Text followers. Such a long lineage additionally suggests that Kang's work on the definition of a Chinese "modernity" cannot be considered as a simple reaction to the impact with the West. Certainly, the late Qing crisis accelerated his thought processes, but the political implications of the New Text School had already been generated by the internal dynamics of intellectual and social discontent. As recently suggested by Samuel Moyn and Andrew Sartori, it may be the right time to study some major intellectual themes both in the Western and the non-Western world by adopting the framework of a still-to-be-defined "global intellectual history," in which "what makes the approach global is not the geographical spread of the concept or the thematic but the fact that a comparison between geographically constrained spaces is possible even without a connection between them."[1] From such a viewpoint, "cultural, social, linguistic, civilizational or geographical boundaries are always occupied by mediators and go-betweens who establish connections and traces that defy any preordained closure":[2] and Kang, with his own form of "intermediation," seems a good candidate for a global intellectual study. More specifically, it would be interesting to compare, for example, the emergence of the New Text Confucianism flowing into Kang's Statism and utopianism, with the European philosophical and social dynamics that eventually created what

---

1 See Samuel Moyn and Andrew Sartori (eds), *Global Intellectual History* (New York NY: Columbia University Press, 2013), esp. Introduction.
2 Ibid.

we call Western "modernity": in this sense, a careful analysis may suggest that they were parallel outcomes of similar global tendencies inaugurated at the end of the eighteenth century (mainly related to new demands of political efficiency, legitimacy, and social representation, together with the emergence of a linear, optimist, and progressive idea of time), rather than simply being the result of one (the Chinese) copying the other (the Western). In this sense, the *Book of Great Concord*—as I tried to point out in Part I—can be considered as one of the most interesting examples of the evolution undertaken by Chinese Classicism between the nineteenth and the twentieth centuries as part of that *global* history.

As far as Western influences are concerned, in Chapter 3 I argued that they are surely abundant in the *Datong Shu*; however, they can be seen as the more superficial elements in Kang's philosophical system. Of course, especially when it comes to scientific, technological, and institutional development, Kang uses Western case studies as universal benchmarks to evaluate each country's stage of progression through the "three ages." As for the relationship between *Datong Shu* and the universal category of "utopianism," I tried to demonstrate how the *Book of Great Concord* is less a Utopia than a peculiar form of "world history" *ante litteram*: the abundance of historical examples from all over the world conveys his huge interest in adopting a global perspective, and it constitutes the platform upon which Kang finally lays out his prophecy; the description of the Age of Concord, then, is more an effort to anticipate *actual* history, rather than the construction of an ideal world *outside* time and space, as happens in the best-known examples of Western utopianism, from Plato to More.

In Part II, I focused on the different threads that connect the "utopian" *Datong Shu* to the political debates of late Qing and Republican China. Issues like the defence of imperial universalism, the concern for social policies and for the "common good," as well as reflection on the possibility of a Chinese democracy, highlight the significance of the book from a purely political point of view: when set alongside and compared with other major (and often neglected) political texts by Kang, such as the *Jiuwanglun* or the *Gonghe Pingyi*, the *Datong Shu* acts as a prism, refracting in different forms the very same grand themes around which modern Chinese intellectual and political history has been gravitating for the last two centuries. And in this sense, together with his book, Kang Youwei really seems to embody the many tensions and contradictions of his time. If the long nineteenth century "was also the starting point for four major trends that would come into their own globally in the course of the twentieth century: nation building, bureaucratization, democratization, and the rise of the welfare state,"[3] then Kang Youwei may be

---

3 Osterhammel, *The Transformation of the World*, 573.

curiously considered as a witness of (and a protagonist in) all these historical trends as they appeared in China. Nation building and bureaucratization were definitely at the core of his Hundred Days Reform project, whereas democracy (*minzhu*) and the welfare state (which in the *Datong Shu* appears in the form of the praise of "common good" or "public-oriented policies," *gong*, as opposed to the selfishness of the private sphere, *si*) are pivotal in Kang's utopianism of Great Concord. However, Kang's shift from an apparently "national" effort to a "global" utopia should not be considered as with a Buddhist sand mandala, in which the Chinese State is built just to be erased. On the contrary, *that* vision of the State is extended so as to encompass the whole world, while retaining those very same characteristics that define a modern State. And technological capacities are the first and foremost instrument of State power, Kang argues. All this again confirms that the *Book of Great Concord* is less a *unique* piece in Kang's production than the "hidden face" (and the most sincere one, perhaps) of his thought, clarifying that very same philosophical framework which he elaborated throughout the whole of his oeuvre.

In the last part of this book, I tried to examine the connection between the political underpinnings of the *Datong Shu* and today's intellectual debates in the People's Republic of China. As I suggested, far from being a "literary" work of the imagination, the *Book of Great Concord* addresses such burning topics as Chinese democracy, the role of religion in a modern society, the dangers of nationalism and the issue of ethnicity and "representation," the pursuit of equality among men and women, and much more. Kang's dream of a united world where Chinese tradition dissolves in a global humanistic identity stands as the monumental legacy of a tormented era in which China started to imagine itself in a new light and within a new world. It is not surprising, then, that Kang's thought has been experiencing a robust revival in recent decades in mainland China. As pointed out in the last chapter, the multifaceted philosophy elaborated by Kang as a response to the challenges of "modernity" is now perceived as conveying a number of equally multifaceted starting points for a discussion on those same questions. As Wang Hui argues, today's China paradoxically seems closer to the late Qing uncertainties than to the dogmas of twentieth-century revolutionism:[4] with the Maoist utopia exhausted, and as the rhetoric of enrichment starts to lose its magic, new ways to keep China together are needed by the CPC leaders. As happened at the end of the nineteenth century, what is at stake is the social compact and the legitimacy of rule, and Kang's solutions seem to resurface in the political and intellectual debate of the present day. His State-Confucianism—as Gan Chunsong explicitly admits—may

---

4   Wang Hui, *The End of Revolution*, 1–3.

be a powerful tool to create a new sense of togetherness in the name of a retrieved Chinese identity. Xi Jinping, through his energetic efforts at revamping tradition in nationalistic terms, seems to be moving in this direction. On the other side, Kang's ideal of democracy as the triumph of public-mindedness against selfish interests serves the new-leftist Wang Hui himself as an inspiration for a political blueprint by which he can denounce the entrenched interests clustered around the Party, while at the same time distancing himself both from neo-liberal approaches and from banal pleas for a "Westernization" of China. Additionally, Kang's comprehensive vision of historical progression, along with his cautious political reformism which demands respectful understanding of the diversity of contexts when judging any given country, is not so distant from the solutions prescribed by scholars like Fang Ning to the major issue of "democracy in China."

And finally, the last stage of Kang's philosophy so vividly described in the *Datong Shu*—a global dream, rooted in the Classics but open to the world—serves as a good example for those who hope to provide Chinese identity (whatever that means) with a sense of globalism and/or internationalism, as demonstrated by the flourishing of articles on Kang's Confucian globalism in the first years of the twenty-first century and, most importantly, by Zhao Tingyang's recipe for a global order inspired by anti-nationalist sentiments. As a Chinese scholar has recently pointed out, the *Datong Shu* can "certainly be considered as an important cultural phenomenon, since its fundamental significance lies in its attempt at using Chinese traditional principle and language to construct a grand narrative of social evolution."[5]

Echoes of Kang's philosophical dream of a stronger China and a harmonious world can thus be heard, albeit diffusely, in today's China, and will probably reverberate throughout the following decades. To quote film-director Evans Chan, perhaps "it is time for the return of Datong, the Great Commonwealth, as the native dream for China's (post)modernity." Though it is surely dubious whether Kang Youwei would have appreciated the twenty-first-century rhetoric of the "Chinese dream" strongly encouraged by the CPC, there is no doubt that the present-day significance of Kang's ideas testifies that China is again, as it was at the end of nineteenth century, at a critical turning point in the definition of its common identity and historical destiny.

---

5 Cheng Boqing 成伯清, "Shijie shehui de Zhongguoshi xiangxiang—Datong Shu zuowei yige wenhua shijian de shehuixue jiedu 世界社会的中国式想象—大同书作伪一个文化事件的社会学解读." (*Jiangsu shehui kexue*, 1, 2009, 20–26), 25.

Bibliography

Bai Rui 白锐, *Xunqiu chuantong zhengzhi de xiandai zhuanxing. Kang Youwei jindai Zhongguo zhengzhi fazhanguan yanjiu* 寻求传统政治的现代转型—康有为近代中国政治发展观研究, Beijing: Zhishi chanquan chubanshe, 2010.

Bell, Daniel, *Beyond Liberal Democracy: Political Thinking for an East Asian Context*, Princeton NJ: Princeton University Press, 2006.

Bell, Daniel and Li, Chenyang (eds), *The East Asian Challenge for Democracy: Political Meritocracy in Comparative Perspective*, Cambridge: Cambridge University Press, 2013.

Bresciani, Umberto, *La filosofia cinese nel ventesimo secolo. I nuovi confuciani*, Città del Vaticano: Urbaniana University Press, 2009.

Buckley Ebrey, Patricia, *Confucianism and the Family Rituals in Imperial China*, Princeton NJ: Princeton University Press, 1991.

Bünger, Karl, "The Chinese State Between Yesterday and Tomorrow," in Stuart Schram (ed.), *The Scope of State Power in China*, London: Soas, 1985: xiii–xxvi.

Chan, Wing-tsit, *Chu Hsi and Neo-Confucianism*, Honolulu HI: University of Hawai'i Press, 1986.

Chang, Garma C.C., *The Buddhist teaching of totality: The philosophy of Hwa Yen Buddhism*, London: London University Press, 1971.

Chang Hao, *Chinese Intellectuals in Crisis: Search for Order and Meaning, 1890–1911*, Oakland CA: University of California Press, 1981.

Che Dongmei 车冬梅, "Datong Shu chengshu shijian kao 大同书成书时间考," *Jiangnan xuekan*, 5, 1999.

Chen, Yong, *Confucianism as Religion: Controversies and Consequences*, Leiden: Brill, 2013.

Cheng Boqing 成伯清, "Shijie shehui de Zhongguoshi xiangxiang—Datong Shu zuowei yige wenhua shijian de shehuixue jiedu 世界社会的中国式想象—大同书作伪一个文化事件的社会学解读," *Jiangsu shehui kexue*, 1, 2009: 20–26.

Chi, Wen-shun, *Ideological conflicts in Modern China. Democracy and Authoritarianism*, New Brunswick: Transaction Publishers, 1992.

Chow, Kai-wing, "Narrating Nation, Race, and National Culture: Imagining the Hanzu Identity in Modern China," in Kai-wing Chow, Kevin Micheal Doak and Poshek Fu (eds), *Constructing Nationhood in Modern East Asia*, Ann Arbor MI: University of Michigan Press, 2001: 47–84.

Creel, H.G., *Confucius and the Chinese Way*, New York: Harper & Row, Publishers, 1949.

Crisma, Amina, "Interazioni intellettuali tra Cina e Occidente dal 1860 a oggi" in Guido Samarani and Maurizio Scarpari (eds), *La Cina. III. Verso la modernità*, Torino: Einaudi, 2009: 859–881.

Crossley, Pamela Kyle, *The Wobbling Pivot. China since 1800: an interpretive history*, Chichester: Wiley-Blackwell, 2010.

Crossley, Pamela Kyle, *A Translucent Mirror: History and Identity in Qing Imperial History*, Oakland CA: University of California Press, 1999.

Cua, Antonio S. (ed.), *The Encyclopedia of Chinese Philosophy*, London: Routledge, 2003.

Czikszentmihalyi, Mark, "Confucius and the Analects in the Han" in Bryan W. Van Norden (ed.), *Confucius and the Analects: New Essays*, Oxford: Oxford University Press, 2002: 134–162.

Darrobers, Roger, "Du confucianisme reformé à l'utopie universelle." *Études chinoises*, 19, 1–2, 2000: 15–65.

Dawson, Raymond, *Confucius*, Great Britain: The Guernsey Press, 1981.

de Bary, Wm. Theodore, Wing-tsit Chan, and Buton Watson, *Sources of Chinese Tradition*, New York and London: Columbia University Press, 1960.

Deng Lilan 邓丽兰, *Rujiao minzhu yihuo xianzheng minzhu—shixi Zhang Junmai yu Qian Mu gyanyu Zhongguo chuantong zhengzhi zhi lunzheng* 儒教民主，抑或宪政民主—试析张君劢于钱穆关于中国传统政治之论争. Tianjin 天津: Nankai Daxue Zhongguo shehuishi yanjiu zhongxin, 2009.

Dikötter, Frank (ed.), *The Construction of Racial Identities in China and Japan*, London: Hurst, 1997.

Ding, John Zijiang, "Li Zehou: Chinese Aesthetics from a Post-Marxist and Confucian Perspective," in Chung-ying Cheng and Nicholas Bunnin (eds), *Contemporary Chinese Philosophy*, Oxford: Blackwell, 2002.

Dirlik, Arif, *Anarchism in the Chinese Revolution*, Berkeley: California University Press, 1991.

Du Enlong 杜恩龙, "Kang Youwei 'Datong Shu' shougao faxian ji chuban jingguo 康有为大同书手稿发现及出版经过." *Wenshi qinghua*, 5, 2002.

Duara, Prasenjit, *Rescuing History from the Nation. Questioning narratives of Modern China*, Chicago IL: University of Chicago Press, 1995.

Elliot, Mark C., *The Manchu Way. The Eight Banners and Ethnic Identity in Late Imperial China*, Stanford CA: Stanford University Press, 2001.

Elman, Benjamin, *Classicism, Politics, and Kinship: The Ch'ang-chou School of New Text Confucianism in Late Imperial China*, Berkeley CA: University of California Press, 1990.

Fan Chaole 樊朝乐, "Kang Youwei 'Datong Shu' de kuleguan 康有为《大同书》的苦乐观." *Chongqing keji xueyuan xuebao*, 4, 2012: 31–32.

Fang Delin 方德邻, "Datong Shu qigao shijian kao—jian lun Kang Youwei zaoqi datong sixiang 大同书起稿时间考—兼论康有为早期大同思想." *Lishi yanjiu*, 3, 1995.

Fang Ning 房宁, *Minzhu de Zhongguo jingyan* 民主的中国经验, Beijing: Zhongguo shehui kexue chubanshe, 2013.

Felber, Roland, "The Use of Analogy by Kang Youwei in Writings on European History." *Oriens Extremus*, 40, 1, 1997: 64–77.

Feng Suqin 冯素芹 and Zhao Tingbing 赵廷斌, "Kang Youwei Sun Zhongshan datong sixiang bijiao 康有为孙中山大同思想比较." *Hunan renwen keji xueyuan xuebao*, 4, 2004: 11–13.

Feng Youlan, *A History of Chinese Philosophy*, Princeton NJ: Princeton University Press, 1953, 2 vols.

Foucault, Michel, "Des Espaces Autres (1967)." *Architecture/Mouvement/Continuité* 1984: 46–49.

Fourier, Charles, *Design for Utopia: Selected Writings. Studies in the Libertarian and Utopian Tradition*, New York NY: Schocken, 1971.

Franke, Wolfgang, *Die staatspolitischen Reformversuche K'ang Yu-weis und seiner Schule*, Berlin: Mitteilungen des Seminars für Orientaliche Sprachen, 1935.

Fung, Edmond S.K., "Nationalism and Modernity: The Politics of Cultural Conservatism in Republican China." *Modern Asian Studies*, 43, 3, 2009: 777–813.

Furth, Charlotte, "Intellectual Change: From the Reform Movement to the May Fourth Movement, 1895–1920," in Ou-Fan Lee and Merle Goldman (eds), *An Intellectual History of Modern China*, Cambridge: Cambridge University Press, 2002: 13–96.

Gan Chunsong 干春松, *Baojiao liguo: Kang Youwei de xiandai fanglüe* 保教立国：康有为的现代方略, Beijing: Sanlian shudian, 2015.

Gan Chunsong 干春松, "Entre connaissance et croyance: Kang Youwei et le destin moderne du confucianisme." *ExtrêmeOrient—ExtrêmeOccident*, 33, 2011: 115–142.

Gao Ruiquan 高瑞泉, "Lun pingdeng guannian de rujia sixiang ziyuan 论平等观念的儒家思想资源". *Shehui kexue*, 4, 2009: 120–129.

Gardner, Daniel K., "Confucian commentary and Chinese intellectual history." *JAS* 57, 2, 1998: 397–422.

Geary, Patrick J., *The Myth of Nations. The Medieval Origins of Europe*, Princeton NJ: Princeton University Press, 2002.

Gernet, Jacques, "Introduction," in Stuart Schram (ed.), *The Scope of State Power in China*, London: Soas, 1985: xxvii–xxxiv.

Gernet, Jacques, *A History of Chinese Civilization*, translated by J.R. Foster and C. Hartman, Cambridge: Cambridge University Press, 1982.

Goossaert, Vincent and Palmer, David, *The Religious Question in Modern China*, Chicago: University of Chicago Press, 2010.

Gray, Jack (ed.), *Modern China's Search for a Political Form*, London: Oxford University Press, 1969.

Henderson, John B., *Scripture, Canon, Commentary: A comparison of Confucian and Western exegesis*, Princeton NJ: Princeton University Press, 1991.

Heuters, Theodore, *Bringing the World Home: Appropriating The West In Late Qing And Early Republican China*, Honolulu, HI: University of Hawai'i Press, 2005.

Holm, Jean, and Bowker, John, *Sacred Writings*, London: Printer Publishers Ltd., 1994.

Hon, Tze-ki, *Revolution as Restoration. Guocui xuebao and China's Path to Modernity, 1905–1911*, Leiden: Brill, 2013.

Hsiao, Kung-chuan, *A Modern China and a New World. Kang Yu-wei, Reformer and Utopian, 1858–1927*, Seattle WA: University of Washington Press, 1975.

Hua Shiping, *Chinese Utopianism: A Comparative Study of Reformist Thought with Japan and Russia*, Stanford CA: Stanford University Press, 2009.

Huang Zhangjian 黄章建, *Kang Youwei wuxu zhen zouyi* 康有为戊戌真奏议, Taibei: Zhongyang yanjiuyuan lishiyuyan yanjiusuo, 1974.

Huang Wende 黄文德, "Gong si lingyu guannian dui Kang Youwei ji qi lixiangguo <Datong Shu> de yingxiang" 公/私領域觀念對康有為及其理想國《大同書》的影響. *Deyu xueban*, 18, 2002: 33–46.

Hui, Victoria Tin-bor, *War and State Formation in Ancient China and Early Modern Europe*, Cambridge: Cambridge University Press, 2005.

Jensen, Lionel M., *Manufacturing Confucianism. Chinese Tradition and Universal Civilization*, Durham NC: Duke University Press, 1997.

Jia Xiaohui 贾晓慧, "Weixin bianfa shibai yuanyin yu Kang Youwei bianfahou de sikao" 维新变法失败原因与康有为变法后的思考. *Zhongguo jinxiandaishi yanjiu* 中国近现代史研究, 8, 1998: 5–9.

Jingpan, Chen, *Confucius as a Teacher*, Beijing: Foreign Languages Press, 1990.

Jordheim, Helge, "Against Periodization: Koselleck's Theory of Multiple Temporalities." *History and Theory*, 51, 2, 2012: 151–171.

Jullien, François, *Traité de l'efficacité*, Paris: Grasset & Fasquelle, 1997.

Kane, Anthony, "The Creation of Modern China: the Nationalist vs Communist Roads." In *Conference on the evolution of democracy in China—sponsored by Carnegie Council on Ethics and International Affairs and Pacific Cultural Foundation*, Taipei: Pacific Cultural Foundation, 1990.

Kang Youwei 康有为, *Datong Shu* 大同书, edited by Jiang Yihua and Zhang Ronghua, Beijing: Zhongguo Renmin Daxue Chubanshe, 2010.

Kang Youwei 康有为, *Riben bianzheng kao* 日本变政考, edited by Jiang Yihua and Zhang Ronghua, Beijing: Zhongguo Renmin Daxue Chubanshe, 2010.

Kang Youwei 康有为, *Wanmucaotang koushuo* 万木草堂口说, edited by Jiang Yihua and Zhang Ronghua, Beijing: Zhongguo Renmin Daxue Chubanshe, 2010.

Kang Youwei 康有为, *Kang Youwei quanji* 康有为全集, Shanghai: Shanghai guji chubanshe, 1990.

Kang Youwei 康有为, *Ouzhou shiyiguo youji* 欧洲十一国游记, Changsha: Yuelu shushe chuban, 1985.

Kang Youwei 康有为, *Kang Youwei Zhenglunji* 康有为政论集 edited by Tang Zhijun, Beijing: Zhonghua Shuju, 1982, 2 vol.

Karl, Rebecca, *Staging the World: Chinese Nationalism at the Turn of the Twentieth Century*, Durham NC: Duke University Press, 2002.

Karl, Rebecca and Zarrow, Peter (eds), *Rethinking the 1898 Reform Period. Political and Cultural Change in Late Qing China*, Cambridge MA: Harvard University Press, 2002.

Kong Xiangji 孔祥吉, *Kang Youwei bianfa zouyi yanjiu* 康有为变法奏议研究. Shenyang: Liaoning jiaoyu chubanshe, 1988.

Koselleck, Reinhart, *Futures Past. On the Semantics of Historical Time*, New York, NY: Columbia University Press, 2004.

Koselleck, Reinhart, *The Practice of Conceptual History: Timing, History, Spacing Concepts*, Stanford, CA: Stanford University Press, 2002.

Kuhn, Philip A., *The Origins of the Modern Chinese State*, Stanford CA: Stanford University Press, 2002.

Kwong, Luke S., "The Rise of the Linear Perspective on History and Time in Late Qing China, c. 1860–1911." *Past & Present*, 173, 2001: 157–190.

Kwong, Luke S., *A Mosaic of the Hundred Days: Personalities, Politics, and Ideas of 1898*, Cambridge, MA: Council on East Asian Studies, Harvard University, 1984.

Laitinen, Kauko, *Chinese Nationalism in the Late Qing dynasty: Zhang Binglin as an Anti-Manchu Propagandist* (Scandinavian Institute of Asian Studies, Monograph Series, no. 57.) xiv, Copenhagen: Nordic Institute of Asian Studies; London: Curzon Press, 1990.

Lau, D.C. (ed.), *Mencius*, Middlesex: Penguin Books, 1976.

Legge, James, *Li Chi: Book of Rites. An encyclopedia of ancient ceremonial usages, religious creeds, and social institutions*, New Hyde Park NY: University Books [1967] (originally published in 1885).

Leibold, James, "Positioning 'minzu' within Sun Yat-sen's discourse on minzuzhuyi." *Journal of Asian History*, 38, 2, 2004: 163–213.

Leonard, Mark, *What does China think?*, London: Fourth Estate, 2007.

Levenson, Joseph Richmond, *Confucian China and its Modern Fate: a Trilogy*, Berkeley, CA: University of California Press, 1968.

Li Aiyong 李爱勇, "Kang Youwei yu 'Datong Shu' zhong de pingdengguan wenti 康有为与《大同书》中的平等观问题." *Xinyang shifan xueyuan xuebao*, 33, 2, 2013: 134–137.

Li Jinxiu 李进修, *Zhongguo jindai zhengzhi zhidu shigang* 中国近代政治制度史纲. Beijing: Qiushi chubanshe, 1988.

Li Yu-ning, *The Introduction of Socialism into China*, New York NY: Columbia University Press, 1971.

Li Zehou 李泽厚, "Datong Shu de pingjia wenti yu xiezuo niandai 大同书的评价问题与写作年代." *Wenshizhe*, 1957. In *Zhongguo jindai sixiangshi lun* 中国近代思想史论, Beijing: Renmin chubanshe, 1979.

Li Zehou 李泽厚, "Lun Kang Youwei de Datong Shu 论康有为的大同书." *Wenshizhe*, 1955. In *Zhongguo jindai sixiangshi lun* 中国近代思想史论, Beijing: Renmin chubanshe, 1979.

Li Zehou and Liu Zaifu, *Gaobie geming: ershi shiji duitan lu* 告别革命：二十世纪对谈录, Taipei: Maitian Press, 1999.

Li Zonggui 李宗桂, *Chuantong yu xiandai zhi jian* 传统与现代之间, Beijing Shifan Daxue Chubanshe, 2011 (English translation, *Between Tradition and Modernity: Philosophical Reflections on the Modernization of Chinese Culture*, Oxford: Chartridge Books, 2014).

Liang Qichao 梁启超, *Intellectual trends in the Ch'ing period, translated with introduction and notes by Immanuel C.Y. Hsu*. Cambridge MA: Harvard University Press, 1970.

Lin Anwu 林安梧, *Zhongguo jindai sixiang jinianshi lun* 中国近现代思想纪念史论. Taipei: Taiwan xuesheng shuju, 1995.

Lin Yutang, *The Wisdom of Confucius*, New York: Random House, 1938.

Lippiello, Tiziana, *Il Confucianesimo*, Bologna: Il Mulino, 2009.

Liu Liangjian 刘梁剑, "Kang Youwei 'Datongshu' yu shijie zhengzhi zhixu yuanli: zhexue xinmeng" 康有为《大同书》与世界政治秩序原理:哲学新梦. *Journal of East China Normal University*, 2, 2013: 52–58.

Lo, Jung-Pang (ed.), *K'ang Yu-wei: A biography and a symposium*, Tucson AR: The University of Arizona Press, 1967.

Lust, John, *The Revolutionary Army: A Chinese Nationalist Tract of 1903*, Paris: Mouton, 1968.

Makeham, John (ed.), *Transforming Consciousness: Yogacara Thought in Modern China*, Oxford: Oxford University Press, 2014.

Mannheim, Karl, *Ideology and Utopia*, London: Routledge, 1936.

Matten, Marc Andre, *Imagining a Postnational World. Hegemony and Space in Modern China*, Leiden: Brill, 2016.

Mazower, Mark, *Governing the World. The History of an Idea*, London: Penguin Press, 2012.

Meisner, Maurice, *Mao Zedong: A Political And Intellectual Portrait*, Cambridge: Polity Press, 2007.

Miles, Steven B., *The Sea of Learning: Mobility and Identity in Nineteenth-Century Guangzhou*, Cambridge MA: Harvard University Press, 2006.

Moeller, Hans-Georg, *The Philosophy of the Daodejing*, New York NY: Columbia University Press, 2006.

Mou Bo 牟博 (ed.), *History of Chinese Philosophy*, London: Routledge, 2008.

Moyn, Samuel and Sartori, Andrew (eds), *Global Intellectual History*, New York NY: Columbia University Press, 2013.

Murthy, Viren, "Modernity against Modernity: Wang Hui's Critical History of Chinese Thought." *Modern Intellectual History*, 3, 1, 2006: 137–165.

Nathan, Andrew, *Chinese Democracy*, New York NY: Alfred Knopf, 1985.

Nylan, Michael, *The Five Confucian Classics*, New Haven CT: Yale University Press, 2001.

Osterhammel, Jürgen, *The Transformation of the World. A Global History of the Nineteenth Century*, Princeton NJ: Princeton University Press, 2014.

Perdue, Peter, *China Marches West*, Cambridge, MA: Harvard University Press, 2005.

Pines, Yuri, *The Everlasting Empire: The political culture of ancient China and its imperial legacy*, Princeton NJ: Princeton University Press, 2012.

Pozzi, Silvia (ed.), *Confucio re senza corona*, Milano: ObarraO edizioni, 2011.

Price, Don, "Popular and Elite Heterodoxy Toward the End of the Qing," in Kwang-ching Liu and Richard Scheck (eds), *Heterodoxy in Late Imperial China*, Honolulu: University of Hawai'i Press, 2004: 431–461.

Puett, Michael, "Centering the Realm: Wang Mang, the Zhouli, and Early Chinese Statecraft." in Elman, Benjamin A. and Kern, Martin (eds), *Statecraft and Classical Learning: the Rituals of Zhou in East Asian History*, Leiden: Brill, 2010: pp. 129–154.

Qian Mu 钱穆, *Zhongguo lidai zhengzhi deshi* 中国历代政治得失, Beijing: Jiuzhou chubanshe, 2012.

Queen, Sarah A., *From chronicle to Canon: the hermeneutics of the Spring and Autumn, according to Tung Chung-Shu*, Cambridge: Cambridge University Press, 1996.

Rhoads, Edward J.M., *Manchus and Han. Ethnic Relations and Political Power in Late Qing and Early Republican China, 1861–1928*, Seattle WA: University of Washington Press, 2000.

Riegel, Jeffrey K., "Li chi 禮記", in Loewe, Michael (ed.), *Early Chinese Texts: A Bibliographical Guide*, Society for the Study of Early China, 1993: pp. 293–297.

Rowe, William T., *China's Last Empire. The Great Qing*, Cambridge MA: Harvard University Press, 2009.

Ryan, Alan, *On Politics: A History of Political Thought, From Herodotus to the Present*, New York NY: Liveright, 2012.

Samarani, Guido, *La Cina del Novecento*, Torino: Einaudi, 2004.

Scarpari, Maurizio, *Ritorno a Confucio. La Cina di oggi fra tradizione e mercato*, Bologna: Il Mulino, 2015.

Scarpari, Maurizio, "Echi del passato nella Cina di oggi: costruire un mondo armonioso," in R. Ciarla and M. Scarpari (eds), *La Cina I. Preistoria e origini della civiltà cinese*, Torino: Einaudi, 2011: xvii–xlvii.

Scarpari, Maurizio, *Il Confucianesimo. I fondamenti e i testi*, Torino: Einaudi, 2010.

Schoppa, R. Keith, *Revolution and Its Past. Identities and Change in Modern Chinese History*, Upper Saddle River NJ: Prentice Hall, 2002.

Schram, Stuart, "Mao Tse-t'ung's Thought to 1949," in Ou-Fan Lee and Merle Goldman (eds), *An Intellectual History of Modern China*, Cambridge: Cambridge University Press, 2002: 267–348.

Schwartz, Benjamin I., "Themes in Intellectual History: May Fourth and After," in Ou-Fan Lee and Merle Goldman (eds), *An Intellectual History of Modern China*, Cambridge: Cambridge University Press, 2002: 97–141.

Spence, Jonathan, *The Gate of Heavenly Peace. The Chinese and Their Revolution 1895–1980*, New York NY: The Viking Press, 1981.

Tang Wenming 唐文明, *Fujiao zaikuan: Kang Youwei kongjiao sixiang shenlun* 敷教在宽：康有为孔教思想申论, Beijing: Zhongguo renmin daxue chubanshe, 2012.

Tang Zhidiao 汤志钧, "Lun Kang Youwei 'Datong Shu' de sixiang shizhi 论康有为《大同书》的思想实质." *Lishi yanjiu*, 1959: 7–20.

Tao Jiyi 陶季邑, "Qingnian Mao Zedong datong sixiang shifou shou Sun Zhongshan yingxiang yanjiu 青年毛泽东大同思想是否受孙中山大同思想影响研究." *Mao Zedong sixiang yanjiu*, 34, 3, 2017: 17–20.

Thompson, Laurence G., *Ta-tung shu. The One-World Philosophy of Kang Yu-wei*, London: George Allen & Unwin, 1958.

Townsend, James, "Chinese Nationalism" in Jonathan Unger and Geremie Barmé (eds), *Chinese Nationalism*, London: M.E. Sharpe, 1996.

Tresch, John, *The Romantic Machine: Utopian Science and Technology after Napoleon*, Chicago IL: University of Chicago Press, 2012.

Wang, Ban (ed.), *Chinese Visions of World Order. Tianxia, Culture, and World Politics*, Durham, NC: Duke University Press, 2017.

Wang Bin 汪斌, "Kang Youwei sixiangzhong de foxue qingjie 康有为思想中的佛学情结." *Heilongjiang shizhi*, 10, 2008: 8–9.

Wang Hui 汪晖, *Xiandai Zhongguo sixiang de xingqi* 现代中国思想的兴起, Beijing: Sanlian Shudian, 2004.

Wang Hui 汪晖, *The End of Revolution: China and the Limits of Modernity*, London: Verso, 2009.

Wang Jing, *High Culture Fever: Politics, Aesthetics, and Ideology in Deng's China*, Berkeley, CA: University of California Press, 1996.

Wang Ke-wen (ed.), *Modern China. An Encyclopedia of History, Culture and Nationalism*, New York NY: Garland Publishing, 1998.

Wang Youwei 王有为 (ed.), *Kang Youwei yu Baohuanghui* 康有为与保皇会, Shanghai: Shanghai renmin chubanshe, 1982.

Wei, Betty 魏白蒂, *Ruan Yuan, 1764–1849: The Life and Work of a Major Scholar-official in Nineteenth Century China Before the Opium War*, Hong Kong: Hong Kong University Press, 2006.

Wei Yixia 魏义霞, "Foxue: Kang Youwei zhexue de zhuyao laiyuan 佛学：康有为哲学的主要来源." *Zhexue fenxi*, 2, 2, 2011: 75–83.

Wei Yixia 魏义霞 and Gao Zhiwen 高志文, "Sun Zhonghsan de datonglixiang ji qi yiyi: jianyu Kang Youwei dengren bijiao 孙中山的大同理想及其意义—兼与康有为等人比较." *Heilongjiang shehui kexue*, 128, 5, 2011: 5–9.

Wielander, Gerda, "Beyond Repression and Resistance: Christian Love and China's Harmonious Society." *The China Journal*, 65, 2011: 119–139.

Wilkinson, Endymion, *Chinese History. A New Manual*, Cambridge MA: Harvard University Press, 2012.

Wong, Young-tsu 汪榮祖, *Beyond Confucian China. The Rival Discourses of Kang Youwei and Zhang Binglin*, London: Routledge, 2010.

Wong, Young-tsu 汪榮祖, "The Search for Material Civilization: Kang Youwei's Journey to the West." *Taiwan Journal of East Asian Studies*, 5, 1, 2008: 33–59.

Wong, Young-tsu 汪榮祖, "Philosophical Hermeneutics and Political Reform: A Study of Kang Youwei's Use of Gongyang Confucianism," in Ching-I Tu (ed.), *Classics and Interpretations. The Hermeneutic Traditions in Chinese Culture*, New Brunswick NJ: Transaction Publishers, 2000: 383–407.

Xia Tingting 夏婷婷 and Du Juhui 杜菊辉, "Mao Zedong yu Kang Youwei shehui sixiangguan zhi bijiao 毛泽东与康有为社会思想观之比较." *Hunan Gongxue Daxue xueban*, 15, 6, 2010: 78–81.

Xie Fang 解芳, "Rethinking Tianxia," Report of the Workshop on 'Culture, International Relations, And World History: Rethinking Chinese Perceptions Of World Order', Stanford University CA, 6–11 May 2011.

Yu Junfang, *The renewal of Buddhism in China. Chu-hung and the late Ming synthesis*, New York NY: Columbia University Press, 1981.

Zang Shijun 臧世俊, *Kang Youwei datong sixiang yanjiu* 康有为大同思想研究, Guangzhou: Guangdong gaodeng jiaoyu chubanshe, 1997.

Zarrow, Peter, *After Empire. The conceptual transformation of the Chinese state, 1885–1924*, Stanford CA: Stanford University Press, 2012.

Zarrow, Peter, "Late Qing Dreams of Modernity. An Interview with Evans Chan." *The China Beat*, December 2011 (www.thechinabeat.org).

Zhang Feng, "The Tianxia System: World Order in a Chinese Utopia." *Global Asia*, 2009.

Zhang Yongle 章永乐, "Bu neng gong ze bu neng he: wanqi Kang Youwei de guojia jiangoulun yu zhengtilun 不能共则不能和:晚期康有为的国家建构论与政体论." *Sixiang zhenxian*, 42, 6, 2016: 55–63.

Zhang Yongle 章永乐, "The Future of the Past: On Wang Hui's Rise of Modern Chinese Thought." *New Left Review*, 62, 2010: 47–83.

Zhao Tingyang 赵汀阳, *Tianxia Tixi: Shijie zhidu zhexue daolun* 天下体系:世界制度哲学导论, Nanjing: Jiangsu Jiaoyu Chubanshe, 2005.

Zhu Min 朱敏 (ed.), *Wujing* 五经, Nanjing: Fenghuang chubanshe, 2012.

Index

Other Works by Kang Youwei

Bu Ren (*Compassion*) 7, 98
Chunqiu Dongshi xue (*A Study on Dong Zhongshu's Spring and Autumn*) 26, 33
Deguo bianzhi ji (*Account of Political Reforms in Germany*) 64
Gonghe Pingyi (*Impartial Words on Republicanism*) 111–125, 179
Jiuwanglun (*Saving the Country*) 93, 99–104, 115, 179
Kongzi gaizhi kao (*Confucius as a Reformer*) 2, 30, 69, 154
Nanhaishi chengji (*Master Nanhai's Annotations*) 35, 38
Ouzhou shiyiguo youji (*A Travel Journal from Eleven European Countries*) 57
Renlei gongli (*Universal Principles of Mankind*) 7, 48
Wanmu caotang koushuo (*Instructions from the Hall of Thousand-Trees Cottage*) 30, 35, 47
Xinxue weijing kao (*A study of the Xin forgeries*) 19

Index of Names, Places, Texts and Concepts

Africa 140
Age of Chaos 21–22, 61, 86–88, 110
Age of Supreme Equality (or of Great Concord) 4, 9, 21–22, 34–35, 44, 49, 56, 66, 77, 86 90–91, 112, 115, 127, 135–136, 138, 152, 154, 176
Age of the Rising Equality (or of Comfort) 21–22, 34–35, 62, 66, 88–89, 115, 174
Agriculture 131–134, 138–141
Alchemy 82
America 42, 170; United States of 62, 101, 105, 106, 114, 116, 117, 118, 123, 132
Anarchism 67
Astral journeys 46, 53
Augustus, emperor 116
Austria 59
Awakening of Faith, the 48

Bai Rui 1, 148
Baopuzi 82
Barbarians 44, 70
Beijing 2
Belgium 104
Benevolence 44
Bentham, Jeremy 74
Boundaries (*jie*) 5–6, 85–86
Boxer Uprising 97
Brahman 43
Brotherhood 35
Buddhism 2, 4, 8, 9, 36, 42–55, 163, 171; Huayan 44–46; Mahayana 38, 49; Tiantai, 45
Bulgaria 104
Bulgaria 104
Bünger, Karl 68

Capitalism 169–170
Cavour, Camillo Benso di 59
Centralization 3, 20, 141–143
Chan, Evans 163
Chang, Garma 46
Chang'an speeches 66
Changzhou 20n24, 23
Che Dongmei 7
Cheng Yi 49
Chi, Wen-shun 161
Chiang Kai-Shek 80
Chinese Academy of Social Sciences 171
Chinese minorities 94
Christianity 50, 106, 129; Catholicism 50; Missionaries 56; Pope 58–59
Chunqiu (*Spring and Autumns, or Annals of Lu*) 14–25, 27, 34, 178
Chunqiu fanlu 17
Chunqiu weiyang gongtu 19
Cixi, Empress Dowager 3, 92, 99
Class struggle 161
Classicism (*Ru*) 2, 9, 18, 31 38–40, 46–48, 53, 129, 151, 163, 166, 178; Esoteric Classicism 18, 33, 44, 54, 178; see also Confucianism, Dong Zhongshu, Mencius, New Text School
Commerce 13

INDEX

Commonality (*gong*)   66, 71, 92
Communism   9, 49, 107, 126–143, 159–161, 178
Communist Party of China   124, 147, 170, 180, 181
Comte, Auguste   73
Confucianism   1, 8, 36, 39–41, 47, 54, 75, 169; and Communism   127–133, 162–167; Confucian Canon   18, 26, 31, 34, 39, 49; Confucian Church   2, 4, 50, 174–177; Confucian modernism   169; Confucian nationalism   174; New Confucianism   175; revival of Confucianism   176–177; see also Classicism, Confucius, Dong Zhongshu, Liji, *Lunyu*, Mencius, Neo-Confucianism, New Confucianism, New Text School, *Shijing*, *Shujing*, *Sishu*, Xunzi, *Zhongyong*
Confucius   36, 52, 56, 132, 135, 163, 174; as a prophet   1, 13–23, 26, 32–33; as "uncrowned king"   13, 17, 27
Constantine, emperor   116
Constitutionalism   101
Cosmology   47, 64
Crossley, Pamela K.   143
Cultural Revolution   159
Czikszentmihalyi, Mark   15

Dai Wang   24
Danwei (units)   173
Daodejing   35
Darrobers, Roger   41n62
Darwinism   63–64, 69, 94–95
Dating of the *Datong Shu*   7–8
Datong (great concord)   4, 9, 38, 41, 46, 50, 66, 68, 71, 131, 135, 171, 175, 178
Democracy   65, 73, 107–125, 154–155, 181; exportability of   120, 122
Deng Xiaoping   169, 173
Dikötter, Frank   94
Ding, John   158
Dong Zhongshu   16, 18, 20, 23, 26–31, 33–34, 36, 178
Du Juhui   162
Du Shun   44n3
Duke Huan of Qi   27, 61
Duke Wen of Jin   27, 61

Dushu   168
Dystopia   80

Elections   62
Elman, Benjamin   18, 20–21
Empathy (*ren*)   35–36, 39, 44, 53, 130
Engels, Friedrich   152
England   42, 116
Equality (*ping*)   25, 128–132
Esperanto   74
Essentialism   57
Ethnic nationalism   9, 69, 86
Europe, early modern   61n4

Fa Zang   44n3
Fang Ning   124, 176, 181
Federalism   24; federations   61–62
Feng Guozhang   116n21
Feudalism   129, 152
Foucault, Michel   5
Fourier, Charles   132n15
France   42, 57, 58, 59, 61, 114, 117, 118, 123; French Revolution   72
Fryer, John   121
Furth, Charlotte   64

Gan Chunsong   174–177, 180
Gao Ruiquan   129
Gaobie geming (*Goodbye to Revolution*)   164
Garibaldi, Giuseppe   59
Ge Hong   82
Gentry   120
Germany   42, 57, 58, 61, 64, 116, 117; German Empire   118
Gernet, Jacques   15n6, 67, 129
Global History   6, 115, 165
Global Intellectual History   39, 166, 178
Gong Zichen   21
Gongli (universal principle)   169
Gongming Yi   30–31
Gongyang Commentary   16–18, 21–26, 29n42, 30–33, 41
Grand Secretariat   20n24
Great Britain   102
Great Leap Forward   147, 164
Greece   42, 64, 104, 114, 117; Greek *poleis*   61
Gu Yanwu   96
Guangdong   1, 23–26, 70

Guangxu Emperor   3, 63n7, 93, 98, 99
Guangzhou   23–24
Gujingjingshe   23
Guliang Commentary   16, 27, 32
Guocui (national essence)   97

Habsburg   94
Hague Conventions   61 n.5
Han dynasty   14, 16, 17
Han Feizi   36
Han nationalism
Han School   23
Hao Jing   20n24
Harmony (*he*)   66; Harmonious society   171
He Xiu   31n44, 34
Hegel, Georg W. F.   35, 57
Heshen   19, 21
History, philosophy of   25–26, 44, 127
Hong Kong   56, 175
Hong Taiji   95
Hsiao Kung-chuan   1, 40–41, 48, 123, 127, 160, 161
Hsü, Immanuel   107
Hu Jintao   173
Hu Shi   93, 160
Huainanzi   32
Human nature (*xing*)   49
Hunan   24
Hundred Days Reforms   3, 8, 24, 72, 97, 158
Huxley, Thomas   94 n.8
Hygiene   80

Immortality   82
Index   000
India   3, 7, 42, 100, 140
Internationalism   71, 171
Italy   57–59, 61, 140

Japan   2, 3, 66, 68, 70, 106
Ji Wenfu   148
Jian Chaoliang   23
Jiangnan   13, 18, 23–24, 26
Jinshi examination   2, 23
Jurchen   94

Kant, Immanuel   159
Kaozheng   20, 24
Karl, Rebecca   168, 177
Katō Hiroyouki   69

Kedilun   97
Korea   94, 140
Koselleck, Reinhart   2, 5, 13, 21; see also *Sattelzeit*
Kropotkin, Pëtr Alekseevič   165
Kuhn, Phillip   18, 21

Laozi   31, 36
Le Corbusier   74
League of Nations   73, 107
Legalism   18, 35
Lenin   156
Li (principle)   49
Li (ritual)   130
Li Jinxi   130
Li Rui   149
Li Si   31
Li Yuning   126
Li Zehou   74, 137, 147–159, 168
Liang Qichao   3, 7, 49, 64, 97, 107, 130, 155, 165
Liao Ping   24
Liberalism   65, 129, 165
Liji (*Book of Rites*)   34, 68, 107, 154
Lin (unicorn)   14, 17, 19, 20, 41
Lin Zexu   139
Linearity, historical   22, 115
Ling Shu   29
Liu Liangjian   171–172
Liu Wenqi   29
Liu Xiang   27
Liu Xin   27, 32 n.45
Liyun   34
Localism   24
Louis XIV of France   100
Lun Heng
Lunyu (*Analects*)   49
Luther, Martin   19

Malqmvist, Goran   66
Manchu   4, 18, 94–95, 113; anti-manchuism   92–99, 109
Mannheim, Karl   5
Mao Jianxun   149
Mao Zedong   9, 131, 159, 161, 165; Maoism   126, 137, 143, 151, 158–169, 180
Marx, Karl   35, 74, 131, 150; Marxism   74–75, 126–127, 147–151, 155, 158
Material progress   65, 73–82

INDEX

Materialism 56, 74, 151, 165
Mazower, Mark 72
Medicine 6, 80–82
Meditation 4, 46
Meiji 3, 63, 66, 69
Mencius 14–15, 23, 27–28, 31–32, 34, 36–37, 68, 129, 151
Miles, Steven 24
Minben 68, 121, 129
Ming dynasty 44, 47, 50, 93, 97
Minquan 130
Minsheng 130
Minzhu 105, 109, 130, 155
Moeller, Hans-George 17 n.14
Monarchy 25; Constitutional Monarchy 3, 4, 124, 153, 155; Empty-monarchy 115
More, Thomas 179
Moyn, Samuel 178
Mozi 31, 36
Multipolar world 173
Murthy, Viren 167
Muslims 94

Napoleon 58
National Assembly 114
Nationalism 3, 57, 85–106, 176–177, 179; Abolition of Nations 60; Alliances among Nations 61
Nazism 80
Neo-Confucianism 50, 121
Netherlands 116, 140
New Kanghism 175
New Left (Chinese) 168, 170
New Life Movement 80
New Text School 2, 8, 9, 13, 18, 20–25, 35, 40, 42, 68, 178
Norway 104

Old Text School 18
One, the 31, 34, 45
Osterhammel, Jürgen 39, 67
Otlet, Paul 74
Ottoman Empire 94
Ouyang Xiu 31n44

Paradise 50
Père L'Enfantine 73

Peter the Great 3, 63
Pines, Yuri 121n29
Planned economy 133–136
Plato 179
Poland 63–64
Politicization, process of 21–22
Portugal 117, 140
Private (*si*) 106, 109, 121, 180
Progress 21, 41, 53, 57, 60, 64, 73–80, 86, 131, 151
Prussia 59
Pu Yi 4; as Xuantong emperor 110
Public (*gong*) 33, 66, 68, 73, 106, 109–110, 115, 121, 125, 128, 170, 180; Becoming Public (*weigong*) 68, 128–139, 152

Qi (ether) 31, 42
Qian (hexagram) 113
Qian Mu 120, 123
Qianlong emperor 19n19, 58, 68, 103
Qing dynasty 8, 13, 19, 20, 22, 24, 40, 47, 74, 93–94, 104–105, 122, 130, 159, 169, 178
Qingdao 4
Qingyibao 97
Queen, Sarah 17n12

Races 85–86, 95, 106, 109, 113; racism 86, 105, 109
Reincarnation (*toutai*) 51
Religion 36, 50
Renxue 38, 47
Republic, universal – 25
Republicanism 4, 112, 116–120
Revolutionary Army, the 93, 98
Richard, Timothy 48
Righteousness (*yi*) 36
Romania 104
Rome 3, 42, 57–59, 69–70, 114, 116, 117
Rowe, William T. 94
Ruan Yuan 23
Russia 116, 140

Saint-Simon, Claude Henri de 72–74, 152
Samsara 36, 49
Sartori, Andrew 178
Sattelzeit (Saddle-period) 1, 13, 18, 21, 39; see also Koselleck, Reinhart
Schram, Stuart 165

Scientific development   65–66, 73–82, 95
Senate   114
Shanghai   56, 111
Shenzi   36
Shi (momentum)   124 n.35
Shijie (world)   57
Shijing (Odes)   17, 26, 31, 37
Shimonoseki, Treaty of   2
Shujing (Book of Documents)   17, 26, 37
Shun (legendary Sage king)   95
Sima Qian   27, 114n17
Sinicization (of Buddhism)   47
Sinocentrism   64
Sino-Japanese War   2, 22, 94
Sishu (Four Books)   26
Socialism   68, 73, 126–143, 147, 167, 170; Introduction to China   126–127; Utopian Socialism   156; Liberal Socialism   160
Society for the Protection of the Emperor (*Baohuanghui*)   3–4, 92
Song Dynasty   18, 28, 49–50, 120, 123
Song Xianfeng   19–20
Sovereignty (*zhuquan*)   68
Spain   140
Stalinism   80
Statism   8, 21, 67, 95, 115, 122, 165; State-building   57–73, 170, 174–176, 179; State unification   107–109
Subao   93, 98
Sun Yat-sen   9, 97–98, 122, 130, 156; Three principles of the people   130–131
Suwang (uncrowned king)   13, 17
Sweden   66
Switzerland   62, 105, 106, 114, 117, 140

Taiping Rebellion   3, 148, 155–156
Taiwan   120, 124, 175
Taixu   47
Tan Sitong   38, 47, 64, 150
Tang Yao   114
Tang Zhidiao   156–157, 162
Technocracy   74
Thompson, Lawrence   4n.6, 13n.6, 8, 50, 133n17, 159, 161
Three Ages   21, 26, 34, 85, 179; see also Age of Chaos, Age of Rising Equality, Age of Supreme Equality
Three Dynasties   28, 32, 61

Tian'anmen Protests   159
Tianxia   28, 57, 64, 110, 130, 171–173, 174
Tianyan lun   21
Tibet   114; Tibetans   94
Ti-yong   121
Tokyo   97
Tong (unity)   6, 25, 34, 73, 92
Tsarist Empire   94
Tsuchida, Kyoson   160
Turkey   140

United States of America   103
Unification   57, 107–109; Global Unification   171
Universalism   41, 63, 65, 70, 176; Universal principle (*gongli*)   169
Utopia   5, 8, 55, 56, 65, 105, 150–152, 173, 179; Utopianism   35, 38, 40, 125, 130, 149, 155, 163, 179

Vegetarianism   53
Vienna, treaty of   61

Wang Ban   171
Wang Fuzhi   96
Wang Hui   106, 124, 168–170, 176, 178, 180
Wang Jingwei   98
Wang Kaiyun   24
Wang Mang   19, 32n45, 127
Wang Yangming   51
Wang Young-tsu   25
Wang Zhongren   28
Wang, Jing   159
Wangguo (death of the country)   99
Wei Yixia   48–49
Wei Yuan   139
Well-field system   32, 127, 130, 137
Wen (legendary Sage king)   26, 154
Weng Tonghe   3
Wenshizhe   147
Westernization   66; Western influences   39–40, 46, 130, 163, 178–179; Western superiority   65, 123
William III of England   103
World War I   61 n.5, 74, 166
Wu (legendary Sage king)   26, 31
Wu Zhao   102
Wudi emperor   16

INDEX

Xi Jinping   171, 173, 181
Xi'an   69
Xia Tinging   162–163
Xinhai Revolution   93, 105, 117
Xuehaitang   23–24
Xunzi   14, 28, 30–31, 34, 129

Yan Anle   27
Yan Fu   21, 64, 94 n.8, 126, 165
Yan Pengzu   27
Yang Fangda   20 n.24
Yang Wenhui   47–48
Yangwu movement   121
Yanlu   22
Yao and Shun (legendary Sages)   36
Yao Jiheng   20 n.24
Yellow Emperor   104
Yijing (Book of Changes)   15, 25, 30–31, 49, 74, 85, 112, 113, 131
Yin and yang   28
Yixin (one mind)   44
Yu (legendary Sage)   14, 26, 31
Yu, Chun-fang   45
Yuan Shikai   110–111, 122

Zarrow, Peter   4n6, 68, 125, 164
Zhan Bai (Tao Hongjing)   82
Zhang Binglin   96–98, 105, 130
Zhang Nanxuan   36
Zhang Xun   110, 115
Zhang Zhidong   64, 121
Zhao Tingyang   171–173, 176, 181
Zhen Bai   82
Zhibao   126
Zhongguo   100
Zhongyong (*Invariable Mean*)   112, 123
Zhongzi (race)   95
Zhou dynasty   18, 20, 28, 114, 137
Zhou, duke of   14, 26
Zhou-Shao Republic   114
Zhu Ciqi   23–24
Zhu Xi   18, 49–50
Zhuang Cunyu   20
Zhuang, lineage   19, 29n42
Zhuangzi   31
Zi Si   31, 34
Zi Xia   16, 30, 34
Zi You   34
Zou Rong   93, 98
Zuo Commentary   16

Printed in the United States
By Bookmasters